The Fabian Society

The Fabian Society is Britain's leading left of centre think tank and political society, committed to creating the political ideas and policy debates which can shape the future of progressive politics.

With over 300 Fabian MPs, MEPs, Peers, MSPs and AMs, the Society plays an unparalleled role in linking the ability to influence policy debates at the highest level with vigorous grassroots debate among our growing membership of over 7000 people, 70 local branches meeting regularly throughout Britain and a vibrant Young Fabian section organising its own activities. Fabian publications, events and ideas therefore reach and influence a wider audience than those of any comparable think tank. The Society is unique among think tanks in being a thriving, democratically-constituted membership organisation, affiliated to the Labour Party but organisationally and editorially independent.

For over 120 years Fabians have been central to every important renewal and revision of left of centre thinking. The Fabian commitment to open and participatory debate is as important today as ever before as we explore the ideas, politics and policies which will define the next generation of progressive politics in Britain, Europe and around the world. To find out more about the Fabian Society, the Young Fabians, the Fabian Women's Network and our local societies, please visit our web site at **www.fabians.org.uk**.

Joining the Fabians is easy
For more information about joining and to learn more about our recent publications, please turn to page **273** or see www.fabians.org.uk

The Solidarity Society

Tim Horton and James Gregory

FIGHTING POVERTY AND INEQUALITY IN AN AGE
OF AFFLUENCE 1909-2009

Commemorating the Centenary of the 1909 Minority Report

In 1909, Beatrice Webb produced her seminal Minority Report of the Royal Commission on the Poor Law. Whereas the Majority on the Commission wanted to reform the Poor Law, the Minority Report sounded a radical call for its abolition and replacement with a modern welfare state to prevent poverty – as well as a wholesale rejection of the assumption that the poor were solely responsible for their own poverty.

Britain was not yet politically ready for Webb's vision of a universal welfare state. But a young William Beveridge worked as a researcher for Beatrice and was greatly influenced by her ideas, which eventually came to fruition in his blueprint for the post-war welfare state. He later said the Beveridge Report "stemmed from what we all imbibed from the Webbs".

This report is the culmination of a research project, conducted by the Fabian Society and funded by the Webb Memorial Trust, to celebrate the Minority Report's legacy, to animate its central values and insights, and to seek to apply them to the challenge of fighting poverty and inequality in Britain today.

Beatrice Webb was not just a social researcher and thinker; she was also an important campaigner and advocate of radical reform. It is in this spirit that we publish this report: as a platform for change.

Fabian Society
11 Dartmouth Street
London SW1H 9BN
www.fabians.org.uk

Author: Tim Horton
Author: James Gregory

A Fabian Special
First published 2009
ISBN 978 0 7163 4110 9

British Library Cataloguing in Publication data.
A catalogue record for this book is available from the British Library.

We would especially like to thank the Webb Memorial Trust for their generous support.

Contents

Acknowledgements

The authors wish to acknowledge the contribution of a number of people towards this project.

Special thanks to Dianne Hayter, Barry Knight, Mike Parker and Richard Rawes of the Webb Memorial Trust. The Trust have not only funded this project, but have provided broader support and advice throughout. We are especially grateful to Barry Knight for chairing the Project Advisory Panel.

The authors owe a large debt of gratitude to the Advisory Panel members who, through their expertise and good will, gave invaluable advice on the project's development. The Advisory Panel included:

Rushanara Ali, Young Foundation
Mike Brewer, Institute of Fiscal Studies
Kate Green, Child Poverty Action Group
Lisa Harker, Institute of Public Policy Research
Peter Kenway, New Policy Institute
Peter Kellner, YouGov
Jane Lewis, London School of Economics
Seema Malhotra, PriceWaterhouseCoopers
Audrey Mullender, Ruskin College, Oxford
Jane Roberts, Parenting UK
Karen Rowlingson, University of Birmingham
Shamit Saggar, University of Sussex

Tom Sefton (before November, 2008), London School of Economics
Nicholas Timmins, Financial Times
Polly Toynbee, Guardian
Stuart White, University of Oxford

Beyond the Advisory Panel, the authors also benefitted from conversations with a variety of experts in related subject areas, among them: Kate Bell, David Coats, Graeme Cooke, Tom Clark, John Denham, Kate Davies, Carl Emmerson, Richard Exell, Simon Griffiths, Marianne Hood, John Hills, Elena Jurado, Stewart Lansley, Adam Lent, Ruth Lister, Ruth Lupton, Martin McIvor, Ed Miliband, David Miller, Sophie Moullin, Jacky Peacock, Nick Raynsford, Howard Reed, Peter Taylor-Gooby, Matthew Toombs, Peter Townsend, Pat Thane, Noel Whiteside, Richard Wilkinson, and Daniel Zeichner.

The authors also wish to acknowledge the contribution of a number of research interns who helped on the project: Ollie Haydon-Mulligan, Debra Hertzberg, Nicole Martin, Veronica Persson, Maddy Power, Oli Sharp, Zoe Sullivan and Anna Wood.

Thanks are also due to several staff at the Fabian Society, especially to Louise Bamfield who helped to conduct the public attitudes research and on whose work on education and life chances we have drawn. Thanks are also due to Tom Hampson, Ed Wallis, Rachael Jolley, Sunder Katwala and Jemima Olchawski for their help and support with the project.

The authors also wish to thank a number of external experts who assisted with, or carried out analysis for, the project research: firstly, to Peter Kellner, Ellen Vandenbogaerde, Jansev Jemal, Sook Yee Choo and Kate Davies at YouGov for their advice and their work in collecting and analysing the survey data we use in this book; secondly, to Sarah Buckley and Oliver Watts at Opinium, along with colleagues at London and Quadrant Housing, for their help in our work on attitudes to social housing; and, thirdly, to Mike Brewer and Robert Joyce at the Institute for Fiscal Studies for their advice and their work on modeling of the tax and benefits system.

Finally, thanks to Teresa Hanley at the Joseph Rowntree Foundation for encouraging us to develop further the public attitudes research and analysis conducted for the Foundation into the research reported here.

The authors have sole responsibility for the content of this report and any views expressed therein are those of the authors alone.

Executive Summary

This report sets out a strategy for how to reduce, eliminate and prevent poverty in Britain – one based on a vision of equal citizenship.

It is the final report of a project to commemorate the centenary of Beatrice Webb's 1909 Minority Report of the Royal Commission on the Poor Law. The Minority Report was original in addressing structural and not only behavioural causes of poverty and in seeing the need to prevent poverty, not simply offer short-term relief. So it argued for the abolition of the Poor Law and the workhouse, making the first call for a universal welfare state as a right of citizenship.

This report addresses how those values and insights can animate and inspire a radical contemporary vision to fight and prevent poverty in modern Britain, and makes immediate proposals which would help to build momentum for deeper change. It also seeks to learn lessons from the successes and failures of post-war welfare history, as well as from international evidence on poverty prevention.

Chapter 1 – 1909-2009: The long view of poverty prevention

Chapter 1 sets out to learn lessons for future poverty prevention by looking at what happened to poverty levels in Britain across the 20th Century and why.

- We show how relative poverty levels through the 20th Century were volatile, swinging from comparatively high poverty in the first half of the century to comparatively low poverty from the 1950s to the 70s, and back to comparatively high poverty again in the 1980s and 90s.

- These trends are explained not primarily by economic or demographic forces, but by politics and policy: the late 1940s and the early 1980s were moments of fundamental change in the nature of our welfare institutions and in the extent to which we decided we were going to prevent poverty. These policy changes, in turn, were driven by significant shifts in public attitudes to welfare and in the underlying quality of social relations, and especially in how people viewed the poorest in society.

- The quality of social relations was itself shaped by how the welfare institutions of the time treated people. The workhouse in Victorian Britain, for example, physically separated the poor and non-poor, generating social segregation. A key lesson is that institutions for successful poverty prevention must attend very closely to the way in which they affect and structure the social relations between individuals and groups in society.

Chapter 2 – Where we are today

Chapter 2 reviews some of the current and future challenges we face for tackling poverty and inequality, including the public and political constraints that the welfare state of the future will need to overcome in order to do this successfully.

- Poverty has fallen in Britain over the last decade. But welcome reductions in child and pensioner poverty have been combined with greater poverty among working-age adults without children, especially those on out-of-work benefits, as well as entrenched disadvantage among those in social housing. And public support for redistribution has fallen sharply.

- Demographic change will drive increases in demand for certain services and benefits, requiring more spending – and public willingness to contribute through taxation. Trends such as ageing and immigration risk putting strain on the solidarity necessary to sustain a generous welfare state.

- Current welfare strategies seem unlikely to reduce poverty significantly below existing levels – where around 20 per cent of people are in relative poverty. Even maintaining these levels may be challenging. Therefore, a new poverty prevention strategy is needed. Restructuring our institutions and changing our public culture of welfare – in particular to ensure the 'welfare contract' is effective and fosters public support for tackling poverty – will be crucial to break out of these constraints.

Chapter 3 – Two dilemmas of welfare

Chapter 3 explores some specific lessons in post-war welfare history about how to design institutions for successful poverty prevention, looking in particular at the tensions between universalism and targeting, and between need and entitlement.

- The very different trajectories of the NHS and social housing since 1945 show how much decisions about universalism and targeting matter. The NHS, which stayed universal, remains popular today, with the public showing a high degree of willingness to contribute towards it. Social housing, by contrast, became ever more narrowly targeted only on the needy, with too much of it also spatially segregated from the rest of society. This has had knock-on consequences for its effectiveness at tackling poverty and exclusion, and for its social image.

● The post-war history of social security shows the tensions that can arise between need and entitlement in welfare policy. Understanding these tensions, Beveridge tried to create a sense of earned entitlement to welfare, but his scheme was structured in a way that made an increasing reliance on means-tested social assistance inevitable. The contributory principle was then further weakened in the 1980s. So we have shifted back towards a need-based framework for out-of-work benefits, policed through a system of conditionality perceived as punitive. This helps to foster the negative views of welfare claimants we see today.

● The evidence suggests that the design of welfare institutions – particularly how far they are targeted or universal in their coverage; and how far who gets what reflects principles of need or entitlement – is crucial for both their effectiveness in tackling poverty and also for their popular legitimacy, which will determine future levels of investment.

Chapter 4 – The dynamics of poverty prevention

Chapter 4 sets out a model of how the design of welfare policy interacts with public attitudes and underlying social relations in order to better understand how we need to restructure our key welfare institutions to tackle poverty sustainably over the long term.

● Public attitudes to welfare exert a significant influence over the development of welfare states. In turn, how welfare institutions operate, by structuring the social contexts in which people evaluate policy, can exert a significant influence over the evolution of public attitudes to welfare.

- Both the coverage of welfare policy and the distributive principle underpinning it are crucial in shaping attitudes to welfare, whether through their interaction with self interest, perceptions of fairness or, more deeply, because of how they structure social relationships between individuals. For example, policies with narrow coverage divide the population into groups, who may then think about their interests and identities in terms of 'them' and 'us', whereas policies with wide coverage align interests and identities so that we are 'in this together'.

- Tensions between how welfare institutions allocate resources, on the one hand, and the effect of these allocation procedures on underlying social relations, on the other, set up dynamic processes that influence how institutions evolve over time – whether expanding and becoming more generous, or contracting and becoming less generous.

- From this analysis, we identify two important paradoxes for poverty prevention: that targeting on the poorest will usually mean less going to the poorest over time; and that allocating purely on the basis of need is not necessarily the best way to help those in need. So getting the underlying design of institutions right is key for effective welfare policy. Perhaps counter-intuitively, welfare systems which are focused on addressing 'poverty' do worse in poverty outcomes than broadly-based systems which aim to reflect a shared sense of citizenship across society. This insight underpins the new welfare settlement we advocate here.

Chapter 5 – Public attitudes to welfare allocation

Chapter 5 looks at some of these dynamics in practice. Drawing on new research, it explores public attitudes to welfare and how they might inform the successful design of welfare policy.

- Many people support progressive tax, benefits and services in principle, but in practice express opposition to redistribution and welfare, particularly if these don't chime with their sense of what's fair. One important reason concerns who is included: in some contexts, people feel uneasy about public spending that is narrowly targeted in coverage, which can create a sense of 'them' and 'us'.

- Another source of opposition to important aspects of welfare is the idea of contribution: a concern that those claiming welfare won't put something back in. People are cooperative by nature, rather than purely self-interested. This is not driven by altruism, however, but by a sense of reciprocity. So people feel concerned about policies where they feel this arrangement is violated.

- Successful poverty prevention requires designing welfare institutions which are both effective and which harness our collective and cooperative instincts, rather than working against them. Tapping into these instincts is key to getting the generous welfare state we need.

Chapter 6 – In this together? Why universalism matters

Taking the lessons of previous chapters seriously means championing universalism and integration in welfare. Chapter 6 looks at what this might mean in some important areas where our welfare state is currently getting it wrong – and doing more to divide than unite us.

With housing, the spatial segregation of much social housing has contributed to poverty and social exclusion for many.

● **The long-term goal should be the full dispersal and integration of social housing across our housing stock.** Local Authorities should have an obligation to ensure that all new private and social housing is genuinely 'pepper potted' and 'tenure blind', with income mix as well as tenure mix; active area management will also be crucial to ensure that mixed communities do not lose their balance over time.

Beyond increasing supply, addressing the 'residualisation' of social housing will also require ending the narrow coverage of financial support for housing.

● **We propose extending the system of financial support for housing further up the income spectrum.** We propose to do this via a Housing Cost Credit, which would bring all forms of housing assistance into the same institutional structure, including extending support to struggling low- and middle-income homeowners.

Tenure distinctions themselves can prove socially divisive, particularly when accompanied by a cultural belief that home-ownership is a morally superior form of tenure.

● **We propose a variety of measures to break down tenure distinctions and blur the polarisation between ownership and 'non-ownership'.** Shared ownership vehicles that allow people to move out of ownership as well as into it could play an important role here, including through a 'right to sell', which would also help to generate housing mix. We also propose a new concept – 'social leaseholding' – to make explicit the way in which private property relies on public goods and public spending.

On taxation, the tax system is bad at tackling poverty because of its partial coverage and the regressive nature of using conventional tax reliefs and allowances for providing financial support.

- **We propose the goal should be a fully integrated tax and benefits system, including by replacing the system of reliefs and allowances with direct transfers, which would be much more progressive.** We propose replacing the personal allowance in the income tax system with a universal tax credit (which, being payable to all, would also be a key instrument for tackling poverty). Tax relief on pensions and savings should be scrapped and replaced with a system of matched payments, providing the same incentives for everyone.

When it comes to benefits and services, the key factor in how successfully welfare states redistribute to those in poverty is not how efficiently they target resources, but the volume of finance flowing through the system. This, in turn, depends on people's willingness to pay tax to finance welfare. So the issue of how generous benefits and services are to middle- and higher-income households therefore becomes crucial.

- **A major focus for poverty prevention therefore needs to be ensuring benefits and services cover middle-income households and are set as sufficiently generous levels to be meaningful to them.** We suggest that the Treasury should explicitly take into account the effect of policy design on people's willingness to contribute when designing welfare programmes and making future fiscal projections.

Chapter 7 – Why we need a new welfare contract

Taking the lessons of previous chapters seriously will also mean shifting welfare policy away from simply responding to need and back towards reciprocity once again, where people earn entitlement through participation in society. Chapter 7 looks at what this might mean in the areas of social security, pensions and welfare-to-work.

The National Insurance system currently excludes many groups in ways that are unjust and which also violate widely-held public perceptions of fairness. These include being too employment-centred and failing to recognise non-work contributions adequately; imposing a floor on the earnings level at which people gain entitlement and a ceiling on the level at which people have to contribute; and tying entitlement quite rigidly to past contribution records.

● **We propose a series of reforms to make the National Insurance system more inclusive and more progressive – changes that would also resonate with public perceptions of fairness.** We propose that caring, studying and certain types of volunteering count as qualifying activities, and are supported by appropriate benefits. We propose the abolition of the Lower Earnings Limit, which means those in part-time or low-paid work do not qualify for entitlements, and the abolition of the Upper Earnings Limit, which currently sees middle-income earners contribute a higher share of their earnings than the richest. And, except for pensions, we propose that other social security benefits should be earned on the basis of current participation, rather than an accumulation of past contribution records.

The motivation behind conditionality is key to whether or not it will help or harm efforts to tackle poverty and inequality.

- **To ensure that conditionality is not used to deter claimants or cut expenditure, we propose that further welfare reforms should be required to demonstrate that they will benefit the prospects or welfare of claimants, and that any savings from reducing welfare caseloads should be hypothecated back into the budget to assist those out of work.** The Government also needs to be clear about those groups for whom there should be no expectation to work or prepare for work, including clarifying the status of caring.

The segregation of people by work status within our welfare system, such as the different status of workers and carers, has long been a source of injustice.

- **Addressing this will require bringing all of working age within the same system.** We propose a single working-age benefit that would not only unite out-of-work benefits and carer benefits, but would also include in-work financial support too.

The current low level of out-of-work benefits means they are not sufficient to keep households out of poverty. At the same time, public support for redistribution and welfare is at a historic low, with widespread negative attitudes towards claimants and those who need help, which create a significant barrier to addressing poverty.

- **We propose a new type of welfare contract which would restore the link between welfare and participation in society. Incorporating public intuitions about fairness and reciprocity would enable benefit levels to be increased in a way that is currently more difficult.** Specifically, we propose to create a system of 'participatory benefits' in which entitlement would be earned through participation in socially useful activities. Such a system would move most claimants out of a need-based framework and into a reciprocity-based framework, whilst avoiding the exclusionary effects of the old contributory system.

● **This system would also increase the value of out-of-work benefits, to bring them up to the poverty line, and link their uprating to increases in earnings. In-work financial support would also be upgraded.** Those refusing to participate would remain on current levels of benefit, rather than the new poverty-prevention levels.

● **We also propose to 're-universalise' social security through a new lifetime welfare contract, which would set out the benefits and services that each citizen could expect at different stages of life, and the types of participation that would be expected in return.** In particular, such a system would end the artificial division at any one moment between 'taxpayers' and 'claimants', by making transparent the financial relationship between citizens and the state throughout their lives.

So the report sets out the principles which could underpin an effective and enduring welfare contract, and how these would open up new space for reform where current approaches make tackling poverty more difficult. The argument is also that these principles of universalism and reciprocity should inform a broader agenda of reform across other areas of public policy.

Introduction

This is an age of austerity – or so we're told. The first General Election after an epoch-making financial crisis will be dominated by arguments about public spending cuts and the fiscal deficit.

So will issues of poverty, inequality and fairness now slide from public view? Politicians of all parties say no. "We are in this together" is a refrain heard across the political spectrum. But those campaigning to reduce poverty fear this may well prove little more than rhetoric. If only limited progress was made during the long boom, can we really hope to do more when times are harder?

Yet compare Britain of 1945 to that of 2009. There can be little doubt which was the age of austerity and which of affluence. One was the era of the ration book; the other of the iPod. After the war, Britain had national debt of over 200 per cent of GDP, compared to 60 per cent today. But that country voted for the vision set out in the Beveridge Report of 1942, created a National Health Service free at the point of need, and pledged 'never again' to the mass unemployment of the 1930s.

Today, even after inflation, our national output is four-and-a-half times greater than it was then.

So the real difference between 1945 and 2009 is not a crisis of affordability. It is a crisis of ambition.

It will be necessary to rebalance the public finances, and debate the different priorities about how to do so. But we should remember too that our societies today, overall, remain the richest the world has ever seen, having long passed the point where aggregate increases in GDP per capita make us all happier. Indeed, our current austerity results from an implosion of that affluence: meltdown in the City has caused economic recession, public debt, growing unemployment and genuine hardship for many.

This should surely remind us that societies have the levels of poverty and inequality that they *choose*. For many that is a subconscious choice because the ability to choose differently often seems beyond our grasp. But we can see how different societies have made different choices. The belief in the American Dream creates a strong tolerance of poverty in the US which would simply be unacceptable in Scandinavia.

Britain has seen uniquely volatile levels of both low and high poverty and inequality precisely because it has been a 'swing battleground' between competing ideas about what's fair. Wartime solidarity created a commitment to full employment which lasted thirty years and an NHS which remains central to our sense of who we are today. On the other hand, the anxiety of the 1970s oil shocks created an individualistic backlash, and the attitudes to tax, welfare and poverty of the Thatcher era which still shape our public debates three decades on.

A decisive moment

This history also reminds us how much decisions made at moments of crisis matter – and can endure for decades to come. The political choices we make about how we balance budgets today could have consequences that last longer than any economic cycle. This report shows why they could well shape the politics of the next half century – and how the crisis we face goes deeper than the current financial crisis and recession.

Today we could be at a 'tipping point' that sends Britain back towards Victorian levels of inequality and social segregation, and, in the process, makes the solidarity which could challenge that social segregation ever more difficult to recover.

Inequality in Britain today, on some measures, is at its highest since the early 1960s. Despite falls in poverty over the last decade, progress is getting harder. Support for redistribution to help those in poverty is at a record low, with public attitudes to those claiming benefits often harsh and punitive. And important parts of our welfare state often seem to be entrenching and reproducing aspects of inequality, rather than tackling them.

There is a good argument that we have now hit the limits of a strategy of incremental progress through quiet redistribution, of doing good when the 'marginal pound' allows. More of the same will now deliver smaller returns, particularly when there is a squeeze on the public finances and increasing demographic pressures on services. If this is not to prove as good as it gets for another generation or more, a different strategy is needed.

It is understandable that anti-poverty campaigners approach the current fiscal squeeze with a defensive 'what we have we hold' mentality. Redistribution to reduce poverty has made a real difference and things would get far worse for the worst-off if current measures were cut back. But that defensive stance is far too limited an ambition, and one which fails to recognise the limits of the current approach.

So this report argues for a new vision of the generous welfare state we need, setting out what would need to change if we wanted to reduce, eliminate and prevent poverty in a sustainable way.

The solidarity settlement

This report commemorates significant moments in our welfare history, to ask what we can learn from them for the future. In particular, it seeks to reanimate the values and insights set out in Beatrice Webb's 1909 Minority Report on the Poor Law, which first argued the (then revolutionary) case to scrap the workhouse and create a universal welfare state as a right of citizenship – a vision that finally came to fruition in the Beveridge Report of 1942 and the post-war welfare state.

But if Britain's welfare state grew out of a society threatened by Hitler and the Blitz, many will doubt whether it is possible to recapture such solidarity today in the modern, diverse, and mobile world in which we live.

Successful poverty prevention in the 21st Century fundamentally depends on showing that we can challenge this view – that we *can* have a sense that we are 'in this together'.

The facts are much less gloomy than most people suppose. In fact, there is strong evidence that most of us are, by nature, cooperative; and that diverse societies can continue to support collective provision as long we think that the arrangements are fair and that others will play their part. But if we want a strong welfare state that eradicates poverty, we must create one which harnesses these cooperative instincts, rather than working against them.

That is why this book argues for a 'solidarity settlement' – a profound re-shaping of our welfare system that would enshrine our equal citizenship and foster a sense of our mutual interdependence.

Anti-poverty programmes which do not do this may have more or less success in reducing poverty over the short term. But they will not eliminate it without being rooted in a much deeper sense of the sort of society we want to be. The poor will indeed always be with us if we think about 'poverty' primarily as a question of 'them' and 'us'.

Too often today our welfare state today fails the test of equal citizenship. It does too much to divide us and too little to unite us.

And there is a risk that this could get worse. Fiscal pressures are leading many to call for greater targeting of anti-poverty programmes. It is easy to understand why: if there is limited cash, surely it would be best to target most on the poorest, which might mean cutting back on benefits and services for the middle class?

In fact, nothing would be worse for the long-term interests of the most vulnerable in our society than taking the middle classes out of the same services the poorest rely on.

Look at what happened to social housing – just as much part of the 'New Jerusalem' of 1945 as healthcare. Yet compared to the popular NHS which still serves us all, today the stigma and separation of too much social housing risks entrenching poverty, while making it all the more difficult to find the support and money to do anything about it. That shows why Richard Titmuss was right to warn 40 years ago that "services for the poor will always be poor services" – an argument which well-meaning advocates of a targeted approach to poverty risk forgetting.

If we need universalism to protect solidarity and common citizenship, the same ideal should also lead us to support the idea of welfare as a contract of shared social responsibility.

An important reason why fighting poverty is hard is that the very idea of 'welfare' has been contaminated by a successful ideological campaign to stigmatise it as the preserve of a feckless and lazy underclass – essentially returning us to the language of the workhouse.

While there are many myths to tackle here, campaigners against poverty will explode these most successfully when we ourselves advocate that welfare should recognise and reward social contribution, not simply respond to need. That is how to make the case for reinvigorating welfare as a badge of full and active citizenship.

Both of these ideas – of universalism and participation in society – are necessary for effective welfare policy. They are also essential to prevent that sense of 'them' and 'us', which makes us so much less willing to contribute to the collective pot.

If we combined them, our welfare system would look very different.

Firstly, we would need institutions that sought to break down the damaging social divisions that our welfare state itself helps to create and deepen – such as those between taxpayers and benefit recipients, workers and carers, and public and private housing. Where the separation of the tax and benefits system divides our interests, for example, an integrated system would give all a stake in a key poverty reduction policy. Similarly, breaking down the deep segregation between public and private housing would give social tenants more access to the same opportunities and status as everyone else.

Secondly, we would need to change the culture of welfare away from merely relieving need and back towards recognising participation and social contribution once again – Beveridge's original vision that was never fully realised. This would involve setting out not just what people are entitled to, but also how they earn that entitlement as citizens. Carers, for example, instead of being treated as second-class citizens, would see their contribution rewarded directly. And those out of work would be expected to participate in activities, whether looking for a job, care work, community involvement or developing skills. But, rather than a negative culture of conditionality surrounding benefits given on the basis of need, recipients would earn these entitlements on the basis of their efforts and contributions. Similarly, the culture of rights and responsibilities would extend across society, including the responsibility to contribute back through taxation, rather than 'responsibilities' seeming only to be demanded from the disadvantaged.

This solidarity settlement cannot be achieved overnight, any more than those of 1909 or 1942 could be.

But anti-poverty campaigners again need a radical strategy for the next 30 years, not the next budget. This report sets out the strategy for long-term reform that we need, and shows how taking important first steps would then create new possibilities to deepen the agenda and build social coalitions for change.

It is an argument for change which speaks directly to the pressures of this moment of economic uncertainty, fiscal crisis and social pressure. Far from watering down our ambitions, now is the right time to begin.

"The question is asked - can we afford it? Supposing the answer is 'no', what does that mean? It really means that the sum total of the goods produced and the services rendered by the people of this country is not sufficient to provide for all our people at all times, in sickness, in health, in youth and in age, the very modest standard of life that is represented [in the National Insurance Bill]. I cannot believe that our national productivity is so slow, that our willingness to work is so feeble or that we can submit to the world that the masses of our people must be condemned to penury"

Clement Attlee, House of Commons, 1946

1. 1909-2009: The long view of poverty prevention

Until income poverty began rising again in 2005, it had been on a declining trend since the late 1990s. Coming after the years of steadily increasing levels of poverty under the Conservative governments of the 1980s and 90s, this was heartening progress. Between 1979 and 1997 child poverty more than doubled; since 1997 it has fallen. This change in the direction of travel matters.

But what do these trends look like when placed in broader historical context? This chapter seeks to put the changes over the last decade into a longer-term perspective in order to look for some deep lessons about poverty prevention. We explore what trends in relative poverty might have looked like over the course of the century, and examine the forces that drove major changes in poverty levels. In particular, we look at the role played by welfare institutions and also the importance of public attitudes in shaping welfare outcomes, and discuss the underlying implications of this for anti-poverty strategy.

What happened to poverty in the 20th century?

Describing trends in poverty throughout the 20th century is difficult, for the simple reason that different studies over the course of the century used different bases for measuring poverty, and adopted different poverty lines.

The introduction of the Family Expenditure Survey in the 1950s – which has been conducted annually ever since

– has provided not only a standardised basis to compare poverty levels in different years, but also a representative national dataset. The reliable measurement of incomes has also allowed modern definitions of poverty in terms of median incomes – something which social research has suggested is a good indicator of living standards and the ability to participate fully in society.

By contrast, in the first half of the 20th century, poverty was usually measured via local surveys focussing on measures of household income and living conditions (the classic examples of which were those of the great social reformer Seebohm Rowntree). Such surveys assessed poverty in terms of the costs of necessities expressed as a defined 'basket of goods'– for example, looking at whether families could afford basic nutrition, clothing and fuel. However, different surveys often used different baskets of goods.[1]

As a result, there are no reliable measures available to compare poverty levels across the whole century. However, where data is available in different surveys which can provide legitimately comparable measures of poverty, one can at least get a sense of how poverty levels might have changed between two dates. And piecing together these 'mini-trends' can – with quite a lot of assumptions thrown in – begin to provide a sense of how poverty was changing throughout the century.

By recalculating the poverty lines used by various historical studies in terms of contemporaneous personal disposable income per capita, and seeing which ones are comparable, David Piachaud has identified some survey results that can be used to provide a snapshot of changing levels of poverty in the first half of the 20th century (Piachaud, 1988). As luck would have it, the Class A poverty line used by Seebohm Rowntree in his 1936 survey of York (Rowntree, 1937) corresponded to 79 per cent of personal disposable income per capita, nearly identical to the 78 per cent of personal disposable income per capita that the 'primary' poverty line for his 1899 study of York corresponds to. In the earlier study, Rowntree found 9.9 per cent of the population below this line; in 1936, he found 8.9 per cent. So (though one can only guess at how representative these two years were), this does correspond to a real fall in poverty between these two dates. In their classic study, *The Poor and the Poorest*, Brian Abel-Smith and Peter Townsend (1965) analysed the results of the 1953 Family Expenditure Survey, estimating the proportion of the population below the National Assistance level. Fortunately, this also corresponded to 79 per cent of personal disposable income per capita at the time, so the 1.2 per cent of the population beneath this mark in 1953 corresponds to a massive fall in relative poverty between 1936 and 1953.[2]

The changes in poverty between the years before and after the Second World War can also be estimated by comparing Rowntree's 1936 survey of York with a further one he conducted in 1950 (Rowntree and Lavers, 1951). Rowntree and Lavers themselves miscalculated the poverty rate from their data (leading them to suggest that poverty had been virtually eliminated by 1950), but subsequent analysis of their data (Hatton and Bailey, 2000) shows there was indeed a dramatic reduction in poverty in York between 1936 and 1950, from 31 per cent in 1936 (according to their main poverty line) to 12 per cent in 1950.

What happened between 1900 and 1936? Again, data is thin on the ground, but a few surveys exist with suggestive results. Arthur Bowley conducted various surveys of English towns and cities, including for a set of five towns in 1912-4, with repeat surveys of the same set in 1923-4. Jo Webb (2002) calculates poverty rates for these studies based on the same poverty line; the results show that for four of the five towns (Reading, Bolton, Warrington and Northampton), poverty rates in 1924 were significantly lower than those for 1912-4 (and in some cases, only around half of the previous level). Several survey studies of big English cities in the early 1930s then show much higher rates of poverty, which is perhaps not surprising given that this was the height of unemployment from the 1930s depression. Indeed, it's clear that unemployment became a much more important determinant of poverty during this time: whereas in Rowntree's 1899 survey just 3 per cent of poor households were headed by an unemployed person (the same proportion as that found by Abel-Smith and Townsend for 1953), Rowntree's 1936 survey showed that 35 per cent of poor households were headed by an unemployed person. If poverty had followed unemployment during this time, then poverty would have indeed risen in the 1920s, peaking in the early and mid-1930s.

The existence of datasets such as the Family Expenditure Survey (now the Family Resources Survey) makes the analysis of poverty in the post-war decades much easier. Fiegehen et al (1977) calculate proportions of individuals and households in relative poverty from the 1950s to the 1970s, using 130 percent of the contemporaneous National Assistance or Supplementary Benefit scale as their poverty line for each year. They find poverty rates relatively low and broadly stable, fluctuating between 6.8 per cent and 4.3 percent for households, and between 5.5 percent and 3 percent for individuals, with poverty rates falling somewhat through the 1970s. This relatively low poverty and stability in the decades immediately following the Second World War, coupled with a slight fall in poverty through the 1970s is also seen in recent analyses of relative low-income from the 1960s through to the present day, as shown in the graph below.

The most striking thing about this graph, however, is the huge increase in poverty that took place during the 1980s and early 1990s – one of the greatest social transformations of modern times, and a central episode of concern for anyone interested in poverty prevention. According to several measures, the proportion of households in relative

Relative poverty levels, 1961-2007

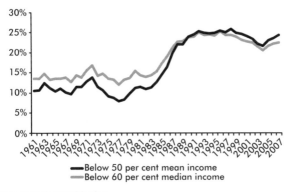

Below 50 per cent mean income
Below 60 per cent median income

Data: Institute for Fiscal Studies

low income more than doubled during this time. (Further details of poverty trends for different households over this period are given in Chapter 2.)

From all this analysis we can begin to build a picture of some of the main movements in poverty levels across the 20th century. As discussed above, it's very hard to make direct comparisons between poverty assessments across the century but nevertheless we believe it's possible to hazard a guess at what the overall trend must have looked like.

If we had to extrapolate from the data we have, then, based on a variety of assumptions, we believe that, for many possible measures of relative low income (or expenditure) that are relevant to thinking about poverty and well-being, the trend in the proportion of the population falling below such measures would have had the general shape shown in the graph below.

What becomes immediately apparent from looking at such a graph is that the kind of movements in poverty levels that have been scrutinised in recent years – while significant and corresponding to real changes in well-being and hardship – are relatively small beer compared to some of the

5

Relative poverty levels across the century

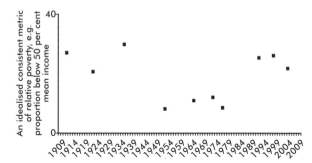

GRAPH: The graph hypothesises what the general shape of the shifts in relative poverty levels across the century might have looked like, for any of a variety of possible measures of relative poverty (such as 50-70 per cent mean / median income or parallel expenditure definitions). The scale on the y-axis is for a measure below 50 per cent mean income. Alternative measures of poverty would require different scales, though the proportionate changes in poverty levels would be roughly similar. Extrapolated from historical studies (particularly Webb, 2002).

changes we've seen throughout the last century. In particular, two large-scale shifts in relative poverty are apparent, creating a giant U-shape: one between the pre-WWII years and the post-WWII years; and one between the late 1970s and late 1990s – shifts that have radically altered the character of our society. Between these moments of radical change there are some important fluctuations, but in the context of the whole century these nevertheless seem like periods of relative stability. The overall pattern is one of shifting from a relatively 'high-poverty equilibrium' to a 'low-poverty equilibrium', and then back to a higher one again.

What caused these changes in poverty levels?

A starting point for thinking about poverty prevention in the 21st century, then, is to ask about the kinds of factors that lay behind these changes in poverty throughout the 20th century. Obviously many factors impinge on the level of poverty and inequality within a society, but chief among them are major demographic and economic forces that shape household incomes and determine their adequacy.

One might be tempted to ask first whether or not *economic prosperity and growth* underpin the variations in the extent of relative poverty suggested by the trend outlined above. Certainly there are times when it must have been a strong contributor, particularly in the post-war boom years. But, equally, there are times when GDP per capita can't have been the main determinant of poverty levels: the 1970s, for instance, where we experienced economic turbulence and recession, but when poverty was historically low and falling; or, conversely, the period since the early 1990s, in which a period of unprecedented economic growth and prosperity has been accompanied only by relatively modest falls in poverty levels.

There is often quite a close correlation between *employment levels* and poverty levels, since employment is the major source of household income for most families. And, sure enough, we can see some important movements in the long-term poverty trend that reflect this: the mass unemployment of the 1930s depression, for example, was almost certainly responsible for higher poverty levels in the 1930s than the 1920s. The huge rise in worklessness during the 1980s and 1990s was also a key driver of the increases in poverty seen then: worklessness rose from 11 per cent of working-age households in 1981 to 19 per cent in 1996 – three quarters of whom were in poverty (Gregg and Wadsworth, 2001).[3]

But, again, while crucially important, there are also times when poverty levels don't move in line with employment levels. Unemployment was around 2.5 per cent in the first half of the 1960s and nearly double that (4.8 per cent) in the second half of the 1970s, but poverty was lower in the latter period than the former. And at various points over the last century, a higher risk of in-work poverty loosened the strong connections between employment and poverty.[4]

Because earnings from work are so important for household income, another factor in explaining relative poverty is *inequality in the earnings distribution*. John Hills (2004a) shows that the large rise in poverty during the 1980s was partly driven by widening earnings dispersion, with the wages of the lowest-paid falling further and further behind the average.[5] But it's also likely that changes in the earnings distribution played a much smaller part in shaping poverty trends throughout most of the century, since evidence suggests there was remarkable wage rigidity for the first three quarters of the century. Hills cites the staggering fact that in 1978 the bottom decile of male earnings for manual workers was still around 69 per cent of the median – exactly the same figure it had been in 1886. So changes in the earnings distribution probably don't account for, say, the large decline in poverty between the 1930s and the 1950s.

Another key factor in determining poverty levels is the *changing composition of households*. Different household structures – pensioner households, couples with children, single-parent households, and so on – have different risks of poverty. This is not only because they have different earning abilities, but also different needs.

There is evidence that this factor has played an important role at times in explaining poverty levels. For example, the rise in single-parent households throughout the 1980s and 1990s was one important driver of the rising number of workless households during this time. But, in general it is very hard to explain many of the changes in poverty throughout the 20th century in this way. The steady growth in the old-age population, for example, did not lead to steadily increasing poverty throughout the post-war decades. Furthermore, the large-scale shifts in the graph occur within relatively short timescales – between the mid-1930s and 1950s, or between the late 1970s and the early 1990s – whereas significant demographic change usually unfolds over much longer timescales.

Of course, in reality, the confluence of all of these factors helped shape poverty at each point throughout the century. But all of the analysis above is missing the point. For while these economic and demographic forces all *underpinned* changes in poverty levels throughout the century, none of them *determined* poverty levels.

What did determine poverty levels, then? The answer is simple: we did. What occurred in the 1940s and in the early 1980s were *fundamental changes in the nature of our major welfare institutions and the associated culture of welfare*. These were moments when we, as a society, decided what all of these economic and demographic forces meant for poverty levels. Unemployment, after all, need only lead to poverty if we want it to. Old age need only lead to poverty if we let it. The reason the rise in worklessness in the 1980s was such a strong driver of rising poverty, for example, was because it also coincided with a continuous decline in the relative value of out-of-work benefits.

So these were moments when we changed our minds about the extent to which we were going to look after each other in society. That is why the overall trend in poverty levels cuts across the myriad of economic and demographic changes outlined above.

These fundamental changes in the character of our society are evident from other similar U-shaped trends in welfare measures across the course of the century. The graph below shows another example: the shares of total personal after-tax income of the top 1 per cent, top 0.5 per cent and top 0.1 per cent of the population from 1937-2000. The shares of income owned by the super-rich were clearly much higher at the beginning and end of the century than in the post-war years.

To summarise, the creation of the post-war welfare state in the late 1940s, on the one hand, and the retrenchment

Share of total income (after tax) of the richest, 1937-2000

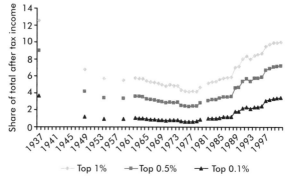

— Top 1%   —■— Top 0.5%   —▲— Top 0.1%

Data from Atkinson (2008)

and restructuring of important areas of welfare in the early 1980s, on the other, were seminal events that shifted us between the different poverty and inequality 'equilibria' we can see in the graphs above.

What were these seismic institutional and cultural changes that led to such dramatic movements in poverty? We examine this briefly in the next section.

A brief history of social policy in the 20th century

Without doubt, the key historical event that we all associate with the 'creation' of the welfare state is the Second World War. In large part, the association is correct. For it was during – and because of – the war that the Beveridge Report was born, with its call to slay the 'five giants': squalor, ignorance, want, disease and idleness. All of these were attacked through a range of legislation in a very short period. In 1944 the great welfare reforms were kicked off with the Education Act. 1945 saw the Family Allowance Act, 1946 the National Insurance and National Health Service Acts, and 1948 the National Assistance Act.

But what was so significant about these Acts? After all, there had been similar flurries of reforming welfare legislation before. Indeed, some argue that the foundations of the modern welfare state lie in the reforms of the Asquith Government. In 1908, the Old Age Pensions Act became the first modern anti-poverty measure financed out of general taxation, and in 1911 the National Insurance Act led to compulsory health and unemployment insurance for workers on low wages. This undoubtedly contributed towards lower poverty levels in the 1920s and mitigated at least some of the misery of the Great Depression in the 1930s (Gazeley, 2001). Nevertheless, these provisions were patchy and ungenerous, and the fact that support was tied to insurance meant that many people – most obviously women – were left out.

Moreover, for all the incremental progress that these measures represent, the fact remains that they did very little to alter the fundamental logic of our welfare institutions. Of the greatest symbolic importance was the continuation of the fundamentally divisive and much hated Poor Law. Beatrice Webb saw this very clearly, so much so that she was compelled to write the dissenting Minority Report when the Royal Commission on the Poor Law reported in 1909. Whereas the Majority on the Commission proposed reforms of the Poor Law, Webb's fundamental objection rested in the very notion of 'reform', as she considered the underlying fabric of the Poor Law to be both socially unjust and ineffective in the fight against poverty. Behind both of these undesirable features lurked the continuing assumption that poverty was mainly the result of poor personal choices or laziness.

The injustice lay in the fact that, to deter 'dependency', assistance was set at a level that ensured that recipients were marginalised from society. This deterrence was even embodied in a formal principle, the principle of 'less eligibility', which stated that the well-being of the 'pauper' must never be greater than that of the poorest working labourer, lest the labourer is tempted to down tools and rely on public assistance instead. The inefficacy came from the same source: the workhouse and Poor Relief were so stigmatised, and so often punitive in practice, that they acted as a real deterrent for those genuinely needing help; and once they did seek help it was far too late for preventative measures. And even when the poor did come forward, their needs were 'met' by just one institution – the workhouse – that was hopelessly ill-equipped to deal with the wide range of needs experienced by its inmates: health needs, educational needs, the particular needs of the elderly, and so on. In this case, one size most certainly did not fit all – and the workhouse was a source of great institutional inefficiency.

Webb thus proposed the complete *abolition* of the Poor Law, and its replacement by, in effect, a universal welfare system that guaranteed everyone a 'national minimum' – judged, by the standards of the day, in relation to what an average household would consider to be the necessities of a 'civilised life'. This included calls for everything from a National Health Service and state pensions to decent family allowances and full employment policy.

Of real importance here was the way in which Webb insisted that this provision was to be met and administered by universal institutions. One of her central proposals was that services for the poor were to be taken out of the workhouse and merged with those provided for the middle classes by local government. The crucial upshot was that services were to be directed at *types of need* rather than at *types of person*. "What is demanded by the conditions," wrote Webb, "is not a division according to the presence or absence of destitution, but a division according to the services to be provided."

What made Beveridge's subsequent reforms so important, then, was precisely their fidelity to this paradigm-shifting mode of thought. Like Beatrice Webb, with whom he worked as a researcher on the Minority Report,

Beveridge sought a national minimum and in many respects a much more universalist approach to the welfare state (which found its clearest expression in the NHS).

Perhaps the largest structural change was the post-war commitment to full employment, closely linked to Keynesian-style demand management to keep the economy and labour market buoyant. A combination of economic growth and proactive government policy ensured that, in the post-war years, unemployment rarely went above 3 per cent, compared with the 11 per cent of the pre-war period. More generally, the state retained the role it had acquired during the war, namely, as a legitimate actor in the public domain (as well as the war-time level of public spending).

The following decades brought incremental changes, with the modification of some benefits and services, and the expansion of others – although bubbling beneath the surface of the welfare consensus was a great deal of debate and dissent, particularly on the right. Some developments during this time were to have important long-term institutional implications. For example, the Conservative Governments of the 1950s actively encouraged as many people as possible to move into private pensions. Thus, when it came to the breaking of the link between the state pension and average earnings in the early 1980s, there was no solid constituency of outrage and protest.

At the same time, a new housing consensus emerged in the 1960s, one which was to have a profoundly negative impact on social housing in the following decades. The new consensus originated in the conservative ideology of a 'property-owning democracy', and had its roots in conservative thinking from the very start of the post-war era. The ideal for the Conservatives was ownership – both to serve the aspirations of the electorate and to encourage the virtues (responsibility and independence) that were said to come with it. Social housing was only to be a temporary stopping point for aspiring citizens, and therefore did not need to be of the highest quality. In 1965, Labour in practice capitulated to this view, with a White Paper that stated that public expenditure was to be targeted only on housing for the needy. The result, over the long term, was that council housing often became a stigmatised tenure of last resort.

Yet there were also instances of pro-collectivist welfare development during these decades. One important moment was the scrapping of child tax allowances (primarily of benefit to those with higher incomes) and the conversion of Family Allowances into Child Benefit – a universal benefit with high take-up that would become a popular part of the furniture of the welfare state. Another was the introduction of Home Responsibilities Protection in 1978 to begin to redress the historic injustice that women and carers had suffered as a result of an employment-based contributory system (particularly the absence of state pension entitlement). However, while such reforms were civilising measures, they were not wide or deep enough to have a transformative effect on our welfare state as a whole.

The next 'paradigm shift' (reforms that, like Beveridge's, made fundamental changes to the nature of a whole set of institutions) was not to come until the late 1970s, with an attack on the welfare state and a significant increase in poverty. Ostensibly driven by the economic 'crises' arising from the 1970s oil shocks, this was a period in which the new right used a sense of crisis to argue for a smaller state not just as an alleged fiscal necessity, but as a virtue as well. Thus, the very idea of demand management and full employment policy was jettisoned: the state, it was believed, crowded out the animal spirits of enterprise, and demand management was ruinously inflationary. Instead, the new economic creed was to be monetarism – a tight control of money supply and inflation. More generally, markets, rather than the state, were to be the key institutional forces shaping society.

The problem was that much of this came at great human cost. The welfare state was rolled back as a means of balancing the books and returning citizens to a state of 'independence' – and, for many, penury. Spending on services did not keep pace with demographic demands, and the Thatcher Government pursued a deflationary policy even in the midst of severe recession. This 'rolling back' of the state meant that those who lost their jobs through economic restructuring were left to waste away, with inadequate benefits and no services to support them in re-training. A whole generation of older unemployed people were shuffled onto Invalidity Benefit and told they should not expect to work again.

At the same time, both national insurance and other benefits were cut back. One of the key moves here was the decoupling of the value of benefits from average earnings in 1981. Another was the removal of earnings-related supplements for out-of-work benefits, thus removing what had in practice been an insurance-based 'right', and greatly reducing the relevance of the contributory system. Instead of a rights-based system, a new era of means testing was launched, all in the name of efficiency and personal responsibility. The great irony was that it was not that efficient, as the costs of means testing were great; nor did means testing necessarily encourage responsibility as it risked disincentivising work and saving.

All this was a recipe not just for poverty, but for great inequality too. At various points throughout the 1980s, tax rates were reduced so as to incentivise work and reward enterprise. These changes not only diluted the tax-and-benefit system's ability to restrain growing inequality, but also in some years actually had a *disequalising* effect (Hills, 2004a): in the second half of the 1980s, inequality in post-tax incomes was actually growing *faster* than inequality in market incomes. As well as cuts in the relative value of benefits, the key changes that contributed to this growing inequality were cuts in the basic and top rate of income tax, and a shift in the burden of taxation from direct taxation (which is progressive) to indirect taxation (which is regressive), such as through the increases in VAT in 1979 and 1992. Our tax system still bears the scars of this today, with the poorest fifth of the population paying more of their income in tax than the richest fifth.

Whilst Margaret Thatcher made a great play of the notion that the state should not be involved in 'social engineering', she was busily encouraging the cultivation of the 'vigorous virtues' through a series of measures designed to force the individual to turn to the market rather than the state. The irony, of course, is that this was a classic piece of social engineering driven through institutions. Indeed, Thatcher very much understood the crucial importance of institutions; it's just that her preferred mode of institutional engineering was through the culture and language of the market. A key measure here was the sale of council houses at often massive discounts – a huge transfer of assets, though one which rarely made it to those in poverty.

The result was that the winners of the Thatcher years drew further and further away from the losers; less tax at the top, and fewer benefits at the bottom – in short, less redistribution. Departing from their low and stable trends of over 30 years, poverty and inequality soon began to race away.

Changing the culture of welfare: the key ideological distinction between left and right

In many respects, the Thatcher revolution did not bring about the same scale of institutional change as Beveridge had. Certainly, the 1980s and 1990s saw significant retrenchment in key areas, notably housing and social security, but nothing quite to match the scale or comprehensiveness of the Beveridge reforms.

Arguably, Beveridge's main achievement had been to redraw the welfare-citizenship boundary. Whereas the Poor Law had separated welfare from the world of work and citizenship (with workhouse inmates physically separated from society and forced to give up civil and political rights), the main instrument of Beveridge's welfare state – social insurance – *linked* welfare and work together (with contributions through employment creating entitlement to benefits).

But this was a cultural change as much as an institutional one. And while the Thatcher revolution was institutionally less radical than Beveridge's, it *did* succeed in changing the culture of welfare again, beginning to separate it from work and citizenship once more. Social insurance was downgraded, welfare benefits became something for a particular need group, and there was a huge emphasis on getting the middle class and more affluent working classes out of 'dependency' on the welfare state. Indeed, the welfare institution that perhaps underwent *least* retrenchment under the Thatcher governments was means tested social assistance; it in fact came to play a much more central role.

At first blush, this might sound strange. Aren't the left supposed to be ones who like allocating things on the basis of need? In fact, while helping those who are in need is a core ideological *goal* of the left, it has, historically, usually been the right who have wanted to *characterise* welfare in terms of need. It has been the left that has generally tried to link welfare to citizenship and work, and the right that has generally sought to separate them.

Why is this? The answer lies deep in the ideologies of left and right. If you are a libertarian, then you have a prima facie objection to coercive taxation (including compulsory social insurance, which you see as taxation) and welfare spending. In such a case, even if you accept the 'humanitarian' case for welfare, you regard being in receipt of welfare as necessarily an 'aberrant' state of affairs – and something to be 'moved off' – hence the right's concept of 'welfare dependency'. By contrast, because for social democrats public spending and welfare provision are not morally objectionable in their own right, there is no logical contradiction between receiving welfare and being a full and equal member of society. Indeed, the very width of welfare institutions assumes a normative importance for the left, as a driver of unity and solidarity.

And this is the key ideological distinction between left and right when it comes to welfare. It might sound counterintuitive, but historically the focus of Conservative governments' retrenchment in welfare provision is less on those programmes that allocate resources to the very poorest who are in dire need – this is in fact the Conservative vision of welfare. Rather, it is always the removal of social protections from the middle class and those who are not in immediate distress, since, for libertarians, the state should play no role here.

What drove policy change?

The role of public attitudes

It's perhaps obvious that these institutional changes were driven by the political ideologies of the politicians that implemented them – the popular socialist collectivism of the Attlee Government, on the one hand, and the radical conservative libertarianism of Margaret Thatcher and Keith Joseph, on the other. Indeed, Thatcher would explicitly reference the work of libertarian philosophers like Hayek to justify her programme. (According to one report of a Conservative strategy meeting, "the new party leader reached into her briefcase and took out a book. It was Friedrich von Hayek's *The Constitution of Liberty*. Interrupting the speaker, she held the book up for all of us to see. 'This', she said sternly, 'is what we believe'.")[6]

In particular, the motivations of the two programmes of welfare reform were totally different: the 1945 Government was trying to slay giants, among them 'want' and 'squalor', whereas Margaret Thatcher was trying to cut welfare expenditure and improve incentives to work. Indeed, for Thatcher it was not that greater inequality might have been an undesirable by-product of welfare reform, it was actually the point – a desirable thing, that would incentivise effort and foster dynamism.[7]

But to locate the explanation for large-scale social reform in the ideological persuasion of political elites is really to beg the question. Saying that governments cause political change is a bit like saying that trains are late because of an earlier delay. The real question is: what permits the governments in question – and what allows them to implement their programmes? It was not ever thus that leaders quoting Hayek won general elections: Churchill's invocation of *The Road to Serfdom* in a 1945 election campaign address (where he claimed delivering the Beveridgean welfare state would require 'a kind of

Gestapo') was widely credited with damaging Tory support and helping Labour to their landslide.

Why were these massive welfare reforms *allowed* to happen, then? As Margaret Thatcher found out over the poll tax, political change requires public consent. It was, of course, crucial shifts in public attitudes towards welfare, producing a critical mass of favourable opinion towards the reform programmes in question, that made reform possible. There is no doubt that a huge groundswell of support for widespread social provision during and after the years of WWII contributed to the popularity of the Beveridge Report and enabled the Labour Party to run on (and win on) a platform to create a modern welfare state. Similarly, it is clear that the ascendancy of the new right in the late 1970s was made possible by a deterioration in public support for key aspects of the welfare state. For example, the number agreeing that benefits and social services 'had gone too far' increased strikingly between 1970 and 1979 (Sarlvik and Crewe, 1983).

There are, however, important qualifications to be made to the classic 'welfare backlash' thesis – that is, that some time around the mid-1970s the British public turned decisively against the welfare state. First, rather than a sudden shift, some evidence suggests there was a more gradual decline in support for welfare that just happened to reach 'critical mass' in the mid-1970s, resulting in a realignment that political leaders could respond to (Butler and Strokes, 1974).

Second, and perhaps more importantly, the evidence suggests that in the late 1970s the public were not falling out of love with the welfare state per se, but rather with particular bits of it. Taylor-Gooby (1985), through an examination of opinion surveys, demonstrated that, far from a generalised backlash against the whole welfare state, support for its underlying principles and many of its institutions remained as strong as ever.[8] The picture was different, though, in attitudes to areas like 'welfare benefits'. Whereas in 1974, 67 per cent had thought 'social services and benefits' should stay as they are or be increased (with 33 per cent thinking they should be cut back), by 1979 only 46 per cent thought this (with 49 per cent now thinking they should be cut back).

So public attitudes had deteriorated towards certain parts of the welfare state, such as social security, but not towards others. Why this was the case will be an important part of our discussion in Chapter 3. For the moment, it is simply worth noting that those benefits and services with deteriorating support proved to be just those services that the Thatcher Government was able to set about restructuring and cutting back. By and large, those services that remained strongly popular – like the NHS – survived the 1980s period of reform.

The quality of social relations

What, in turn, drove changes in public attitudes to welfare? Was it that people's underlying sense of fairness changed? The evidence suggests not. Surveys at the time suggest strong support for the underlying principles of the welfare state, but concern at its practice. A survey conducted in 1981 (Taylor-Gooby, 1982) found 93 per cent agreeing that the welfare state 'is good in principle, but needs reform'. It was not that people thought the unemployed, for example, should not be supported, but rather that they thought something was going wrong with the policy as it was currently administered. In particular, people seemed to have very negative views of claimants, which in turn seemed to be the overwhelming driver of antagonism towards these areas of policy.[9]

And this is a finding that has been observed time and again in welfare history: strong support for the *principles* of welfare policy, but opposition to policy itself, arising from the view that, in practice, those benefiting are somehow unworthy of it. Large numbers of studies during the 1970s and 1980s (Deacon, 1978; Townsend, 1979; Golding and Middleton, 1982) pick up this 'scroungerphobia' as the key driver of antagonism towards welfare.

So it is partly the quality of social relations that underpins attitudes to welfare, particularly how people tend view those in poverty. Are they deserving or not? Are they to blame or not? Are they my responsibility or not? The answers to these questions depend, as well as on rational evaluations of welfare recipients' behaviour, on factors like the perceived social identity of those in poverty and the perceived social distance between those in poverty and everyone else (van Oorschot, 2000). And different possible answers tend to lead to very different attitudes towards welfare policy.

Looking back through the 20th century, especially at these formative moments of institutional change, it's clear that a range of forces were at work in shaping social relations, whether solidaristic or individualistic. In the early 20th century, the operational concept was not so much 'poverty' as 'pauperism': a condition of the individual (including a failing of 'character') for which they were squarely to blame. As well as this moral distancing, there was also often a spatial separation of those in poverty from the rest of society in concentrations of slum dwellings. But perhaps the most potent mechanism of segregation was the predominant welfare institution itself – the Poor Law.

The essential logic of the Poor Law was the labelling of the recipients of assistance as the 'undeserving poor', and often their physical separation from society in the workhouse. Indeed, stigma and separation were consciously employed as an explicit policy tool: the stigma of having to enter the workhouse was intended to deter vast hordes from calling in the assistance of the state. For those entering the workhouse, their citizenship status was literally revoked, with both the loss of freedom and the loss of important political and civil rights (such as the right to vote).

The attitudes that this created are striking. In 1905 the *Daily Mail* ran a story that would be very familiar today, in which it lamented the existence of a 'Workhouse de Luxe' – a 'poverty palace' in Camberwell (April 12th 1905). The complaint was that inmates were given quality bread and were allowed to venture out in the day. With the very literal separation of 'poor' and 'non-poor', it should come as no surprise that Victorian society regarded those in poverty as alien 'others', a 'submerged residuum' that was the object of fear and fascination in equal measure. Just as we have Vicky Pollard and voyeuristic reality shows, so well-to-do Victorian ladies would go on covert tours of East End slums.

These attitudes and relations were perpetuated in various social behaviours through the 1920s and 1930s. In the 1930s Britain saw perhaps the first aspirational generation of former council house tenants intent on owning their own home, not just for the sense of control that it could bring, but because of a conscious desire for distance from 'the poor'. This was evident in the design of houses pitched at the new buyers, with mock Tudor gables and the like, built with the conscious aim of distinguishing them from the council house (Power and Houghton, 2007).

Perhaps the most symbolic expression of this social separation came with an extraordinary episode on a housing estate in north Oxford. In 1933, the new Cutteslowe council estate was opened, all of it quality housing and well connected to local services and jobs. But almost as soon as it housed its first tenants, the private developer on the adjacent land erected a wall across the road, complete with revolving spikes on top, to physically segregate the social tenants from the private ones. (It only came down in 1959.)

The 1930s, however, also saw the Great Depression with mass unemployment on a frightening scale. This period, perhaps more than any other in the first part of the 20th century, had the effect of highlighting bleakly the structural causes of unemployment and generating some empathy for those in distress.

But it was arguably the Second World War itself that had the most transforming effect on social relations in Britain. Whether inspired by nationalism or simply through being forced to suffer the same experiences, this was undoubtedly a time of stronger collective identity and greater solidarity. And the category of 'deserving' citizens expanded rapidly, with the suffering of many (not least those returning from the Front) clearly attributable to forces beyond their control.

Once again, we see the welfare institutions of the time both reflecting, but also reinforcing, these more solidaristic relations. Indeed, during and after the war there was a genuine institutionally-driven trend away from the segregation and social distancing of those in poverty. We saw this not only in Nye Bevan's historic vision of the 'living tapestry of the mixed community', in which the doctor was to live side by side with the labourer, but also in the creation of the National Health Service, which remains a powerful force of integration today.

By the 1970s, however, it's clear that a weakening of social bonds, including a rise in individualism and geographical mobility and a decline in participation in collective institutions, provided the backdrop for a deterioration in support for key aspects of welfare.

Conclusion: the relational component to poverty prevention

So we can trace a particular causal chain, seeing how welfare outcomes are determined by welfare institutions that are shaped by public attitudes and, in turn, by the underlying quality of social relations. We have also seen hints at another link in this chain: social relations are themselves partly a by-product of welfare institutions themselves and welfare outcomes (the resulting pattern of equalities or inequalities). In Chapter 4 we will argue that the design of welfare policy is a key determinant of how people view the recipients of welfare and of the quality of social relations between recipients and everyone else. But it's worth noting here the implication of this: there is a 'feedback loop' between the way in which our institutions structure our society and the sort of institutions that our society will permit. Getting the dynamics of this right is therefore an essential aspect of anti-poverty strategy.

A broader conclusion, then, is that there has to be a 'relational' component to poverty prevention as well as simply a distributional one. Without a sensitivity to the way in which policy structures social relations, you won't successfully tackle poverty over the long term. An important question for later chapters will be how we need to reform our welfare institutions in order to get this relational component of poverty prevention right.

2. Where we are today

The previous chapter looked back across the 20th century for lessons about successful poverty prevention. This chapter looks at where we are right now, and what the current and future challenges are for tackling poverty and inequality in the 21st century.

In particular, we look at some of the economic, demographic and political pressures that our welfare institutions will face over coming decades and ask how they will need to respond. Given the importance of solidarity for sustainable welfare policy, we also look at how some of these pressures will impinge on the quality of social relations in the UK and the challenges this might present.

A progressive moment?

In September 2008, for many of our banks at least, twenty-two-and-a-half years of systemic under-regulation finally came home to roost. The response of governments worldwide – bailouts and nationalisation – gave the lie to the ideological dogma that had underpinned financial reform in the 1980s: that successful financial markets would somehow be all about the absence of government. Indeed, the response showed that we never had a government-free 'free market' at all; we were just pretending it was. Financial institutions like banks provide such core economic functions (notably the provision of credit) that they

simply could not be allowed to fail. All the time, benefi-
cent government was sitting underneath it all, ready to
step in if things went belly up. And we were only happy
to do (and allow) all of the things we have over the last
two decades because we knew it.

On a practical level, the credit crunch tipped almost every
advanced economy, like the UK, into recession, while the
necessary government responses to it have increased national debts and budget deficits. UK economic output is forecast
to drop by 3.5 per cent in 2009, with world economic output
falling too (the first in-year contraction in the post-war period). This year, public sector borrowing is projected to rise to
12 per cent of GDP, falling back to 5 per cent by 2014. And
although the UK did enter the credit crunch with substantially lower debt than a decade ago (37 per cent of GDP in
2008, compared to 43 per cent in 1997), the national debt is
projected to rise to nearly 76 per cent of GDP by 2014.

We believe, from the perspective of poverty prevention,
that there are right and wrong responses to the fiscal con-
solidation that will need to happen over the coming years.
What mixture of reduced expenditure, increased taxation
and increased borrowing should we pursue? What areas
should be prioritised for spending or taxation? Of course,
different visions of society mean balancing budgets in different ways. And, as we will argue later, we believe that
different political choices today could define the shape of
our welfare state – for good or ill – for decades to come.

It may seem as if the current crisis poses an intractable barrier to a more ambitious anti-poverty strategy. Perhaps. But a
crisis can also be an opportunity. Many on the right are
already planning to use the need for fiscal tightening to scale
back the welfare state. We would argue, by contrast, that now
is a moment for major institutional restructuring that could,
over time, put us on a path to a more equal society.

This is not to play down the real difficulties that deteriorating public finances present for social policy. But nor
should we overestimate the constraints. After all, we built

the NHS and post-war welfare state at a time when the national debt was over 200 per cent of GDP. It's amazing what's possible when the (public) will is there.

In particular, we think there are two aspects of the current climate that, far from making a collectivist leap forward more difficult, make it much more viable.

First, times of instability and recession tend to make people focus more on risks to their own security and well-being. At times like this, many middle-class households are thinking less about aspiration and more about survival. And this, in turn, tends to unite their interests and concerns with those of low-income households. The expansion of important social protections becomes not only more relevant at such moments, but also more politically viable too.

Second, we suspect one of the most important legacies of the credit crunch will be to further reinforce public beliefs about the necessary role of government in guaranteeing welfare. For the last thirty years we have been spoon-fed a litany about the failures of government and the benefits of markets. But ever since the Government had to step in to prevent the collapse of the banking system, the idea that markets can somehow guarantee welfare and security by themselves seems more far-fetched than ever. We think the recent financial crisis has been another nail in the coffin of attempts to wean the British public off the collective protections and services that they are rather attached to. And for some time to come, it will be hard for any politician to repeat with a straight face Reagan's mantra about government being the problem not the solution (though many will try).

Before the crunch: progress on child and pensioner poverty since 1997

What was happening before the credit crunch? For the first time in history, we were seeing a period of sustained Labour governance. The twelve years of opportunity for progressive social policy that we have enjoyed so far since 1997 (twice the length of Labour's previous longest spells in government) should therefore have been a real testing ground for what can be achieved. How has it turned out? In short: good, but not yet 'game changing'.

In 2007 (the last year for which figures are available) around 22 per cent of the UK population (about 13.5 million people) were living in poverty (below 60 per cent of median income, after housing costs).[10] There had been a period of substantial falls in poverty between 1997 and 2005 – down from 14 million to 12 million people – the longest continual decline since records began in 1961. Over the last three years, however, there have been increases in poverty once more.

This overall trend since 1997 masks a variety of different trends for particular groups.

Pensioner poverty has fallen very dramatically since 1997, from 29 per cent of pensioners (2.9 million) to 18 per cent (2 million) today. The key driver of this has undoubtedly been huge increases in welfare benefits for pensioners (increases in the basic state pension, the introduction of the Pension Credit, the introduction of the Winter Fuel Payment, the introduction of free TV licences for the over-75s, and so on).

As a result of these measures, pensioners are now less likely to be in poverty than non-pensioners, a remarkable reversal of the situation that has existed throughout our history, when living into old age was for most a passport to poverty. From the early 1960s to the late 1970s the risk of poverty for a pensioner was around 40 per cent, compared to around 14 per cent for the population as a whole. Today, the risk of poverty for a pensioner is 18 per cent, compared to 22 per cent for the population as a whole. Ironically, if Labour had committed to similar targets on eradicating pensioner poverty as it did for child poverty in 1999, then it would have met the first target for 2005, and be much closer to meeting its target for 2010.

One group whose plight is worth singling out is that of single female pensioners. Because of the historic unfairness in our pensions system, depriving many women of entitlement to a full state pension – they have long had a higher risk of poverty than other pensioner households, and this remains the case today. The policies mentioned above, particularly the Pension Credit, have had a huge impact for this group: poverty rates for single female pensioners *halved* from 41 per cent in 1997 to 20 per cent in 2005. But it remains the case that 1-in-4 single female pensioners (23 per cent) are in poverty today.

Having more than doubled between 1979 and 1997, *child poverty* has also fallen since 1997, though a smaller fall than that for pensioner poverty. Four million children (31 per cent) are currently in relative poverty, around half a million less than in 1997. Child poverty fell more substantially up until 2005, but has been rising again over the last three years, leaving the Government adrift of its 2005 target to cut child poverty by a quarter from 1999 levels, never mind its 2010 target to halve it.

Conservative critics, it's worth pointing out, usually draw exactly the wrong conclusion from this situation – arguing that stalled progress shows the failure of government policy levers such as tax credits. In fact, precisely the opposite is true: the years of progress, from 1999-2005, were precisely when the Government *were* investing in these policies. Progress began stalling after the 2005 election when the Government abstained from increasing tax credits markedly.

The reason financial support is so important is because, for most households around the poverty line (in the second and third income deciles), income from benefits and tax credits constitutes a sizeable amount of their overall household income. So when the level of financial support rises faster than the poverty line, then (all things being equal) households will exit from poverty; when it rises more slowly than the poverty line, households will move into poverty.

Tax credit increases announced in the last two years should once again result in substantial falls in child poverty, with several hundred thousand households expected to be lifted out of poverty over the coming years (Brewer, Browne, Joyce and Sutherland, 2009). But with much smaller increases in financial support announced in Budget 2009 than were needed to meet the 2010 target, it seems likely that the Government will fall well short of it.

Finally, we should note that single parents have a particular risk of poverty. The poverty rate among couples with children, at 23 per cent, is around that for the population as a whole. This looks small, however, behind the 50 per cent poverty rate among single-parent households. So Britain's single-parent households have a 1-in-2 chance of being in poverty.

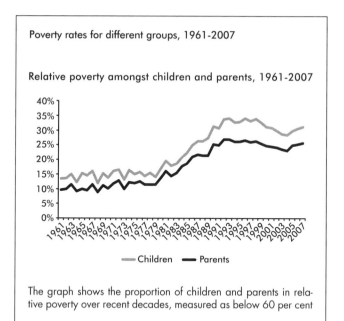

Poverty rates for different groups, 1961-2007

Relative poverty amongst children and parents, 1961-2007

— Children — Parents

The graph shows the proportion of children and parents in relative poverty over recent decades, measured as below 60 per cent of median income, after housing costs. As might be expected, poverty rates for both groups tend to move in parallel. After relative stability up until 1979, there is a huge increase throughout the 1980s and early 1990s. Since 1998, poverty rates declined up until 2005, though in recent years have been rising again. Data: Institute for Fiscal Studies.

Relative poverty amongst pensioners, 1961-2007

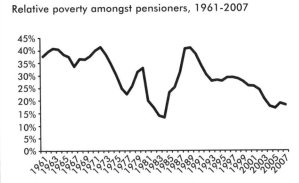

The graph shows the proportion of pensioners in relative poverty over recent decades, measured as below 60 per cent of median income, after housing costs. The huge volatility that can be seen from the mid-1970s to the mid-1990s reflects economic turbulence. Pensioner poverty tends to fall in recessions as incomes amongst the working-age population stagnate or fall, whilst pensioner incomes are maintained; conversely, pensioner poverty has tended to increase during times of economic growth. Behind this volatility is a fall in pensioner poverty from around 35-40 per cent in the 1960s down to 25-20 per cent in the mid-1990s. This was almost certainly driven by the growth of private and occupational pension provision for increasing numbers of pensioners over this period, with this effect outweighing that of the declining value of the basic state pension relative to average earnings. What is extraordinary is the subsequent fall in pensioner poverty since 1998, during a time of strong economic growth, in part driven by large increases in benefits available to pensioners. Data: Institute for Fiscal Studies.

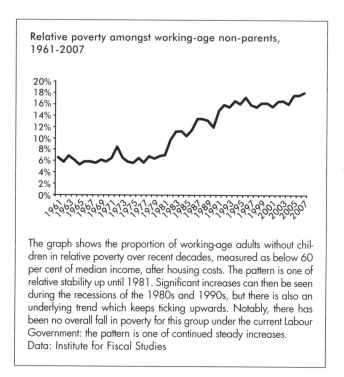

Relative poverty amongst working-age non-parents, 1961-2007

The graph shows the proportion of working-age adults without children in relative poverty over recent decades, measured as below 60 per cent of median income, after housing costs. The pattern is one of relative stability up until 1981. Significant increases can then be seen during the recessions of the 1980s and 1990s, but there is also an underlying trend which keeps ticking upwards. Notably, there has been no overall fall in poverty for this group under the current Labour Government: the pattern is one of continued steady increases.
Data: Institute for Fiscal Studies

Some current poverty challenges

The unspoken subject: poverty amongst working-age adults

While pensioner households and households with children have seen a fall in poverty rates over the last decade, the plight of working-age adults without children has been rather different. Poverty amongst this group has *risen* from 3.5 million to 4.2 million since 1997 (enjoying no fall in Labour's early years), and is now at its highest since records began in 1961 (Brewer et al., 2009). In particular, 1-in-4 single working-age adults without children are now in poverty – a higher risk than for couples with children or even single female pensioners.

Changes in the number of people in relative poverty for different groups over the last decade

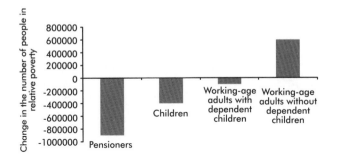

The graph shows the change in numbers below 60 per cent of median income, after housing costs, between 1995-7 and 2005-7. Data from The Poverty Site (www.poverty.org.uk)

In many ways, despite the faltering progress, tackling child and pensioner poverty is *politically* quite easy. Both groups are seen as relatively 'deserving' of help and spending on these groups tends to rank relatively high in terms of public support. Many can easily imagine the ways in which children and pensioners in poverty aren't fully responsible for their situation, or at least deserve to be supported.

By contrast, talking about adult poverty is difficult. In the media and in our popular stereotypes – just like a century ago – working-age adults in poverty, particularly workless adults, are the 'undeserving poor'. Their poverty is seen as their own fault.

Of course, in the real world, it's virtually impossible to separate poverty among working-age adults from child or pensioner poverty. Because poverty is a household phenomenon, tackling child poverty is really about tackling parental poverty.[12] And pensioner poverty in future will be determined in part by saving behaviour today; yet the biggest reason people cite for not saving is not having enough income to save.[12] Nevertheless, both the Government and campaigners have clearly found it more viable to focus attention on children and pensioners. Not that there aren't compelling reasons of fairness and justice to tackle child and pensioner poverty, of course. But this has meant that adult poverty has been the unspoken subject of the last decade (let alone in the years before that).[13]

Ever since the Thatcher Government broke the earnings link for social security benefits in 1981 (and linked them simply to prices), the value of such benefits has declined relative to average incomes (and in some cases also relative to certain measures of prices).[14] While the decline in value of the basic state pension has probably received most political attention, this has to some extent been offset since 1998 by increases in other pensioner benefits (including a more generous (means tested) minimum income guarantee for pensioners, most recently in the form of Pension Credit). But for many years now, often under the radar, the value of the key income-replacement benefits – Jobseeker's Allowance, Incapacity Benefit and Income Support – has been slipping further and further behind average incomes (and therefore further and further behind the poverty line). Because benefit income constitutes a significant proportion of household income for poorer households, the falling value of such benefits relative to average incomes has been a central driver in the rise in poverty amongst working-age adults without children (Brewer et al., 2009).

The result today is an appallingly low level of out-of-work benefits – just £64 a week, or £90-95 if you are unable to work through illness or disability. As well as being far, far below the poverty line (even with Housing Benefit and Council Tax Benefit on top), according to recent assessments of minimum income standards (Bradshaw, 2008) these amounts are also totally inadequate to get what most people regard as basic necessities. As the charts below show, for working-age households without children – the UK has some of the lowest levels of income-replacement benefits in the OECD.[15]

Financial position of a single person on unemployment benefit as % of the average wage for a selection of OECD countries

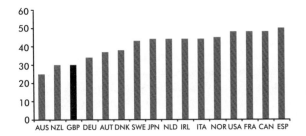

Data from OECD (2007)

Financial position of a couple with two children as % of the average wage, where the first spouse is on unemployment benefit and the second spouse is employed full-time at 67% of the average wage

Data from OECD (2007)

It's hardly a surprise, then, that the risk of poverty for those receiving out-of-work benefits is huge. A massive 73 per cent of households where an adult receives Jobseeker's Allowance are in poverty; 65 per cent of households where an adult receives Income Support are in poverty (DWP, 2009).

While no charity will ever raise much funding with a photo of an adult in poverty, talking about adult poverty is now as important as ever.

Social housing and life chances

During the last five years there has been a growing body of evidence that confirms what many have long suspected: that living in social housing can be not just a symptom of poverty, but part of the causal story as well. A large part of this is due to the high unemployment levels associated with social housing. In a landmark review, John Hills found that, "even controlling for a wide range of personal characteristics, the likelihood of someone in social housing being employed appears significantly lower than those in other tenures"(Hills, 2007). Even more interesting is the result of a robust longitudinal study that found that whilst those born into social housing in 1970 suffered from a range of subsequent disadvantages closely correlated with the tenure, for those born into social housing in 1946 there was no such effect (Feinstein et al., 2008).

It is important to stress that, although the statistical analysis upon which this is based cannot itself yield any hard causal conclusions, by factoring in a wide range of variables and controls, the analysis does rule out the most seemingly obvious explanation of the poverty-housing correlation: that the poverty simply reflects the fact that social housing is allocated to those on low incomes. In other words, it is not just that the most disadvantaged are filtered into social housing, there is also something about the tenure that then maintains their disadvantage.

On the flip side, of course, this analysis shows there is nothing *intrinsic* about social housing that causes this disadvantage: the 1946 cohort suffered no such disadvantage from it. Rather, it is the way in which social housing provision came to be structured during the following decades.

A key process at work here has been the growing 'resid-ualisation' of social housing: the process in which an ever diminishing stock of housing has to be targeted ever more narrowly on those with low incomes, thus increasingly concentrating poverty in the tenure. Today, a fifth of all households are in the social rented sector, a significant fall since the late 1970s when over two-fifths were (Hills, 2007). And whilst in 1979 over 40 per cent of social hous-ing tenants were in the top half of the income distribution, this figure has now halved (Hills, 2004a).

This residualisation has combined with a second type of 'concentrating process': historically, much social hous-ing has typically been physically and spatially concentrat-ed. The overall result has not just been the concentration of poverty in a particular tenure, but in particular areas and neighbourhoods as well. Analysis of the characteris-tics of electoral wards has found a close correlation between area poverty and concentrated social housing: two-thirds of electoral wards with over 60 per cent social housing are 'poverty wards' (Lupton and Power, 2002).

There are some very tangible explanations as to why spatial segregation makes for poverty – above and beyond the increased targeting on those at the bottom of the income spectrum. Often social housing estates are very poorly connected to both labour markets and serv-ices, and typically households will have to pay a premi-um for many commercial goods and services, often because of a lack of competition in areas with a poor supply of shops (National Consumer Council, 2004). Stigma also plays a part, with postcode discrimination in the job market (Fletcher et al., 2008). But there are also more complex social and cultural explanations for entrenched poverty. As one might imagine, the role of expectations is important: living in an area where very few people work can 'normalise' worklessness, and without people working there are fewer potential links to labour markets and word-of-mouth opportunities.

There is in fact evidence to back this up. A study of Swedish social housing found that, even controlling for a range of other factors, the concentration of poverty is strongly correlated with further disadvantage: living in such areas makes it far harder to then *exit* poverty (Musterd and Anderson, 2006). The study found the following correlation between area and unemployment: the risk that a person unemployed in 1991 would still be unemployed in 1995 and 1999 is only 16 per cent if that person lives in an environment with 0-2 per cent unemployment, whereas this doubles to 32 per cent if he or she lives in an environment with 14-16 per cent unemployment. The concentration of poverty is not just a symptom and collective aggregation of individual circumstance; it is part of the causal process too.

Two sets of facts illustrate the impact that all of this can have on individual lives, not just in terms of unemployment, but more broadly. Firstly, a variety of research has found demonstrable 'tenure effects'. For example, those now living in social housing are more likely to suffer from mental health problems than those in other tenures (Singleton et al., 2000). Other evidence suggests that those living in social housing at the age of 30 (once again, controlling for the fact that the disadvantaged are filtered into the tenure) are eleven times more likely than those in other tenures to be not in employment, training or education; and nine times more likely to live in a workless household (Feinstein et al., 2008). Secondly, there is similar evidence for 'area effects'. For example, electoral wards with concentrated unemployment are more likely to be populated by people that go on to suffer chronic mental health problems after a physical illness, and they are less likely to recover from these mental health problems in a reasonable time (Fone et al., 2007).

All this amounts to a serious indictment of social housing in the UK as it is currently organised. It is of course not to say that social housing is intrinsically bad, or that we should do away with it. On the contrary, our analysis will lead in the opposite direction: the poverty of social housing is closely associated with its concentration and residualisation. The correct response, as we shall discuss later, is to supply more of it, and to thoroughly mix it in with other tenures in order to break self-perpetuating concentrations of poverty.

The looming welfare crisis? Public attitudes to the welfare state

It appears the UK welfare state is fast approaching a crisis of legitimacy. The last two decades have been characterised by declining support for 'redistribution' in general, and for specific aspects of welfare in particular. The graphs below illustrate this with respect to two questions from the British Social Attitudes Survey, showing changes in support for redistribution 'from the better off to those who are less well off' and changes in support for spending more on 'welfare benefits for the poor', respectively. The drop-off in support in each case is marked: in 2007 (the most recent data available), for example, just 32 per cent agreed that 'Government should redistribute income from the better-off to those who are less well off', down from 51 per cent in 1985.

Trend in support for redistribution of income to the 'less well off' (calculated from the British Social Attitudes Survey)

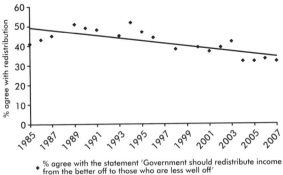

♦ % agree with the statement 'Government should redistribute income from the better off to those who are less well off'

Data from NatCen's British Social Attitudes Survey.

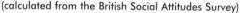

Trend in support for government spending more on welfare benefits 'for the poor'
(calculated from the British Social Attitudes Survey)

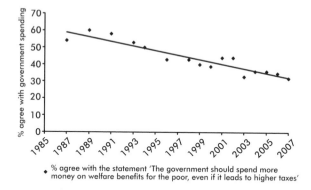

♦ % agree with the statement 'The government should spend more money on welfare benefits for the poor, even if it leads to higher taxes'

Data from NatCen's British Social Attitudes Survey.

These trends are evident when people are asked about specific types of provision too. Sefton (2009) notes that the numbers agreeing it should 'definitely' be government's responsibility to provide 'a decent standard of living for the unemployed' has – rather ominously – fallen from 42 per cent in 1985 to 10 per cent in 2006.

And we shouldn't comfort ourselves that such attitudes will necessarily soften in a recession. While recessions can increase support for social protections (because people are feeling more insecure) and increase sympathy for the unemployed (because people can more clearly see the structural causes of unemployment), the squeeze that recessions place on family finances can also make people more 'hard-nosed' in how they approach tax and spending.

Surveys also suggest that, since the mid-1990s, public attitudes have been hardening towards those in poverty or those receiving out-of-work benefits (Taylor-Gooby and Martin, 2008). One question from the British Social

Attitudes Survey asks people about what causes poverty. In recent years – for the first time – the numbers saying poverty is due to laziness have overtaken the numbers saying poverty is due to injustice.

As we saw in Chapter 1, the constraints such attitudes place on our ability to entrench a long-term poverty prevention settlement are huge. And unless policymakers can find ways to challenge or overcome such attitudes, the underlying trends augur very badly for tackling poverty in the years to come.

Three challenges for the future of poverty prevention

Increasing life expectancy and demographic change

It was growth in life expectancy that was originally one of the major drivers behind the creation of modern welfare states, particularly social security systems. More and more people were living beyond an age when they could work and needed support.

Over the coming years and decades, population ageing and demographic change will be a major driver of welfare expansion once again. If past trends continue, the UK's population will reach some 67 million by 2020, driven by both increasing life expectancy (which is going up by two years every decade) and also net inward migration.[16] With the share of older people rising gradually, the 'age structure' of the population will change considerably.

Already – for the first time ever – there are more people over the age of 65 than there are under the age of 18. Over the next 10 years, the number of those aged over 65 will increase by over 30 per cent (to 12.7 million) and the number aged over 85 by 50 per cent (to 1.9 million).

There will be several consequences to this. First, the growing size of the old age population will mean a growth in demand for existing benefits and services, particularly health and care services, housing and pensions, as well as the development of new areas of service provision, from telecare services to training programmes for those working past retirement age.[17]

Second, this service expansion will be expensive and require a higher proportion of national income spent on such benefits and services. Indeed, the Treasury estimates that simply to 'stand still' in terms of service provision with our growing and ageing population will require spending on health, long-term care, education and pensions alone increasing by 3.3 per cent of GDP over the coming twenty years (though this would still leave overall spending well below that of many EU countries today) (HM Treasury, 2008). The alternative would be to require individuals to finance more of their needs privately, which would produce serious inequities, including (in all likelihood) increasing poverty. Assuming this is not to be met from borrowing, this will require a larger tax take – and public acceptance of a larger tax take.

Finally, even with increased inward migration (which tends to lower the average age of the population), an ageing population will increase the *old-age dependency ratio* – the ratio of pensioners to working-age people. Today, for every person in retirement there are four people of working age. In 50 years time, there will be just two (DWP, 2006). To some extent this can – and will – be offset by longer working lives and a later state pension age. But there will also be an increased burden on those of working age to finance welfare for older generations.

This, it should be noted, is simply an extension of how the welfare state already works. The first graph below (from Sefton, 2002) illustrates the value of services received per head at different ages. In terms of the direct value of services to individuals, we benefit significantly from the welfare state in childhood (because of education), less so in working age, but then hugely in older age (particularly through health and care). The second graph (figures from Rachel Smithies, personal communication) illustrates the *net* pattern of contribution and receipt throughout life – that is, when tax is taken into account. The pattern is one of being net recipients in childhood and old age and net contributors during working age.

Average annual value of services received per person in 2001 (for health, education, housing and personal social services)

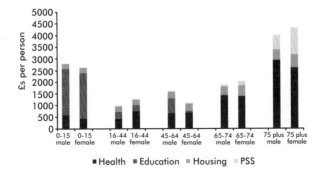

The chart above shows the average annual value (£) of services received per person in 2001, by age and sex, in the areas of health, education, housing and personal social services (PSS). From Sefton (2002)

Pattern of net receipt from, or contribution to, the welfare state by age cohort (2001)

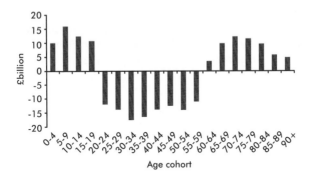

The chart above shows the net amount received from (bars above the x-axis) or contributed to (bars below the x-axis) the welfare state by different age cohorts in 2001 in the areas of health, education and social security, on the one hand, and taxation on the other. (Note that these are figures for the whole cohort, rather than per capita, and the cohorts are of different sizes.) The basic pattern is one of being a net beneficiary in childhood and retirement, and of being a net contributor during working age. (Smithies, personal communication, 2009)

So tax-funded welfare redistributes money across people's lives, from working age to childhood and old age. One estimate (Hills, 2004) suggests that as much as 75 per cent of the redistribution that the welfare state does is effectively 'life-cycle redistribution' (shifting resources across an individual's life span) and only 25 per cent is 'vertical redistribution' (moving resources from richer individuals to poorer individuals).

But in reality the welfare state is more than a piggy bank. Its pay-as-you-go nature means that working-age generations will always be funding the welfare of younger and older generations, linking individuals together in contributor-recipient relationships (explored further in Chapter 7).

Future demographic change will intensify this pattern. This will not only require that those of working age will need to pay more in tax. In order for them to be happy to do so, there will also need to be strong *intergenerational solidarity*, so that individuals are happy with the idea that they are paying tax today to support other generations. And there will need to be a robust expectation by those of working age that they will receive similarly decent provision when they are older (financed by younger generations of working-age people). So taxpayers will need to perceive the existence of a secure 'welfare contract' across the life-course.

Increasing returns to skills and the changing labour market

Global economic competition means competitiveness will increasingly lie in comparative specialisation and high-value-added production. These trends have already meant increasing economic returns to skills over recent decades, a trend that will continue over coming decades. On the flip side, the doubling of the global labour force as a result of the integration of China and India into the world economy will create downward pressure on both the employment and earnings of less skilled workers.

These pressures, moreover, are being exerted in an area – the UK skills base – where we have historically struggled. Though there has been real improvement in educational attainment over the last decade, the UK has a legacy of low adult skills, and compares badly with some of its international competitors in intermediate skills: 35 per cent of UK adults have low skills, compared to just 13 per cent in the US and 17 per cent in Germany; and only 37 per cent of UK adults have intermediate skills compared to 49 per cent in the US and 59 per cent in Germany.[18] It is therefore no surprise that the UK currently has a long 'tail' of low qualified workers (Leitch, 2005).

Technological progress is also driving changes in the labour market – though not quite in the way people imagined 30 years ago. Technology (such as computers) doesn't necessarily replace low-skilled jobs, but routine jobs (Autor et al., 2003). And many of these *routine* jobs are (or were) to be found not at the bottom of the employment distribution (where jobs often require non-routine manual skills, for example, cleaning), but in the *middle* (such as clerical work or certain skilled manual tasks). The result has been a growing 'hour-glass' shape in the employment distribution, nicknamed the 'disappearing middle', with growing numbers of high-skill and low-skill jobs ('MacJobs and McJobs' – see Goos and Manning, 2003), but dwindling numbers of intermediate ones.[19] And this process of *job polarisation* has significant consequences for poverty and inequality.

Many of these low-skill jobs are also low-paid, so job polarisation risks significant and growing earnings inequality. A 'hollowing out' of the middle also reduces opportunities for many on low pay to progress to better jobs and higher wages.

So with high employment and decent wages crucial for poverty prevention, skills must be a key focus over the coming decade – the area where social justice and economic competitiveness collide. The last decade has seen real progress through a range of new free entitlements to training, including employer-led training. But it's clear that the welfare state of the future will need to go much further in both directly supporting adult skills and also encouraging work-based training.

However, there's a hard truth to be faced here. While the Government is absolutely right to focus on improving the supply of skills (for social as well as economic reasons), there is no guarantee that this *by itself* will be sufficient to create the better-skilled jobs we need. Indeed, recent increases in the supply of skills have not been matched by more skilled jobs: there are currently many more jobs requiring no qualification than there are workers with no qualification. This could partly be because of a mismatch between the qualifications gained and the actual skills required in the workplace (meaning demand-led approaches to skills and well-designed qualifications are key). But it is probably also a result of wider factors such as firms getting locked-into particular production strategies or a lack of pressure on firms to innovate. If so, simply improving the supply of skills is not enough: we will need a more proactive industrial strategy to help firms compete by making better use of their employees' skills and by shifting to higher-value production strategies.

Ultimately, however, no-one knows how the employment and earnings distributions are going to evolve in future. The real fear is that, for some sectors, it might actually be economically sustainable to pursue low-skill and low-value-added production strategies. Let's hope not. But there is no guarantee that 10, 20 or 50 years from now, we will not still have a minority of the population reliant on low-paid jobs. And while we can and must place upward pressure on wages through the minimum wage – getting employers to tackle poverty through becoming more productive – there may well be limits to the extent to which this can offset inequalities in the future earnings distribution.

Many will find the implications of this difficult. It may well be the case in future that, for some, wages alone cannot be expected to provide a route out of poverty. That would not necessarily stop there being important value in work, nor remove the requirement for all who can to work. But it would mean that income from work would need to be supplemented by further income from the state – much as happens at the moment with the Working Tax Credit.

We believe there is much that government can do to ensure that wages do provide a route out of poverty, particularly through a more proactive industrial strategy and maintaining a generous minimum wage. But nor do we find the concept of in-work financial support objectionable, as some on the right do.

Part of their objection comes from an ideologised distinction between being 'independent' through work and being 'dependent' on the state. But this distinction holds neither in practice nor in theory. The phenomenon of in-work poverty has always existed – something neither the Poor Law nor Beveridge could get to grips with – and those on the right have often had very little to say about it. And the independence–dependence distinction itself reflects a kind of naïve libertarianism that does not stand up to scrutiny. While part of your salary from work may reflect your own efforts and talents, part of it will reflect value of public goods that make your employment possible: from roads, to a system of public law, to an educated population. The fact that this value is being extracted via an income stream from your employer doesn't necessarily make you 'independent' from the state.

Of course, real independence is the independence to do things. And by ensuring people have better incomes, in-work support substantially increases independence. Indeed, later on we argue that the scheme of in-work support should be widened to embrace more citizens.[20]

47

Increasing diversity and mobility and the strains these place on solidarity

A third challenge for the future of poverty prevention will be the increasing diversity and mobility that will characterise society over coming decades. Economic restructuring has created greater labour mobility both within and between countries. Domestic labour mobility has already led in some parts of the UK to more 'transient' communities, with people feeling less rooted and knowing fewer of their neighbours (Dorling et al., 2008).

But it is immigration that has been the most politically salient aspect of this phenomenon. While the UK has a long history of inward and outward migration, we only became a country of net immigration (that is, with the inflow exceeding the outflow) in the mid-1980s. Since then, net inflows have risen to around 200,000 people a year. The foreign-born population in the UK rose from 2.1 million (or 4.2 per cent of the population) in 1951 to 4.9 million (or 8.3 per cent of the population) in 2001 (Rendall and Salt, 2005). And even though migration rates fluctuate upwards and downwards, this aspect of our demographic evolution looks set to continue.

Why should this be a challenge for the welfare state? After all, immigration brings immense benefits to both our economy and society. Many immigrants bring with them valuable skills our economy needs. Employment rates for many migrant groups are high (in 2006, for example, the employment rate was 85 per cent among Polish migrants, 84 per cent among Filipino migrants and 80 per cent among Ghanaian migrants – compared to 78 per cent for the UK-born population) (Sriskandarajah et al., 2007). And the migrant population also tends to reduce the UK's overall 'economic dependency ratio' (the number of those not in work supported by those in work).

However, immigration also presents challenges for the welfare state, some practical, some political. On a practical note, population growth of any kind has to be managed in the right way. Without appropriate planning, high levels of immigration may put pressure on public services in particular areas of the country. And there may be certain migrant groups which require particular help and support. The Somali migrant community, for example, are clearly struggling in terms of education, employment and housing outcomes (Sriskandarajah et al., 2007).

However, much greater are the political challenges that immigration brings to the welfare state. As the graph below shows, even though the recent recession has begun to eclipse other issues, immigration has been rising steadily up the political barometer over the last decade – perhaps culminating in the Conservatives' unsavoury *'Are you thinking what we're thinking?'* 2005 election campaign.

Views of 'most important issue' facing country 1995-2009 (% selecting issue for 'What would you say is the most important issue facing Britain today?')

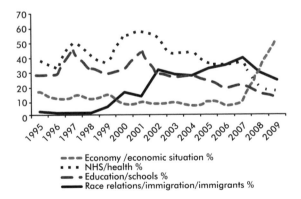

Data from MORI.

Some have speculated that increasing diversity necessarily weakens the social relations and solidarity that underpin the welfare state. In his famous 2004 essay *Discomfort of Strangers*, David Goodhart argued that, "the left's love affair with diversity may come at the expense of the values and even the people that it once championed".[21] In fact, we will argue later that immigration needn't mean declining public support for welfare, provided the right institutional conditions are in place. But clearly there are situations where diversity can place strains on solidarity.

A more fluid citizenry also raises the question of our obligations to one another, putting pressure on the need for a welfare contract that is perceived to be fair. Again, a failure to ensure that all who benefit from public services – including those recently arrived in the UK – are contributing back to society (where they can), and are seen to be doing so, could risk eroding public support for collectively-provided welfare. This dilemma – of how to reconcile need with entitlement in an age of international mobility – is one of the key challenges facing the 21st century welfare state.

Conclusion: overcoming political constraints

One might be forgiven for thinking the material reviewed in this chapter makes for pretty grim reading. Good but incremental progress in reducing child and pensioner poverty seems to be getting harder (and clearly vulnerable to reversals). Demographic change and the evolution of the labour market could (and almost certainly will) create more demand for state welfare, which will be expensive. Furthermore, both increasing life expectancy and increasing mobility (including immigration) will potentially put more pressure on the welfare 'contract' and the solidaristic relations that should underpin collective provision. Declining support for redistribution and declining sympathy for those in poverty seem to be reaching crisis proportions. And this all comes at a moment when the state of the public finances seems to preclude any more ambition in poverty prevention.

In fact, none of these things presents an insurmountable problem. It only looks like they do within the confines of our current welfare institutions. Certainly, the issues listed above all present political pressures. But the problem is that the structure of our welfare institutions means that all these pressures currently work *against* the objective of tackling poverty.

It is, however, within our grasp to reshape our institutions in such a way as to make these pressures work *for* us – and towards a more equal society. Imagine if the way to help taxpayers squeezed by the recession was the same way to help those struggling on a low income. Or if youngsters entering the job market felt that fears about future residential care were actually about them.

In the rest of this book we explore how you might go about trying to achieve this. What emerges are proposals that don't look very much like tackling poverty (and certainly not like the most efficient way of tackling poverty in year 1). But, over time, they would transform the way in which the attitudes and institutional constraints Labour has struggled with over the last decade impinge on the strategy of equality, turning them from obstacles into resources.

But, while they would be of long-term strategic importance, such changes are also urgent. As the analysis above shows, from inadequate benefit-uprating conventions to geographically segregated council housing, too often the problems we face in poverty prevention lie in the underlying structure of our welfare institutions. Too often we seem to have to fight against the dynamics they set up.

Ultimately, it should be clear that we can't keep going forever on a strategy of doing good when the marginal pound allows. Labour has in fact done much better than many people think over the last 12 years at reducing poverty and keeping inequality in check because they've been doing it within the institutional structures that Margaret Thatcher bequeathed. They've been running up the down escalator.

It's now time to get off the escalator.

3. Two dilemmas of welfare

The previous chapter highlighted some instances where our major welfare institutions seem not only to be ineffective at preventing poverty, but too often seem to be reproducing and entrenching it.

What is it that makes institutions effective or ineffective at tackling poverty and inequality? And what accounts for whether they remain effective or ineffective in the long run? In this chapter, we look back at welfare history since the Second World War for some lessons about how to design institutions for effective poverty prevention. In particular, we explore two classic 'dilemmas' of welfare through some case studies: the dilemma of targeting versus universalism, and the dilemma of need versus entitlement. Both are aspects of institutional design with profound consequences for anti-poverty strategy.

Dilemmas of universalism and targeting

As discussed in Chapter 1, precisely *who* welfare policy is supposed to apply to very much depends on your underlying philosophy. Is welfare provision a necessary evil, a temporary phenomenon for those in need, or is it a positive mode of social provision and interaction, which, far from undermining citizenship status, also helps to create it?

Regardless of where you stand on this question, it is nevertheless possible to scrutinise the practical consequences of different choices about institutional coverage for the effectiveness and sustainability of policy. Below we compare two examples which provide an important contrast.

A tale of two services: social housing and the NHS

Invited to choose a single institution that embodies the values of a universal welfare state, the chances are that the great majority of people would turn immediately to the National Health Service. Instantly popular from its inception in 1945, its approval ratings have rarely fallen below 80 per cent (Lowe, 1999).

In a sense there should be no surprise here, at least not when we consider the context in which the NHS was created. Prior to the war, health coverage had been incomplete and uneven. Non-working wives (and children) were typically not covered at all, and thus had no access to a GP, and very often hospital treatment was either not provided for or strictly means tested. So it is small wonder that the NHS proved immediately popular. It met a real and desperate need, and almost instantly emancipated huge numbers of people from the kind of pain and incapacity that required the simplest of treatments. In the first weeks of service queues for dentures and spectacles could stretch for miles.

But, in fact, it was not this desperate sense of need that secured the future of the NHS. Certainly it was not desperation that embedded its enduring popular and political legitimacy. There was also a growing desire amongst the middle classes for a new form of provision, driven in no small part by concern at the rising premiums of private health insurance. Thus, from the very beginning, a large swathe of the British population saw the NHS as being for 'them' – not for 'the poor', or some other group. And so the NHS was protected by the interests (and electoral preferences) of the middle classes. And it was this group that proved a key source of its resilience through the subsequent decades.

Perhaps the best illustration of this resilience in practice is the way in which the values of the NHS survived the twin onslaught of the 1979 to 1997 Conservative administration. First starved of cash in the 1980s, the NHS was then vulnerable to a perverse logic that stipulated that the subsequent decline in standards was proof of its own inherent failings. It was in this context that, in the early 1990s, the principle that treatment should be free at the point of need was placed under sustained pressure by a Government hell-bent on introducing market reforms. The fierce resistance, and ultimate failure, that this met is testament to the fact that the vast majority of the population had a vested interest in maintaining the NHS and its values.

Although Tony Blair had reservations about whether or not people would accept a rise in taxation to increase spending on the NHS (Hyman, 2005), he turned out to be unusually out of touch on this issue: the 2002 Budget, which increased National Insurance Contributions by one per cent to pay for this, was the most popular budget since the 1970s – dwarfing the popularity of the famous tax-cutting budgets of the 1980s.[22] The NHS thus provides a very important demonstration of how universal services – through popular legitimacy – are resilient to political and economic pressure.

Indeed, such is the strength of the NHS that we tend not to think of it as a 'welfare' institution at all. Often it is simply taken for granted as part of the very fabric of our society. In more conscious moments it is viewed by many as a simple right of citizenship. Though there are groups who access the health service less than they should, none of this is because of a negative image of the organisation's clientele, and there is certainly no sense of stigma attached to using it. Indeed, the very fact that the NHS is a universal service means that questions about entitlement and the 'deservingness' of recipients are quickly 'closed down' (Larsen, 2008).

In this sense, the NHS provides an excellent example of what Bo Rothstein (1998) identifies as the ability of welfare institutions to create and sustain 'narratives' about a country's history and values, which persist in collective memory – sustaining popular support for, or opposition to, an institution – and which profoundly influence subsequent *social norms* towards a particular type of provision. For many Brits today, healthcare just *is* something that should be provided to all free at the point of need.

Social housing: a case study in residualisation

The history of housing policy in Britain offers a perfect illustration of the difficulties we face when confronted by the need to target (relatively) scarce resources. Not only can the excessive targeting of a service like social housing undermine support for the institution itself, but historically it has also been done in a way that has undermined its effectiveness in poverty prevention.

In fact, the starting points for the post-war histories of the health service and social housing are both ones based on a profoundly universalistic ideal. For housing, this was best encapsulated in Nye Bevan's promise of the 'living tapestry of the mixed community', in which the doctor, grocer and labourer were to live side by side, with no status difference signified by quality or type of housing.

But the subsequent trajectories of these services could not have been more different. Whereas the NHS is embedded in a collective sense of what it means to be British, 'council housing' has in many people's minds become a byword for exclusion and even an ascription of social and individual failure. And whereas the NHS remains a universal service, social housing came to be ever more steeply targeted; ever more narrowly a good only for the 'needy'.

As we saw in Chapter 2 the perverse outcome of targeting is that it has helped to entrench poverty and disadvantage. So as a policy lever aimed at poverty reduction it has failed in its intended purpose.

This of course is not to say that there should not be targeting in social housing; on the contrary, it always was – and always will be – a rationed good. In the original ideal of mixed communities, there was never any suggestion of the universal provision of social housing. The point, rather, was that those who needed state assistance would not be systematically and visibly separated from those who did not. Council housing was not be to be a mark of inferior status, and the homes themselves were to be of the highest quality (as, indeed, they often were). Indeed, it is these two principles of quality and integration that have been systematically dishonoured over the last sixty years. For 'council housing' has come, in the popular imagination at least, to be closely associated with mono-tenure high-rise estates of poor design quality.

What happened? The central process in this historical trajectory has been what is often described as the 'residualisation' of social housing – which has been both an economic and a spatial phenomenon.[23] The more tightly rationed social housing has become, the more it has come to be identified only with the neediest in our society. The association is then firmly cemented by the concentration of a significant proportion of social housing in huge estates. Cut off from the rest of society and the opportunities that it brings, these clearly identifiable concentrations of poverty have often been an instant recipe for stigma and exclusion. Post-war sociological naivety was little excuse for this, as the large-scale council estates of the inter-war years had come in for precisely the same kind of criticism as today.

There were perhaps two key causes of residualisation that we can single out. The first is the 'rush to volume' that the huge post-war demand for housing led to, with larger subsidies for high-rises and a belief in the great utility and social vision of 'system build'. The result was the huge concrete jungles that so are now so engrained in the popular imagination as a symbol of social decay and decline.

The second cause was deeper and based upon shifting attitudes (first amongst political elites, and then the wider public) about the virtues of public and private housing. The defining feature of this process was the Conservative vision of a 'property owning democracy', held by the Conservative Party right from the start of the Beveridge settlement all the way to this vision's fruition in the 1980 Right-to-Buy legislation and beyond. The impact of this programme has been well-documented: not only did it lead to the loss of the best council stock – without allowing councils to keep sales receipts in order to replenish it – but it was also predicated on a very specific view of citizenship. 'Freedom from the state' through ownership was not just an opportunity but also a moral duty – the virtue of 'the good citizen', in contrast to 'the dependent and feckless poor'.

Moreover, the loss of housing stock was compounded by an earlier development. In 1977, Local Authority housing departments became obligated, by statute, to house the homeless. Clearly, this was a means of addressing the neglected rights of the homeless, who prior to this were ostensibly under the care of local social services departments. But without a simultaneous rise in the supply of social housing, what happened in practice was that a rationing system was created, in which the most needy and vulnerable households went to the top of the waiting list. Thus, not only was there less social housing to meet the needs of the population, but what remained was ever more narrowly targeted at households at the bottom of the income spectrum.

Despite the Conservatives being the driving force behind the ideology of a property-owning democracy, Labour had also been increasingly complicit in an elite consensus that endorsed the logic behind this. A key turning point in Labour's thinking about the role of social housing had occurred as early as 1965, when Richard Crossman's housing White Paper stated that, "The expansion of the public programme now proposed is to meet exceptional needs...the expansion of building for owner-occupation on the other hand is normal; it reflects a long-term social advance that should gradually pervade every region".[24] Bevan's vision of a living tapestry – a progressive universalism in housing provision – had given way to the logic of targeting.

There are various lessons that we should take from this brief history of social housing. The first is that extreme or ineffective targeting can 'devalue' the good that it seeks to distribute efficiently and fairly; the very process of distribution ensures that, often, the good itself changes in nature and is no longer a 'good' at all. We see this very clearly in the worst examples of social housing: not only are these highly unpopular and often 'hard to let'; there are also more objective grounds for thinking of these homes as part of the problem of social disadvantage rather than, as they are intended to be, a central part of a solution.

A related lesson is that residualisation can undermine the effectiveness of institutions for poverty prevention. The isolation of much social housing from labour markets and services (both public and private) is a major contributory factor in individual household poverty, and the same concentration of social housing that makes it so easy to stigmatise can also act as a deeper barrier to opportunity and social mobility.

A third lesson is that highly targeted services directed only at the poorest risk fostering feelings of resentment

towards recipients. Clumsy targeting makes for social separation and distance (beyond the very physical separation
in the case of some social housing). The result is a sense of
'them' and 'us' that is deeply corrosive of the ideal of
equality of citizenship and status. In the case of social
housing, we can see that this separation sets up a circular
process: targeting leads to negative perceptions of recipients, which weakens public support for the institution of
social housing, which leads to greater targeting, and so on.

Had housing policy after the Second World War
remained true to Bevan's original vision and followed the
universalist ethos of the NHS more closely, it may have
been possible to prevent this vicious circle from developing in the form that it did. But then we should not under-
estimate the extent to which the NHS ran against the grain
of the inherited history of welfare in Britain.

Dilemmas of need and entitlement

Many aspects of the welfare system have the delicate task
of balancing criteria of entitlement with the function of
responding to need. Sometimes eligibility for policy is
defined precisely in order to match a particular social
need. In other situations, however, eligibility might be
linked to behaviour or to a variety of external criteria,
whether to incentivise action on the part of the recipient or
to satisfy public perceptions of fairness.

Below we look for lessons in perhaps the most obvious
arena in which these tensions have been played out in the
post-war welfare state: social security.

The re-emergence of social assistance: the legacy of Beveridge's model

Few policymakers have thought about the perceived public legitimacy of their proposals to quite the same extent as
Beveridge did in formulating his plans for social security.

Indeed, the primary motivation behind a scheme of social insurance was Beveridge's belief that it would be this model that would prove most palatable to the public. In particular, his model was one where there was a very clear link between putting into the system and taking out: by linking welfare and work, it enshrined a sense of reciprocity.[25]

But various features of Beveridge's insurance proved to be serious structural flaws (Glennerster, 2004). Some of these created injustices in their own right. Others proved strategically fatal for fostering a sustainable and popular system. Below we look at each of these problems in turn.

A particular injustice was that the notion of contribution was restricted to that of paid employment. Those who were unable to contribute in this way were not fully included. Disabled people, for example, had to rely on the means-tested system of National Assistance, a particular disgrace. Similarly, many women and carers were, at a stroke, relegated to the status of second-class citizens, eligible for support, not by virtue of their caring activities, but only as dependents of their husbands.

The result was an institutional segregation of people depending on their work status, profoundly undermining equal citizenship. When they needed support, the insured received welfare on the basis of their contribution to society; another group (the disabled, lone parents, etc.) had to receive welfare on the basis of their need; yet another – married carers – had to receive welfare via their 'dependency' on their partners.

Later, there were attempts to correct this treatment of carers. In 1976 the Invalid Care Allowance (now Carer's Allowance) was introduced, followed by Home Responsibilities Protection in 1978. These measures meant that caring full-time for a child or disabled person was taken into account in calculating pension entitlement. Yet the fact remains that Beveridge's model created serious gender inequality from the very start: today, only 30 per cent of women reaching the age of retirement are entitled to a full state pension, compared to 85 per cent of men (and only 23 per cent of women are entitled to a full state pension *on the basis of their own activities*) (DWP, 2005).

Other features of Beveridge's model resulted in inadequacy in the level of support provided, 'locking in' the system's future decline from the beginning. This partly arose from the structure Beveridge chose for financing the scheme (and which he persisted with, even in the absence of an adequate contribution from the Treasury). National Insurance was based on quite a rigid 'classical' conception of social insurance; Beveridge originally envisaged a tight link between the amounts paid in and the benefit levels paid out.[26] In this context, a particularly unfortunate decision was the decision to structure the scheme on *flat-rate contributions* (with everyone having to pay in the same amount regardless of income). This meant that the resulting benefit levels were therefore tied to what the poorest could afford to contribute in the first place. The upshot was that the level of benefits available was too low to meet living costs (particularly when housing costs were taken into account).

As a consequence of this, many of those within the National Insurance system also had to rely on National Assistance to 'top up' their awards. For example, when the pension was introduced, over 600,000 people over 60 had to supplement it with National Assistance (Thane, 2006). Beveridge had originally hoped that his reforms would see means-tested social assistance becoming a smaller and smaller part of the welfare state. In fact, it became a growing part of welfare.[27]

Occasional attempts were made to try to increase National Insurance in order to 'float' people off means-tested National Assistance, such as in the mid-1960s. However, the fact that the population were already divided between two different benefits proved detrimental to subsequent attempts to rebalance the system (Glennerster,

2004): increases in National Insurance needed to be balanced with corresponding increases in National Assistance to stop those without National Insurance (often the poorest) falling further behind.

So increasing numbers of people grew increasingly reliant on a need-based benefit for their social security. And as unemployment grew in the 1970s, so did the numbers on social assistance. By 1974, the number of unemployed with insurance also having to claim National Assistance – by then called 'Supplementary Allowance' for those under state pension age – stood at 73,000, up from 19,000 in 1948. And they were joined by increasing numbers of unemployed without any insurance, some 228,000 in 1974 (up from 34,000 in 1948) (Lowe, 1999).

It was perhaps no accident, then, that the mid-1970s was also the height of 'scroungerphobia' hysteria in the media. Some of this was due to rising unemployment itself, with growing public suspicion about the causes of unemployment and an increasing tendency to blame the individual. But it is important to recognise that such questions only become pertinent when coupled with an underlying sense of unease about the fairness of the benefits regime that supports the unemployed.

Supplementary allowances seemed particularly vulnerable here. In their seminal study of the media portrayal of poverty (*Images of Welfare*, 1982), Peter Golding and Sue Middleton found that "the fraud theme was present in 53.2 per cent of supplementary allowance stories. No other category of benefit attracted similar association with fraud". Similarly, a 1978 research report into attitudes to supplementary benefits (Schlackman, 1978) found that "It was the almost universally declared belief of informants of all types that those who were in least need would be the most likely to claim, and the most successful in obtaining Supplementary Benefit; while those who were in most need, and most deserved to receive help, would be the most reticent in claiming, and the least likely to receive help. This belief is the lynch-pin of attitudes towards the Supplementary Benefits scheme."

Tabloids seized upon the sense that the system was not reciprocal, and made the unjustified leap from the general unease that this engendered to specific instances of actual benefit fraud. Headlines – which today would not seem the least surprising – included 'Get the Scroungers' (*Daily Express*, 15 July 1976). But the outrage that continued to grow was a more general resentment of the unemployed themselves, with the anger directed no longer at just the fraudulent, but at all of those considered to be a drain on public resources – all of those perceived not to be contributing. This is perhaps the greatest danger for a system that separates entitlement from the logic of contribution. The result is that claimants are perceived as 'takers' and not 'contributors'.

Ironically, then, the rather rigid constraints Beveridge had placed on the operation of the contributory system in order to satisfy public perceptions of fairness led to the system evolving in a way that eventually put the very idea of a fair contract under strain. Quite arbitrary structural features of Beveridge's original scheme resulted in a large and growing group reliant on social assistance. Not only did this prove ineffective from the perspective of poverty prevention; it proved fatal for fostering a more benign notion of welfare linked to participation in society.

The decline of the contributory system: the effect of the Thatcher Governments

The re-emergence of means tested social assistance as a central plank of the welfare state not only continued on into the 1980s, but was greatly accentuated. Reducing welfare expenditure was a major objective of the new Thatcher Government, and over the 1980s and 1990s this led to an increasing reliance on Supplementary Benefit (later renamed 'Income Support').

In particular, the abandonment of a commitment to full employment and a deep recession in the early 1980s resulted in a dramatic increase in the number of workless households – and with it a dramatic increase in welfare spending. Out-of-work benefits therefore became a major focus for budget savings (something that reinforced another objective of the Thatcher Government: to improve work incentives). Hence a variety of cuts in unemployment benefit, including breaking the earnings link in 1981, and multiple restrictions on eligibility for it.

But as well as budgetary savings, there was a crucial change in the *nature* of out-of-work benefits, with a major shift away from contributory benefits and towards income-based ones. The earnings-related supplement to contributory unemployment and sickness benefits was removed, and the value of contributory benefits was subsequently equalised with that of their income-based equivalents. In the 1990s, this downgrading of the contributory system went further, with a limitation in duration of these contributory benefits to six months (before people were transferred onto the income-based versions). The result was a profound change in the relationship between taxpayers and benefit recipients, from one of reciprocity and risk pooling, to one of providing transfers to others on the basis of need.

It also meant that welfare went from being about 'all of us' to being about 'other people'. The great thing about an insurance system framed in terms of risk is that the major life risks apply to all of us – they're universal. Though at any one time 'the unemployed' will only constitute a small proportion of the population, the possibility of being unemployed applies to everyone. So this downgrading of the contributory system also changed the conception of welfare from being something that insured everyone across their life-cycle to being something that helped a particular 'need-group'. Culturally, we went from paying into a system and rightfully claiming benefits if we were unlucky enough to suffer from a particular contingency, to large-scale moral panic about a mass of workless people who we had to constrain and cajole, and whose claim on the welfare state seemed much less legitimate.

There was more than one driver of this downgrading of the contributory system (Hills, 2004b). One was external: a large rise in the numbers of workless with insufficient con-tributions records to be entitled to contributory benefits. And those in this position clearly had to be supported. (Indeed, this phenomenon meant many of the left were not especially attached to the contributory system either.) But we'll argue later that an income-based benefit was not the only possible response to this situation. Rather than breaking any link between putting in and taking out, and transferring support onto a need-based footing, an alter-native would have been to shift entitlement criteria away from a simple link to past contribution records.

But another important force behind the downgrading of the contributory system was simply a desire to cut spending and 'target' resources as effectively as possible on the neediest. Non-means-tested benefits, earnings-related supplements and wide entitlement clearly did not sit well with this retrenchment agenda. The shift from a concept of insurance to one of means testing and targeting was a direct result of a desire to bear down on welfare expenditure.

This went hand in hand with a more profound agenda: a new type of thinking about welfare and poverty. As dis-cussed in Chapter 1, a desire on the political right to limit welfare spending springs from a belief that receiving col-lectively-provided welfare is an undesirable state of affairs (and certainly not a legitimate aspect of citizenship). Reflecting this, the 1980s saw a real shift in the culture of welfare, one that began to separate it from citizenship once again. Charles Murray, the American sociologist, visited Britain and asserted that, just as in the US, there were two 'types' of poverty: actual material hardship caused directly by lack of income, and the self-induced poverty that was driven by individual failings.

A related phenomenon was the resurgence of the notion of an 'underclass' – which of course has a long history in Britain, stretching back through Charles Booth's language of the 'residuum' ('a submerged tenth') to the very origins of the Poor Law in the sixteenth century. But its reappearance in the early 1980s was particularly strong; and it was at this time that 'welfare' came to take on the very negative connotations that it had in the US, where it has always been contrasted with the respectable, contributory 'social security'. Combined with the language of welfare 'dependency', this created the toxic conditions in which the ideal of the welfare state was to come under constant attack for nearly two decades, and was to emerge on the other side with different political expectations of what the state could and should be expected to achieve.

From 'contribution' to conditionality

The system that emerged out of this shift from contributory to need-based welfare therefore placed the burden of enforcing any kind of 'contract' on the moment of claiming welfare itself. And the consequence of this has been a growing framework of 'behavioural conditionality', with far more emphasis on individual behaviour while out of work, and with more and more conditions attached to receiving welfare.

As Clasen and Clegg (2007) observe, the UK has not been alone in an increasing focus on behavioural conditionality; many other OECD countries, such as Denmark and Germany, have introduced reforms along these lines. And from the perspective of labour market policy, this is perfectly legitimate. Conditionality is one element of a set of 'activation' policies (along with training, advice, etc.) which evidence suggests can be very effective in helping people move into work. In particular, appropriate conditionality can help claimants themselves by ensuring they maintain contact with the labour market and take up opportunities available to them, thereby improving their future life prospects.

What is more of a problem, however, is when conditionality becomes the sole vehicle for maintaining public perceptions of fairness. The types of conditionality that emerge from this situation can be wholly detrimental to the well-being of claimants. An example would be the type of 'workfare' schemes that have emerged in the US since the late 1980s, where claimants are forced to work in return, not for a wage, but for benefit payment, and are typically given no additional assistance with work-search or work-preparation in order to help them find other opportunities (as shown in the table below).

But just as conditionality for the wrong reasons can be damaging, so can the absence of conditionality for the right reasons. If appropriate conditionality and support can be beneficial for those at risk of becoming detached from the world of work or who would not otherwise take up opportunities that would be in their long-term interests, then a failure to provide such a framework can be just as irresponsible. This is essentially what happened to many elderly unemployed in the 1980s, who were intentionally placed on Invalidity Benefit (thereby reducing the unemployment figures) and told they should not expect to work again – one of the most socially irresponsible aspects of how economic restructuring was managed at the time.

This specific case of neglect is part of a more general issue. A commitment to fair reciprocity in welfare thus involves more than the desire to ensure that all who can should contribute to society; government must also step up to its responsibilities to help them do so. Far too rarely in welfare reform debates do we seriously interrogate what the Government's side of the bargain should be in welfare conditionality – and not only at the moment of claiming (in terms of providing advice, training, support with childcare, etc.), but also in terms of providing individuals with a decent set of opportunities in the first place (from education to local economic regeneration).

Ultimately, getting conditionality right means that we must recognise – both institutionally and morally – that a welfare contract is a two-way process. And if conditionality is really there to help claimants rather than simply to assuage public anxiety, then we must look to other aspects of policy design to address public concerns about fairness.

Table: Different possible policy mixes for labour market policy		
	Support	*No support*
Conditionality	Classical active labour market policy	Classical workfare
No conditionality	Appropriate mix for those on whom there should be no requirement to work or to prepare for work	What happened to Invalidity Benefit claimants in the 1980s

The 1948 National Assistance Act opened with the words, "The existing poor law shall cease to have effect". And it was certainly Beveridge's great hope that the prominent role in the British welfare system of a stigmatised and residualist model of social assistance would become a thing of the past. It is perhaps ironic, therefore, that relatively arbitrary choices Beveridge made about the structure of his National Insurance scheme were to prevent it ever fully superseding provision through social assistance. Indeed, among welfare historians, some of Beveridge's firmer critics have even argued that his long-run contribution to British welfare history was to essentially preserve the prominence of social assistance in our welfare mix.

However, there is a more specific irony here. For it was some of the rigid constraints that Beveridge imposed *precisely in order to satisfy what he perceived to be popular attitudes to fairness* (an employment-centred conception of 'contribution', subsistence benefits, flat-rate contributions, and so on) that led to the subsequent structural problems which, in turn, rendered the system incapable of forming the basis of something the public would perceive as a fair welfare contract.[28]

To summarise, the problem with Beveridge's original scheme was that in trying to create the link between welfare and contribution too strictly, the system became sufficiently exclusionary as to lose its purchase in many debates about welfare and fairness over the subsequent decades. And the notion that inadequate insurance payments could be topped up painlessly with means-tested social assistance hugely undermined the potential moral legitimacy a contributory system might have had. The result was a precarious situation that left National Insurance highly vulnerable to retrenchment under an incoming Thatcher Government. The reforms of the 1980s were to shift the culture of welfare further away from an inclusive system based on participation and equal citizenship and back towards a residual system targeting need. The legacy has been that the lever of conditionality has not only been used for 'activation' strategies, but has had to bear the brunt of responsibility for policing public perceptions of fairness – a dangerous state of affairs.

Conclusion: the importance of institutional design

By tracing through some key moments in recent welfare history, this chapter has explored two fundamental 'dilemmas' in social policy: the tensions between targeting and universalism, and the tensions between need and entitlement.

The deep lesson that emerges is that the underlying design of welfare institutions is of paramount importance for poverty prevention. Tackling poverty isn't a simple issue of channelling as many resources as you can to the most disadvantaged, but depends very much on *who is included* within a policy and *how they are characterised* by it. And when policy is designed in the wrong way, the results can be disastrous.

In particular, we have seen how residualised systems, which target only the poorest, can often end up being part of the problem, rather than part of the solution – a point the Webbs understood so well. Excessive targeting can seriously undermine the effectiveness of measures to tackle poverty and inequality, creating stigma and exclusion, while also leaving the service in question bereft of the widespread political support that is needed to maintain and improve quality over the long run. That is why we had a successful campaign for a penny on National Insurance for the NHS, but never will for social housing – as it is currently organised, at least.

We have also seen how important it is to create welfare institutions where the public feel that the contract underpinning them is fair. Despite Beveridge's efforts, a failure to get this right within social security led to the resurgence of a reliance on social assistance and a culture of welfare marked by stigma and suspicion. And, as we see in current debates over the fairness of need-based allocation in social housing, there are many other areas of public policy that are testament to this fact.

Much here depends on whether policies are perceived to give support to people purely on the basis of their need – in effect, for being perceived to fall short of being a full member of society – or rather on the basis of their participation – that is, as fully signed up members of society. The lesson is that, while effective poverty prevention must of course respond to need, if the institution in question makes neediness the primary characterisation of recipients then the resulting welfare contract can soon come under strain. The holy grail for progressive welfare policy is therefore a system that bases awards on participation, but does so in a way that can encompass the vast majority of those who need support.

In the next chapter, we analyse the processes underlying these tensions between targeting and universalism and between need and entitlement. There, we elucidate a model of the dynamic interactions between welfare institutions and the social context in which they operate, one that helps to explain the logic behind the historical episodes described in this chapter and the different evolutionary paths that different institutions take.

Chapter 1 suggested there was not only a distributional dimension of poverty prevention, but also a 'relational' one, which relies on strong social relations between those in poverty (or at risk of poverty) and the rest of society. To anticipate our conclusion in the following chapter, targeting and universalism, on the one hand, and need and entitlement, on the other, are both welfare dilemmas because they are aspects of institutional design where these distributional and relational dimensions can work *against* one another.

4. The dynamics of poverty prevention

The previous chapters have highlighted the crucial role of welfare institutions in explaining poverty outcomes, and also the importance of getting the design of these institutions right for effective poverty prevention. In particular, Chapter 3 explored two 'dilemmas' of institutional design, tensions between universalism and targeting, and tensions between need and entitlement, in order to look for some general lessons here.

In this chapter, we investigate in detail how welfare institutions interact with public attitudes and underlying social relations, and investigate how the different possible structures of welfare programmes can set up different social dynamics. The analysis also makes clear how these dynamics, over long timescales, can exert a significant influence on how welfare institutions evolve.

Two vignettes

In his seminal 1949 Cambridge lecture 'Citizenship and Social Class' – delivered shortly after the abolition of the Poor Law and the creation of the NHS – the great sociologist T.H. Marshall declared that the 20th century 'war' between citizenship and 'the capitalist class system' was being won decisively by citizenship; for citizenship had now 'invaded' the sphere of contracts and had 'subordinated' market prices to broader social aims and individual rights.[29] In Marshall's historical account of the evolution of citizenship, the *social* rights of the welfare state were finally joining civil and political rights in the lexicon of modern citizenship.

Marshall was, in effect, retrospectively 'theorising' the impulses behind the creation of the post-war universal welfare state, called for by the Webbs in 1909 and finally delivered through the Beveridge report in 1942. But his analysis of its emergence was distinctively teleological in flavour, even deterministic: social rights were "the latest phase of an evolution of citizenship which has been in some continuous progress for some two hundred and fifty years" (1950). This inevitable march of progress was arriving at its logical endpoint of comprehensive welfare. A consensus had formed around the idea that the state should provide extensive social protections to its citizens.[30]

Just 30 years later, Margaret Thatcher was elected and began rolling back the post-war welfare state. Entitlements were diluted, protections were cut, and – far from being seen as a higher state of citizenship – receipt of welfare, and the 'dependency' that resulted, were seen as the hallmark of failure.

The welfare retrenchment of the 1980s was in fact seen by many economic commentators as the first instalment in another phase of the evolution of welfare states: that of globalisation.

The so-called 'third wave' of globalisation (the first two were in the industrial revolution and mid-twentieth century) began properly in the 1980s, marked by increasing trade flows, the entrance of developing countries into global markets, rapid developments in information and communications technology and transport, increasing industrial specialisation and accelerating migration. In this context, 'globalisation' was invoked by many commentators as a kind of 'bogeyman' for welfare spending within advanced industrial economies, coming to crash the welfare party.

These economic forces, we were told, would inevitably lead to pressures on welfare spending: international economic competition and the possibilities of mobility and 'capital flight' would force states to reduce their social expenditures and the taxation that made them possible (for example, Pfaller et al., 1991). Indeed, some right-wing commentators actively welcomed this anticipated reduction in the 'social-policy sovereignty' of national governments (for example, Ohmae, 1996).

Looking back, three decades into this latest wave of globalisation, what has happened? Most OECD countries have actually *increased* their overall welfare spending as a proportion of national income (and nearly all of the others have at least maintained their spending levels) (OECD, 2007).[31] Certainly, there have been significant cutbacks in many countries within particular types of welfare programmes, notably unemployment and sickness benefits. But not in overall welfare spending, which is what the 'globalisation' thesis predicts. As one recent review of contemporary welfare states put it, "We can only conclude that the 'race to the bottom' is a crisis myth rather than a crisis reality." (Castles, 2004).

Why didn't most governments reduce their welfare spending (and why did many increase it) in the face of the economic pressures of globalisation, then? Recent studies suggest that an important part of the answer is quite straightforward: because their citizens didn't want them to.[32] Similarly, as we saw in Chapter 1, Margaret Thatcher was able to dismantle key planks of Marshall's 'historically-inevitable' social rights simply because these particular areas (like unemployment benefits) had lost their base of popular support.

These two tales – the tale of the inevitable evolution of welfare rights, on the one hand, and the tale of inevitable welfare retrenchment, on the other – provide a salutary reminder of the importance of public opinion in explaining the evolution and sustainability of welfare states. The fatal flaw in these and other deterministic accounts of welfare state development lies in their failure to take into account the fundamental role of public attitudes in shaping policy output – and the ability of attitudes to change (in the first tale) or to persist (in the second).

In the next section we will go on to look at this further, but first it is worth stressing the basic implication of the tales above: nothing is inevitable. *We can choose our welfare future*. We are not simply buffeted around by economic winds, nor do we stand helpless in the face of 'one-way' evolutionary social forces. The issue of how we go about choosing the right way is the subject of this chapter – and, indeed, the remainder of this book.

The importance of public attitudes for poverty prevention

It seems a bland truism to say that public opinion exerts strong pressure over the development of social policy in democracies. Elections provide a regularly occurring opportunity for voters to influence the shape of policy by determining the composition of governments.[33] If a government does something you don't like, you can kick them out and replace them with a government who will undo it. Ask Kim Campbell, the Canadian Prime Minister whose party was reduced from 151 seats to just 2 in the 1993 election.[34]

But public opinion also exerts a much more subtle influence over policymaking. Politicians have a strong incentive to accommodate and respond to the policy preferences of voters in order to reduce the risk of future electoral defeat or of public protests or disobedience. And this phenomenon, which academics call *policy responsiveness*, is the key to explaining how public attitudes shape welfare states: not an expression of opinion at election times, but a continuous invisible constraint on policymaking, exerting pressures one way or the other. It is why, for example, the Conservatives' ditched their most electorally successful leader in 1990, and replaced the poll tax with council tax.

And, sure enough, many studies find a substantial and patterned variation in public attitudes towards welfare across different countries, with support for welfare spending higher in higher-spending 'social-democratic' and 'Christian-democratic' welfare states than in lower-spending liberal-democratic regimes (Svallfors, 1997).[35]

Brooks and Manza (2007) in fact demonstrate a strong relationship between the policy preferences of national publics in one year and the size of welfare spending *in subsequent years*. And the magnitude of this apparent effect of preferences on welfare spending is substantial when compared with that of other factors that are known to influence the shape of welfare states (such as the extent of women's labour force participation or 'left party control').

Using a statistical model, the authors also show that differences in attitudes between countries are important in accounting for the differences in welfare spending between countries. For example, they estimate that one third of the overall difference in spending between social-democratic regimes (like Sweden) and liberal regimes (like the US) is accounted for by differences in attitudes. And they suggest public attitudes account for nearly *two-thirds* of the difference in spending between Christian-democratic regimes (like Germany) and liberal regimes (like the US).

As a thought experiment, Brooks and Manza use sophisticated modelling to explore what would happen to a country's welfare state if you magically gave its population the policy preferences of another country's population (while holding all other factors constant). For example, if, during the 1990s, Norwegians had miraculously developed the policy preferences of Americans, the result would have been a dramatic decline in welfare spending in Norway from 25 per cent of GDP to just 18 per cent of GDP – in other words, major retrenchment. Conversely, if Americans had developed Norwegian policy preferences the result would have been an increase in US welfare spending from 15 per cent to 21 per cent of GDP – which would have had a huge influence on poverty levels within the US. As the authors conclude, "Future efforts to alter policy preferences among citizens could, if successful, readily induce a shift in overall welfare output within democracies" (2007).

So in order to understand differences between welfare states, we must understand the role of public attitudes in shaping social policy. This has always been the 'achilles heel' of economically-oriented theories of welfare state development – as many historical accounts have been. For example, the 'logic of industrialisation' thesis (Wilensky, 1975) explains the emergence and development of welfare states as an inevitable by-product of industrialisation and the increased life expectancy that rising prosperity brought in its wake. Alternatively, neo-Marxist accounts (such as O'Connor, 1973) view welfare states as responses to inevitable crises or class struggles generated by the evolution of capitalism.

Such theories, of course, contain many important insights about welfare state emergence and development. But, by themselves, it should be clear that they are severely inadequate. In particular, they are unable to account for the remarkable *cross-national variation* in the long-term development of welfare states (even though these different nations are subject to many of the same economic and social forces). The basic point is that factors such as the level of economic development within countries, the age structure of the population or levels of 'class conflict' cannot, by themselves, account for cross-national differences in social policy development and welfare state output (see Orloff, 1993, for a review).

The same holds when considering different welfare institutions within a single country. If economic forces such as recessions and oil shocks have such causative power, why is it that the NHS survived them all? Or, more specifically, why has the NHS survived the eight economic cycles since the Second World War, whereas a commitment to full employment only survived five of them? (A more pertinent question might be why the NHS has survived the 15 or so *electoral* cycles since the Second World War, whereas a commitment to full employment only survived eight of them.)

Of course, public attitudes are not fixed or immutable, but susceptible to considerable influence. So holding them up as an explanatory variable really begs another question: where do attitudes come from in the first place? We look at this further in the following section.

Before proceeding, however, there is one further result about the relationship between public attitudes and welfare state output that is worth noting. Brooks and Manza's study also shows that mass preferences have a significant impact on policymaking *independently of the partisan control of government*. In other words, public opinion will constrain governments from doing certain things and force them to do other things regardless of whether parties of the left or right are in power. That is why, for example, Margaret Thatcher found it impossible to scrap the NHS and why Labour found it impossible not to scrap the fuel duty escalator. While a good deal of the effect of mass preferences is mediated by elections, much of it is ethereal, an invisible hand that guides and constrains policymaking across the political cycle.

This is something to remember for those who invest hope in a simple notion of 'political leadership': yes, leadership is necessary, but over the long term public preferences will probably determine the shape of your welfare state independently of who gets elected. That does not absolve politicians from responsibility for their decisions: public attitudes are never an excuse for making the wrong decision (as Labour did on inheritance tax in 2007). And politicians can and should be ahead of public opinion with policy reform. But the point is that if you don't shift attitudes as well, then often it turns out that you might as well not have bothered (witness the fate of Bill Clinton's progressive reforms). Real leadership isn't doing what you think is right regardless of public opinion; it is doing what is you think is right *and taking the public with you*.

The crucial role of institutions

Granted, then, that public attitudes matter in shaping social policy. But what factors shape public attitudes? Many different underlying perceptions, beliefs and sentiments shape attitudes to welfare, ranging from self interest to principled judgements about fairness and desirability to a range of more practical issues such as the perceived necessity of a policy, perceived affordability, perceived effectiveness, trust in government, and so on. And, in turn, multiple factors (economic, social, cultural, personal) weigh on these kinds of perceptions and judgements.

But as we suggested in Chapter 1, a crucial factor in understanding where welfare attitudes come from is the *social context* in which they are formed, especially the perceived identities of individuals and groups within society (whether common or different) and the quality of social relations between them. Chapter 1 also hinted at a deep relationship here, by observing some of the ways in which *welfare institutions themselves* can be responsible for shaping the social context in which policy is evaluated – for example, by both reflecting and reinforcing the prevailing climate of social relations at any one time.

In what follows, it will be our contention that the design of our welfare institutions is a key part of the social context in which attitudes are formed – and therefore a key determinant of such attitudes. Specifically, the current design of welfare institutions within a society will structure the contexts in which people make subsequent judgements about welfare policy. Institutions can align or de-align the interests of particular groups in society, they can impose particular social identities on individuals and groups, they can mould the social relationships between individuals and groups, and they can help to generate social norms about fairness. Through these dynamics, they play a significant part in constructing and sustaining the very attitudes which, in turn, sustain them.

The next section goes on to explore these issues in detail by looking at a model of the dynamics of welfare policy. In the final section of the chapter, we then ask what the significance of this is for understanding how to entrench an anti-poverty settlement for the long term.

The dynamics of poverty prevention: a causal model

1) A naïve view of poverty prevention

While there are a variety of types of policy that welfare institutions can employ to tackle poverty and inequality – regulating markets, providing information and advice, and so on – in this context it is primarily their role in allocating resources (benefits and services) that concerns us, that is, their distributive (or *re*distributive) role.

The most efficient way of allocating resources to tackle poverty would be to target them efficiently and unconditionally on the basis of need (see the figure below). And, historically, some policies (such as means tested social assistance) have sought to do just this.[36]

Figure: A simple approach to anti-poverty policy. The grey arrow emanating from the 'welfare institutions' box represents the allocation of resources to individuals in a society, with an effect on the social positions they occupy (in this case, channelling resources to the poorest). By 'social positions', we mean the relative positions individuals occupy in some spectrum of outcomes – in this case, in the distribution of household incomes.

However, there are good reasons to think (and real historical examples which suggest) that, for many types of need, such an arrangement would not endure. Even though there may be certain types of need, for example, disability-related needs, for which such an arrangement might indeed command popular support, in most instances, such a policy is likely to be highly unpopular (as the history of social assistance shows). And, as we've seen, public attitudes would constrain the future course of policy: its unpopularity would result in much lower investment than necessary.

2) Bringing public attitudes in

When we take into account this role of public attitudes in sustaining or undermining social policy, then, the dynamics look more like that in the figure below.

The result is a 'feedback loop', with policy affecting public attitudes, which in turn determine the political viability, and influence the evolution, of the policy itself.

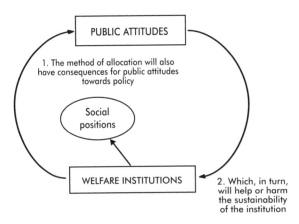

Figure: As well as affecting individuals' social positions, the welfare allocation represented by the grey arrow also has an effect on public attitudes (represented by the larger black arrow emanating from 'welfare institutions' and leading to 'public attitudes'. Clearly, the salient attitudes here concern both perceptions of the underlying fairness of the policy and perceptions of the beneficiaries of the policy. Public attitudes, in turn, will shape social policy output through the responsiveness of politicians and governments to public attitudes (represented by the corresponding black arrow emanating from 'public attitudes' and leading to 'welfare institutions').

3) How do institutions influence public attitudes to welfare?

There are several ways in which the design of policy can interact with public attitudes:

- *self-interest*, namely, people considering how they would fare under the policy in question, and judging it accordingly;

- *direct fairness judgements about the structure of the policy*: all other things being equal, people will presumably be less supportive of a policy whose underlying principles they regard as unfair; and

- *indirect perceptions of fairness,* mediated by how social policy influences the social identities of individuals and the social relations between individuals. As we will see shortly, these factors can exert a sizeable influence on judgements about the fairness of policy.

It will be our contention that all three of these issues are strong drivers of support for, or opposition to, welfare policy – and, crucially, of people's willingness to contribute to that policy through taxation. For each, we will see that welfare institutions have the potential to shape attitudes profoundly because they structure the context in which citizens evaluate policy.

In what follows, we investigate these issues through the lens of two important properties of the way in which welfare institutions allocate resources:

- the **coverage** of a policy – that is, the extent of the group that receives something from the policy (usually determined by criteria of eligibility); and

- the **distributive principle** by which resources are allocated – that is, the factors that 'justify' receipt of an award. This can refer to factors that determine eligibility for an award, or factors that determine the size of award, or both. These factors could include: whether and how an award is sensitive to need; whether it is conditional or unconditional; whether and how an award might be determined on the basis of previous behaviour or on the basis of some external criterion (such as identity and citizenship); and so on.

The reason why we have divided up the allocation process in terms of these two properties is because they correspond to the two distinct dimensions along which welfare institutions structure social relations: determining group membership (in the case of coverage) and the nature of the interrelationships between individuals (in the case of the distributive principle).

For each property we shall explore the three linkages between social policy design and public opinion set out above. In particular, we'll look at why attempts to redistribute, if structured in the wrong way, can often fall foul of the electorate.

3a) Coverage

Self interest

The relationship between coverage and self-interest is relatively straightforward: those who do not benefit as recipients of a policy will support it less than those who do.[37] Consequently, policymakers have the opportunity, through choosing the coverage of policy, to align or counterpose the interests of key electoral groups. Thus, policies that are targeted only at the poorest will fail to secure the self-interested support of key middle-class constituencies; they will rely instead on fairness motivations to achieve majority public support. Of course, many targeted policies of this type *do* enjoy widespread public backing for just such reasons (such as support for disability benefits). But it could be argued that, by missing out on self-interested sources of support, such policies will be much more vulnerable to partisan criticism and retrenchment than those with wider coverage. And, sure enough, it is often just such targeted policies (like social assistance) that have suffered historically from failing to achieve sufficient generosity or to keep pace with rising living standards.

In particular, while narrowly targeted policies will fail to draw on the strength of middle-class political pressure to defend welfare, policies with wider coverage actively recruit 'the sharp elbows of the middle class' to protect the provision the poorest rely on. When Margaret Thatcher froze child benefit in 1987, the ensuing disquiet ensured it was unfrozen again by 1990. The declining value of income support since the 1980s has met with no such clamour, however.[38] The *Daily Mail's* recent attack on the Conservatives' proposal to take upper-middle-class households out of tax credits ('Tory Tax War on Middle Classes', *Daily Mail*, 27/07/09) shows this dynamic is still very much alive and kicking.

There are many examples in history of important welfare policies failing to garner middle-class buy-in, and suffering as a result. More pernicious than the missed opportunities, however, are policies that actively *counterpose* the interests of the middle class against those in poverty. Here, majoritarian sentiment actually becomes a driver of retrenchment. For example, the use of tax reliefs to channel support to middle-income households, and the subsequent pressure for more generous reliefs, can put tax revenues under strain, with knock-on consequences for welfare spending. Such policies *increase* the vulnerability of low-income households and create socioeconomic cleavages, generating conflict and damaging underlying social relations.

This situation is illustrated in the figure below.

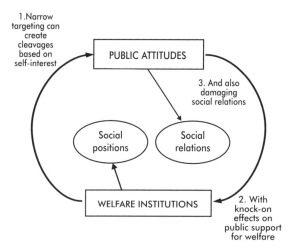

Figure: This figure illustrates the way in which a policy such as narrow targeting can not only affect public attitudes, in turn undermining support for welfare, but, through its effect on public attitudes, can generate social cleavages (the grey arrow emanating from 'public attitudes' and leading to 'social relations').

Direct perceptions of fairness

The coverage of welfare policy can also be influential in determining perceptions of how fair the underlying structure of the
policy is. It could legitimately be argued, given the existence of
unmet needs across a large proportion of the population, that
while the needs of some may well be greater than others – and
therefore resources will be more heavily directed towards
those with the greatest needs – it is simply unfair to allocate
resources in a way such that many of those with smaller unmet
needs nevertheless receive *no* award.[39] Correspondingly, whatever threshold is drawn may itself seem morally arbitrary – the
fact that someone with £(n) of household income is entitled to
help, but someone with £(n+1) is not.

Social identity

Beyond these basic points, however, there is a deeper way
in which the coverage of a welfare policy may affect perceptions of fairness: by structuring the social relations
between different groups in society.

Targeting resources divides the population into distinct
groups of recipients and non-recipients. This is a process
that can lead to the categorisation of people (into one group
or the other), imposing a particular *social identity* upon
them. If salient, these different social identities can create
social distance between individuals. This, in turn, under-
mines the social relations between citizens, potentially
weakening feelings of interdependence and solidarity.[40]

In particular, we know that categorising people into
groups with a salient social identity tends to stimulate a
desire to perceive a sense of positive group distinctiveness,
where the 'ingroup' is favoured over the 'outgroup'. This
leads people to look for dimensions on which their own
group is perceived to be superior to the outgroup – and to
place greater emphasis on these dimensions. The result is
negative evaluations of those in outgroups, at its worst lead-

ing to stigmatisation (Tajfel and Turner, 1986). We have seen this time and again throughout welfare history, with narrow targeting leading to the 'othering' of welfare recipients, resulting in judgemental attitudes towards them.

Stigmatisation is not only objectionable for its detrimental effect on an individual's confidence and self-esteem (Lister, 2004); it has practical consequences too, of great significance for poverty prevention. Stigmatisation influences social behaviours in ways that can directly affect policy effectiveness; for example, resulting in low take-up of benefits or lack of compliance with policy on the part of the stigmatised.

But it is in its effect on social relations, and the resulting negative attitudes towards welfare recipients, that stigma exerts its most pernicious effect. In the immediate term, this could be manifest directly in discrimination and excluding behaviours towards the stigmatised (such as discrimination in job applications) (Heatherton et al., 2000). And over the longer term, the weakening of social relations and increased social distance between recipients and non-recipients can result in reduced public willingness to redistribute to the disadvantaged group (and to contribute through taxation to the policy in question).

At its most extreme, sharp group divisions can generate 'moral exclusion' for outgroups, where people simply do not see the disadvantaged as part of their 'community of responsibility' (Optow, 1990; Montada and Schneider, 1989). More generally, the social distance created by institutional cleavages can itself affect individuals' evaluations of fairness in welfare, including their willingness to redistribute (Brewer and Kramer, 1986). For example, social distance may reduce perceptions of the 'deservingness' of welfare recipients, thereby reducing support for welfare policies targeted on them (van Oorschot, 2000).

The figure below illustrates this situation, where attitudes to welfare policy are mediated by the perceived social identity of the beneficiaries of policy.

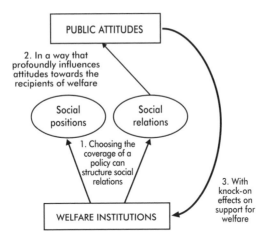

Figure: This figure shows how the distributional aspect of a policy (the grey arrow emanating from 'welfare institutions' and leading to 'social positions') can also have consequences for the social relationships between individuals (the grey arrow emanating from 'welfare institutions' and leading to 'social relations'), for example, creating social distance between recipients and non-recipients. This social distance, in turn, affects public attitudes to the disadvantaged group (the grey arrow emanating from 'social relations' and leading to 'public attitudes'), which, in turn, can undermine support for welfare policy (the big black arrow emanating from 'public attitudes' and leading to 'welfare institutions').

It's an important claim here that the way in which policy divides up a population can actually *constitute and shape* the social relationships between individuals. Of course, pre-existing social cleavages (defined by class, geographical and other boundaries) can give rise to policy structures that are aligned with these cleavages. But here we're claiming that the causality works the other way around too: that choices about coverage actually *create* groups within society with their own social identity.

By contrast, policies with universal coverage, by integrating everyone into the same system, automatically define recipients of welfare as part of the same group as everyone else, thereby reducing social distance, and potentially enhancing willingness to redistribute. No-one suffers stigma for using universal institutions and increased spending on universal institutions is usually quite popular. Indeed, whereas selectivity 'opens up' a range of questions about who benefits from welfare policy and how deserving they are, universalism tends to 'close them down' (Larsen, 2008). That's why, when the tabloid press hit upon some ne'er-do-well with no intention of working or behaving in a socially responsible way, they will invariably be described as a 'benefits scrounger', but never as an 'NHS scrounger'.

3b) Distributive principle

As well as the issue of who actually gets welfare, there is also the question as to the basis on which it is distributed. Is it sensitive to need, and if so how? Is it conditional or unconditional? Is it dependent on behaviour? This section explores the institutional and social dynamics set up by different distributive principles, and how different choices of principle might help or harm public support for welfare.

Self-interest

Distributive principles offer an impartial basis for allocation that is by definition not self-interested. So they mainly interact with self-interest through what they imply for the coverage of a policy or its generosity to a particular group: protagonists might self-interestedly opt for a distributive principle that would maximise their own award. The choice of distributive principle is therefore partly susceptible to some of the dynamics discussed in the previous section – about how self-interest interacts with the design of welfare institutions and what this means for their sustainability.

Direct perceptions of fairness

The distributive principle by which a particular benefit or service is allocated mainly interacts with public attitudes through perceptions of fairness. Are institutions justified in allocating via a particular principle? And is the resulting distribution of resources fair or not? Such perceptions of fairness are a strong driver of public support for policy, including willingness to contribute (Azjen et al., 2000).

In practice, what is regarded as fair is highly sensitive to the specifics of any situation. People are essentially *pluralistic* in the fairness principles they apply, recognising the validity of a range of distributive principles and trading them off against one another in any particular context (Miller, 1999). Unconditional need-based allocation may be seen as fair in healthcare but not in income replacement. Someone may feel that school places should be allocated regardless of ability, but not university places. And so on.

As discussed in detail in Chapter 5, many people's attitudes to welfare seem *not* to be driven primarily by self-interest, but rather by a deep-seated sense of *reciprocity* or *conditional fairness* (Fong et al., 2005). The classical economist's view of humans as utility-maximisers applies to only a small proportion of the population. Most people do care – often very deeply – about what happens to others and (though they don't like the 'r-word' itself) are often quite relaxed about distributive arrangements that result in substantial 'vertical' redistribution (that is, redistribution from richer individuals to poorer individuals).

This doesn't mean they are simple altruists, though: support for redistribution is often conditional on people feeling that those who are benefiting are making some reciprocal effort to contribute back. This has a very important consequence. Behavioural criteria like reciprocity introduce a 'procedural' element to judging fairness (as well as an 'outcome' element). The result is that even if a need-based policy has the same distributional consequences as a reciprocity-based policy, the former will be perceived as unfair for being blind to procedural criteria. As Fong, Bowles and Gintis (2005) put it, reviewing US literature on attitudes to welfare, "egalitarian policies that reward people independent of whether and how much they contribute to society are considered unfair and are not supported, *even if the intended recipients are otherwise worthy of support and even if the incidence of non-contribution in the target population is rather low*" (italics mine).

To summarise, there will be numerous contexts – some of which we will examine later – in which targeting resources unconditionally on the basis of need will be perceived as unfair, leading the policy in question to be seen as illegitimate, and therefore jeopardising its sustainability. That is why the 'naïve' approach to poverty prevention discussed at the outset is naïve.

Social identity

Beyond direct judgements of fairness, however, the distributive principle chosen also shapes public attitudes through a more subtle process, once again via the effect of policy on social relations. The criteria by which resources are allocated (such as need, desert, or equality) will categorise people accordingly and, in doing so, impose a particular character onto the relations between individuals (Miller, 1999). For example:

- allocation by desert both implies and engenders competitive relations between individuals, with an emphasis on rewarding performance;

- equal allocation implies and engenders more solidaristic relations, with an emphasis on equal social status and common identity;

- allocation by need implies and engenders sympathetic relations, sometimes solidaristic, but on other occasions with a potentially distancing quality (emphasising the way in which recipients differ from each other).

The way in which the choice of distributive principle structures social relations becomes further apparent when we take into account the financing of welfare through taxation. A system where people pay tax into a central pot, and the resources are subsequently allocated as welfare spending, sets up a system of potential 'exchange' relationships between individuals (albeit mediated by the state). Tax-financed welfare that effects 'vertical' redistribution (from richer individuals to poorer individuals) therefore automatically links members of society in a system of contributor-recipient relationships. And this, in turn, means that the basis on which resources are allocated (and also the basis on which individuals are taxed) can shape the type of relationships that result. For example, progressive taxation combined with unconditional need-based allocation will result in fairly straightforward redistributive transfers from one group to another, with those contributing assuming an apparently 'altruistic' position and those receiving assuming an apparently 'dependent' position. By contrast, with conditional need-based allocation or desert-based allocation, those contributing to the welfare pot are essentially contributing in return for a particular behaviour on the part of the recipient, and those receiving are reciprocating the contribution of the taxpayer in some appropriately fitting way.

Note that, as with the coverage of welfare policy, it is our claim here that distributive principles can both *reflect* and also *create* social relations. For example, societies with strong solidarity between different social groups might be more predisposed to support universal benefits.[41] But it may also be the case that universal welfare institutions are more likely to make individuals regard each other as being of equal status and therefore more likely to foster solidaristic relations. Indeed, social psychology experiments show that the *experience* of working cooperatively helps to shift people from supporting allocation by desert toward greater support for allocation by equality (Deutsch, 1985).

The point is that policies may not be regarded as fair if there is a mismatch between the quality of felt interrelationships within society and the way in which welfare policy characterises these relationships. A move to allocation by desert in a highly solidaristic society may be perceived as unfair; conversely, a move to need-based allocation might be perceived as unfair in a group with only weak social connections.

So it is clear that the choice of distributive principle impinges very clearly on a policy's perceived legitimacy and therefore on its long-term sustainability. In the case of unconditional allocation on the basis of need, quite apart from the question of whether or not this would be regarded as fair in its own right, it is clear that there is a tension between the sympathetic relations which may underpin its legitimacy and the potentially distancing effect of focussing policy on a dimension where recipients will differ from non-recipients. It is our contention here that, if framed badly, the ongoing application of such a policy might risk creating the very same social distancing effects as discussed earlier.

This section has elucidated a model of the dynamic interactions between welfare institutions, public attitudes and social relations. The figure below illustrates the full range of possible processes.

Some other important interactions that have not been previously discussed are evident here. First, is the way in which the social positions people occupy (for example, in the income distribution) can themselves affect social relations and public attitudes (represented by the small black arrow emanating from 'social positions' and leading to 'social relations', and the small grey arrow emanating from 'social positions' and leading to 'public attitudes'). For example, the more unequal incomes become, the weaker social relations will be (Wilkinson, 2009).

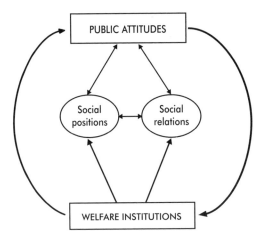

Figure: The possible dynamic interactions between welfare institutions, social positions, social relations and public attitudes.

And, worth commenting on is the way in which public attitudes and social relations can directly affect social positions – the distribution of outcomes – in the context of hierarchies of social status. (This is symbolised here by the small black arrow emanating from 'social relations and leading to 'social positions', and the small grey arrow emanating from 'public attitudes' and leading to 'social positions'). Lister (2004), for example, discusses how negative or distancing attitudes towards other social groups can create inequalities of social status and self-esteem.

Having explored the ways in which the coverage of welfare policy and the distributive principle underpinning it can shape public attitudes to the policy itself, we will conclude by discussing how these factors help to shape the evolution of welfare institutions.

Path dependency and welfare institutions

The discussion above highlights the ways in which welfare institutions both shape, and are shaped by, public attitudes to welfare policy. In this way, the social policy output of a government can be seen as both cause and effect. The result, as the figure above clearly illustrates, is a 'feedback loop', with welfare institutions influencing public attitudes, which in turn influence the future state of welfare institutions, which in turn further influence public attitudes, and so on.

Note that many possible examples of feedback within this causal chain are 'positive feedback': welfare institutions, public attitudes and social relations all influence each other in ways that reinforce the original dynamic. In this way, the design of welfare institutions can set off a train of evolutionary processes that produce *increasing returns* (Pierson, 2000).

Certain retrenchment dynamics provide classic examples of this feedback process. For example, introducing a targeted benefit, or cutting the coverage of an existing benefit, may lead people to perceive it as unfair; it may affect social relations by leading people to regard recipients as different from them; the resulting unpopularity may therefore produce pressure towards further cuts in expenditure, met by narrowing the coverage still further, which, in turn, amplifies the social distancing of recipients, and so on.

Alternatively, wide coverage could create an 'expansion dynamic': spending more on a benefit or service by increasing its coverage may well increase its popularity, producing pressures for further increases in investment and extensions of coverage, and so on.

The upshot is that *different institutional structures will give rise to different evolutionary pathways over time*, ultimately stabilising at different 'equilibria'. The welfare retrenchment dynamic described above, for example, would keep reinforcing itself and then ultimately stabilise at a low-expenditure, residualised policy structure. The expansion dynamic described further above would stabilise at a higher-expenditure, more universal policy structure. These are examples of a more general phenomenon, called *path dependency*, whereby a system's previous states or decisions influence the direction in which its subsequent states evolve (North, 1990).

Note that this is not a deterministic account of welfare state development. Sudden institutional or attitudinal changes can happen that alter a policy's evolutionary path or disturb an existing equilibrium (which is what happened in 1940-1945 and 1974-1979). But it does mean that, if things are left undisturbed, then – all things being equal – institutions (and the associated public attitudes and social relations) will tend to evolve in a particular direction or remain at particular equilibrium. In particular, with the wrong institutional design, we can get 'locked in' to a path which will produce undesirable future outcomes.

And, of course, different sets of attitudes and different institutional designs will lead to different possible welfare futures. We can see this most clearly by looking at the different paths along which welfare programmes develop in different countries. One school of thought over the last two decades has been that increasing global economic integration, and increasing political integration (for example, through the European Union) will bring convergence between welfare states (for example, Kosenen, 1995; Tsoukalis and Rhodes, 1997). In fact, a close look at what has actually happened reveals something quite different. In some areas there has been a small amount of convergence in welfare spending between OECD welfare states, but this trend is entirely down to similar types of welfare state becoming more like each other (see, for example, Castles, 2004; Brooks and Manza, 2007). So, for example, the social-democratic welfare states like Sweden, Finland and Norway have come to resemble each other more over time; as have Christian-democratic welfare states. In fact, *countries with different types of welfare state have become less similar from one another.* So the difference, say, between the Scandanavian social-democratic welfare states and the Anglo-American 'liberal' welfare states has actually become greater. The trend has been divergence, not convergence.[42]

Conclusion: reshaping our welfare institutions

If the analysis in this chapter is right, then the name of the game with long-term poverty prevention is not about how we spend our next pound bringing about the largest possible reduction in poverty, but rather about *getting the underlying institutional design right* (something the Webbs understood so well).[43] Structuring institutions in a way that will generate a 'high-redistribution equilibrium' is paramount. For those existing institutions that have evolved in a way that means they are ineffective at tackling poverty, the key must be to correct the path we're on. And this will require restructuring our institutions in the right way.

Later chapter will explore some possible strategic institutional reforms we need to make in existing areas of provision in order to entrench a long-term poverty prevention settlement, focussing on areas which are not only essential for poverty outcomes, but whose underlying institutional structure is now working against tackling poverty and inequality.

The analysis here also suggests why, as we saw in Chapter 1, welfare trends across the 20th century were U-shaped, showing two great moments of change (1945 and 1979), with relative stability in between. These were the two 'game-changing' moments in the design of our welfare institutions and the framing of our welfare culture, shifting the UK between higher-poverty and lower-poverty equilibria. While welfare states certainly have their own inertia, there will be formative historical moments that shift them from one path onto another. The year 1909 could have been one of these, but ultimately wasn't. In 1945, a huge surge of attitudinal change permitted massive institutional restructuring. In the late 1970's, the weakening of support for certain elements of the welfare state – and the election of a radical – allowed enough restructuring to definitively change our welfare path back again.

5. Public attitudes to welfare allocation

Previous chapters have highlighted the importance of public attitudes for the effectiveness and sustainability of welfare institutions. In particular, Chapter 4 set out a model of how public attitudes interact with welfare institutions to shape the evolution of welfare policy.

This chapter explores some of these attitudes and dynamics in practice, presenting the results of our own research on attitudes among the UK public, as well as reviewing existing survey and experimental evidence about the beliefs, values and psychological mechanisms underlying people's views about fairness in welfare. Understanding the factors that drive support for, or opposition to, welfare policy can then help us in thinking more strategically about how to reshape our welfare institutions.

Supportive in principle, but opposed in practice

Attitudes to fairness in welfare present something of a paradox. As we saw in Chapter 2, the last decade has seen growing opposition to redistribution and other aspects of welfare policy. In our own polling in 2009, people were asked to agree or disagree with the statement: "The Government should increase benefits for the poor, even if it leads to higher taxes for everyone else." Only 24 per cent agreed, with 49 per cent disagreeing.

So one might expect people to be broadly opposed to progressive tax and benefit systems (where those on higher incomes contribute a larger share and those on lower incomes get more help), or to services which give more to those in need. But this is far from the case. When asked about the *principles* underlying welfare, people are hugely supportive of a range of progressive – and, indeed, redistributive – policy measures.

In our focus groups, when participants were shown how the system of direct taxes and benefits affects household incomes for each income group – one of progressive redistribution (see table below) – they found the overall redistributive nature of the system utterly unobjectionable; it was just what they thought a tax and benefits system *should* do.[44] Similarly, when participants were shown the proportion of household income paid in taxes when the effect of *indirect* taxes (like VAT) were also taken into account, they were shocked to discover that the overall impact of the tax system was *regressive*, with taxes taking a higher percentage of gross income for the bottom fifth (39 per cent) than for the middle fifth (37 per cent) or the top fifth (35 per cent), a situation variously described as 'impossible', 'unbelievable' and 'crazy'.[45]

Table: Summary of the effects of direct taxes and cash benefits, by quintile groups of non-retired households, 2006-07[46]

Quintile	Bottom	2nd	middle	4th	top
original income	**£7,760**	**£20,660**	**£32,380**	**£46,060**	**£81,110**
plus cash benefits	+5,960	+4,640	+2,530	+1,610	+1,090
less direct taxes	-1,590	-4,320	-7,380	-11,270	-20,710
disposable income	**£12,130**	**£20,980**	**£27,530**	**£36,400**	**£61,480**

Alan Hedges (2005), on whose illuminating research our own work draws, has characterised this as the difference between *implicit* and *explicit* support for redistribution.

Most people seem to support systems based on 'progressive' principles (where richer individuals are effectively contributing more and poorer individuals are effectively receiving more) and which are therefore highly redistributive in effect – in other words, they 'implicitly' support this redistribution. But many people also shrink from the idea of 'redistribution' itself (which they tend to conceptualise as direct income transfers from richer individuals to poorer individuals), and often demonstrate strong opposition to policies that are redistributing income in a way that looks like this.

So if people are so committed to progressivity in welfare, why do they seem so opposed to important aspects of welfare policy? Deliberative research conducted by the Fabian Society in 2008 and 2009 found two key sources of this opposition:

1. Qualms about the distributional fairness of key welfare policies. In particular, there was *a belief that benefits or services with narrow coverage were unfair.*

2. A belief that the primary beneficiaries of welfare policy (those in poverty or those receiving benefits) did not deserve this support, which then fed through into a belief that the underlying policies which supported them were therefore unfair. In particular, there was *a strong belief that those claiming out-of-work benefits would not necessarily go on to make a reciprocal contribution back to society.*[47]

The sources of discontent with welfare highlighted here – qualms about distributional fairness and a perceived failure of reciprocity – therefore relate to the two aspects of welfare allocation analysed in Chapter 4 – coverage and distributive principles. In later chapters, we will go on to ask how policy can confront and address these attitudes in ways that can entrench popular support for welfare institutions. In order to do that, in this chapter, we set out in more detail what people think about these issues and why.

Universalism, distributional fairness and welfare

Perceptions of fairness

Our deliberative research explored attitudes to policy coverage by showing participants the design of some benefits and tax credits with different structures (Child Benefit, Child Tax Credit, and an example of Housing Benefit) and asking whether or not they thought them fair. Two things were noticeable each time we did this exercise. First, there was strong support for progressive expenditure in general. But, second, there was considerable unease about narrow targeting. The example of Housing Benefit given (shown by the black line in the figure below), in particular, was viewed as unfair for being so narrowly targeted.

This was highlighted further in exercises where participants were given the opportunity to increase expenditure on these benefits. Virtually no participants thought that extra expenditure was best spent by targeting it *solely* on the poorest households. The vast majority focused more on topping up the awards of those groups who were seen to be hit most by the initial phase of withdrawal (middle- and lower-middle-income households). This is illustrated in some typical participant diagrams for extending Housing Benefit, given below.

Note that these middle- and lower-middle-income 'top-ups' were for most participants about making the overall distributional structure of the benefit *fairer*, rather than about eliminating the disincentives of steep withdrawal – hence the extensions being roughly equally divided between reducing the taper gradient (the first figure) and increasing the earnings disregard (the second). A further important observation is that these types of extensions did not seem especially motivated by self-interest: in particular, participants in higher income bands did not necessarily distribute this extra expenditure across an income range that went up to their own income band. It was more often motivated by sympathy for those who were felt to be just missing out.

Public attitudes to welfare allocation

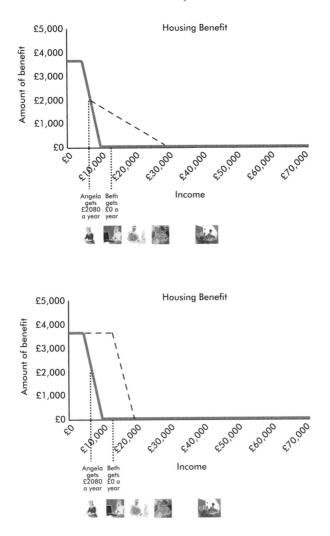

Figure: Typical diagrams of how many participants chose to allocate extra expenditure on Housing Benefit (for a particular example). The black dashed line shows the allocation of increased expenditure.

In a related exercise, participants were asked to design their own generic benefit 'to help with living costs'. While nearly all participants tapered their benefit progressively with increasing income, the vast majority gave it wide coverage: considerable attention was focussed on ensuring that those perceived to be in the 'middle' got something from it (Bamfield and Horton, 2009).[48]

The term 'universalism' is sometimes used to refer to the universal coverage of a policy (like the NHS), and on other occasions to refer to the flat-rate allocation of resources (like with Child Benefit). The implication of this research is that, of these two conceptions of universalism, wide coverage is much more important to people than flat-rate awards.

Survey research also points towards this conclusion. In fact, what polls tell you about perceptions of fairness in benefit design is highly dependent upon the wording of the question. When a decision about targeting or universalism is presented in the context of limited expenditure and only two options are given for how money should be spent – a flat-rate award with universal coverage or a (larger) award targeted only on those with low incomes – unsurprisingly, many people opt for targeting: 68 per cent in the case of Child Benefit, compared to just 29 per cent opting for universal coverage (Sefton, 2005).

However, when more options are presented, a different picture emerges. Our survey asked people about the best option for spending an extra £1 billion on families with children, so again in the context of limited expenditure, but this time giving people four different options for the coverage of a flat-rate award: 100 per cent, 75 per cent, 50 per cent and 25 per cent. As shown in the first table below, only 30 per cent were prepared to target the money maximally (on the bottom 25 per cent); 54 per cent of respondents chose one of the options for wider coverage (although only 17 per cent chose full coverage). Again, it's

Table: Preferences for targeting and universalism by socioeconomic position

Question: "Suppose the Government has decided to spend an extra £1 billion a year on increasing financial support to families with children. If you had to choose, how do you think it should prioritise this spending?"

		All	ABC1	C2DE
Give extra support to *all families* with children – for example, by using child benefit to give all families with children *an extra £2.75 a week*	%	17	19	14
Give extra support to *the bottom three quarters (75%) of families* with children (who, after tax and benefits, currently have household incomes less than about £29,000) - for example, by using the tax credit system to give these families *an extra £3.66 a week*	%	13	13	13
Give extra support to *the bottom half (50%) of families* with children (who, after tax and benefits, currently have household incomes less than about £20,000) - for example, by using the tax credit system to give these families *an extra £5.50 a week*	%	24	24	25
Give extra support *to the bottom quarter (25%) of families* with children (who, after tax and benefits, currently have household incomes less than about £14,000) - for example, by using the tax credit system to give these families *an extra £11.00 a week*	%	30	29	30

interesting to note there were only minor differences between the preferences of ABC1 and C2DE groups, again suggesting the responses were about more than simply self-interest.

Another survey question (Sefton, 2005) asked people for their preferences about how benefits should be designed, giving them options of varying the award by income as well as limiting coverage. As shown in the

second table below, only 8 per cent thought that Child
Benefit should be restricted to low earners; rather, 44 per
cent argued that low earners should get more (within
universal coverage) and a further 42 per cent opted for
everyone getting the same. Even smaller numbers were
willing to restrict the coverage of disability benefits and
state pensions by income group.

Preferences for benefit designs for different types of benefits.
Data from Sefton (2005)

	State pension	Disability benefit	Child benefit
	% agree	% agree	% agree
High earner should get more	12	10	4
Both should get same amount	56	55	42
Low earner should get more	27	30	44
Only low earner should get benefit	4	2	8

Interestingly, despite the basic underlying commitment
to progressivity shown by most participants, a degree of
support for flat-rate universal benefits such as Child
Benefit was also in evidence in our focus groups (though
participants were often split on this issue). Partly, this was
because people did not necessarily apply a single criterion
of distributional fairness in all cases; most recognised the
validity of different principles for different benefit structures.

But more nuanced attitudes towards targeting and
universalism also emerged when the discussion moved
away from thinking simply in terms of the allocation of
limited resources on a single benefit and instead towards
considering the benefit in the context of the tax and benefits system as a whole. More details are given in the box
below.

**Deliberative research on benefit structures: spontaneous
arguments put forward in defence of flat-rate universalism**

Of the arguments put forward by participants in favour of flat-rate
Child Benefit, some justified the design by reference to Child
Benefit's place within the larger system of tax and benefits (where
an overall progressive effect was still seen as desirable) or in terms
of the net effect of the whole system. So some highlighted the fact
that Child Benefit was only one benefit, and that you could use
other benefits in order to get more to those on lower incomes.
Others highlighted the fact that those on higher incomes were paying more in tax, which is what created a progressive system, so it
was fine for them to get a flat-rate benefit too.

*It should be the same for everybody, but people on
lower incomes should then be getting extra.*
(Woman, London)

*But, then again, you should look at the fact that
someone earning £150,000 is paying however much
back to the system in tax, so why shouldn't they get Child
Benefit?*
(Woman, Sheffield)

Another set of arguments offered in defence of flat-rate distribution were more instrumental: that equal awards promoted solidarity, for example, or that higher-income groups also receiving
the benefit would be happier to contribute to it through taxation.

*By making it flat-rate, it's seen as a socially accepted
benefit. Anything that's targeted is seen as less acceptable.*
(Man, Bristol)

Social identity

Chapter 4 highlighted how the strategy of targeting
resources, by dividing the population into groups, can effectively impose an identity on the targeted group, categorising
recipients and non-recipients as different. If salient, this division can increase social distance between members of

society, influencing perceptions of recipients and potentially leading to more negative evaluations of them.

A variety of evidence exists for such effects. Larsen (2008) compares a group of countries (Scandanavian countries) with similar types of welfare state; examining the same type of benefit across different countries, he shows that more selectivity generates greater stigmatisation. The table below illustrates this for two types of benefit: housing allowances and social assistance.

Table: The link between benefit coverage and stigma (from Larsen, 2008). Norway targets housing assistance on far fewer people than in the other countries, and there is correspondingly greater stigma attached to recipients. By contrast, the coverage of social assistance is greater in Finland than in the other countries, and there is correspondingly less stigma attached to recipients.

		Denmark	Finland	Norway	Sweden
Housing Allowance coverage (% of the population receiving it)	%	5.7	7.5	**1.1**	8.0
Stigma associated with Housing Allowances (% of population saying Housing Allowance recipients are looked down on)	%	10	17	**23**	12
Social Assistance coverage (% of the population receiving it)	%	5.8	**9.0**	4.5	5.5
Stigma associated with Social Assistance (% of population saying Social Assistance recipients are looked down on)	%	73	**49**	70	68

Table: How social distance can affect attitudes to welfare policy and service users. (The survey questions are paraphrased here.)

	Of those who feel they have 'a lot' / 'a little' in common with those living on council estates...	*Of those who feel they have 'not very much' / 'nothing' in common with those living on council estates...*
People living on council estates are working hard to get on in life...		
Agree	50	24
Disagree	13	30
People living on council estates make responsible decisions about spending and saving money...		
Agree	32	13
Disagree	21	40
Do you think mixed communities are a good idea?		
Good idea	59	36
Bad idea	37	60
The Government should spend more on welfare benefits for the poor, even if it leads to higher taxes...		
Agree	43	30
Disagree	35	47

Identity cleavages and increased social distance between recipients and non-recipients can in turn lead to negative evaluations of recipients and reduce non-recipients' support for the policy in question (van Oorschot, 2000).

Survey research for the Fabian Society conducted in 2008 reveals clearly the links in this process in the context of social housing. A significant minority (around a third) of the population felt that those living on large council estates aren't like them (including 38 per cent of people who don't have a large council estate in their area). Those who felt this way ranked such tenants low in terms of 'deservingness' (see the first two questions in the table below), with knock-on effects on both their attitudes towards wanting to mix with social tenants and their willingness to support redistribution generally (see the last two questions).

These findings are not simply a testament to income targeting; as we saw in Chapter 2, the geographical segregation of many tenants into large mono-tenure estates creates a very literal sense of social distance. Further analysis of our results shows that this geographical dimension also played an important role in responses: the further away the respondent lived from a large council estate, the less likely they were to think they had anything in common with tenants, and the less likely they were to perceive them as deserving of support.

This seems to reinforce the hypothesis of Chapter 4: that institutions which divide the population into groups can increase social distance between recipients and non-recipients, with knock-on consequences for support for welfare – and for willingness to contribute to welfare through taxation.

Reciprocity and welfare

As discussed at the outset of this chapter, a second key source of opposition to welfare policy was a widespread belief that 'benefit recipients' would not necessarily go on to make a reciprocal contribution back to society (through work, caring, etc.). Indeed, this emerged in the focus groups as perhaps the strongest source of punitive attitudes towards those receiving out-of-work benefits. In turn, this sense that there was a general failure of reciprocity in the system fed through into opposition to welfare policy more generally.

Our survey evidence backed this up. The survey found only 25 per cent believe that 'Most people who receive benefits now will make a contribution back to society in the future, through activities like employment or caring for others' (with 46 per cent disagreeing). And, as the table below shows, this belief was very, very strongly associated with support for, or opposition to, increasing benefits 'for the poor'.

		Agree	Disagree	Net agree (agree – disagree)
The government should spend more on benefits for the poor, even if it leads to higher taxes for everyone else.	%	24	49	**-25**
Most people who receive benefits now will make a contribution back to society in the future, through activities like employment or caring for others	%	25	46	**-21**
Support for increasing benefits 'for the poor', by views about benefit recipients...				
...of those *agreeing* that most people on benefits will make a contribution to society in future	%	49	27	**+22**
...of those *disagreeing* that most people on benefits will make a contribution to society in future	%	11	72	**-61**

In the remainder of this chapter, we wish to explore in more detail some aspects of people's attachment to reciprocity in welfare. In order to do this, we briefly review some experimental evidence for lessons about how reciprocity-based sentiments might map onto the design of welfare policy.

Reciprocity: experimental evidence

Ever since the creation of the welfare state – indeed, the Poor Law – many progressives have harboured a secret fear: that public opposition to redistributive welfare stems from narrow middle-class self-interest, and that such self-interest will prove an enduring barrier to significant redistribution. Such fears were compounded by the success of 'New Right' governments in the 1980s in the UK and US, who swept to power on a programme of tax cuts and welfare retrenchment. Repeated electoral success seemed to validate the political message with which these governments narrated their policy programmes: that people are fundamentally self-interested and individualistic so we should structure society in a way that recognises this. Collective tax-and-redistribute welfare programmes were, apparently, doomed to failure.

In fact, in the 1960s and 1970s, just as this political ideology was being seeded in the think tanks and political institutions of the right, a range of academic research programmes were being seeded in psychology and economics departments that would comprehensively falsify this ideology's underpinning assumptions. And as these research programmes have matured over the last twenty years, they have generated a set of results that have fundamentally challenged the classic economic model of the rational self-regarding actor.

It turns out that people care about much more than their own potential outcomes and payoffs in interactions. People also care about what others gain and lose too (and not just for strategic reasons). They also care deeply about the fairness of the procedure that led to the outcome, as well as the outcome itself. And it turns out that a substantial fraction of people demonstrate such social motives, or 'social preferences', in their behaviour.

Perhaps the most famous studies of reciprocal behaviours are experimental games in which several agents interact within rules that produce particular patterns of costs and benefits. Below we look at two of these.

The ultimatum game

In the ultimatum game, two players interact in a single round. One, the 'proposer' gets a certain amount of money and can offer (only once) any proportion of this to the other player, the 'responder'. If the responder accepts this offer, the money is divided accordingly. If the responder rejects the offer, neither player gets anything.

The key point is that self-interest should lead the responder to accept any amount of money, as the alternative is receiving nothing at all (and, knowing this, a self-regarding proposer should offer the minimum amount). However, only a minority of participants (around a quarter) behave in a purely self-regarding manner. Most proposers offer substantial amounts (50 per cent is the most common offer). And responders routinely reject offers of less than 30 per cent (The figure below illustrates this for an 80-20 offer).

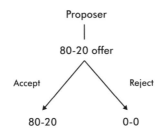

Why do responders reject low offers when it would be in their own self interest to take the money? Because they want to punish what they perceive to be an unfair offer. This behaviour is a classic example of 'altruistic punishment', where people punish non-cooperators even at substantial cost to themselves. And this pattern of results is robust across different cultures around the world.[49]

Altruistic punishment constitutes important evidence the people are not motivated by self-interest, but by reciprocity. Though progressives rarely think about punishment in these terms (because it's not nice), it often constitutes important evidence of 'other-regarding' behaviour. When Daily Express readers clamour for government to spend more of their hard-earned cash on building prisons to punish people whose crimes have nothing to do with them, this is a display of profoundly non-self-interested behaviour.

The public goods game

Another game – perhaps more akin to welfare – is the 'public goods game', played with several players over multiple rounds.[50] Each player starts with a certain amount of money and in each round can choose how much of her money to put into a public 'pot'. Each player keeps the money they do not put into the pot, whereas the money in the pot is shared out equally among all players after being multiplied by a certain factor (reflecting the gains to cooperation). So placing money into the public pot has a cost to the individual, but if other players do this too then each member of the group can gain more by contributing to the pot than they would get simply by keeping what is in their private account.

Self interest would predict zero contributions, retaining one's own money privately whilst benefiting from the contributions of others. In fact, only a fraction of subjects behave in a self-regarding manner. Initially, many do in fact make contributions to the pot (on average about half of their money). However, in subsequent rounds of the game the level of cooperation tends to decay. The reason for this is that subjects become angry with those who are free-riding on the rest of the group and retaliate in the only way available to them – by withdrawing cooperation.

By contrast, when subjects are allowed to punish free-riders (by fining them) at a cost to themselves (through paying a fee), significant numbers do. (Again, this contradicts the self-interest hypothesis, which predicts no punishing behaviour.) Since being fined costs free-riders money, the possibility of punishment induces them to cooperate. In this situation, cooperation is not only maintained through repeated rounds, but tends to increase steadily until by the final rounds almost all participants are contributing their full endowment. If the punishment option is removed, cooperation deteriorates.

The heterogeneity of the population

By no means everyone exhibits such 'social preferences'. A significant proportion of the population, around a quarter, typically behaves in a self-interested manner in such interactions. But some 40 to 50 per cent of the population do exhibit the reciprocal behaviours outlined above; they are what is called 'conditional cooperators'. A further minority of the population are unconditional altruists – always cooperating and never punishing.[51]

Given the heterogeneity of the population, how these different groups interact is essential to understanding the dynamics of human cooperation. The presence of reciprocators changes the incentives for self-interested types, by punishing free-riding and rewarding cooperation. This will induce selfish types to behave in a 'cooperative' way and make collectively beneficial decisions (as it will now be in their own interest to do so).

The role of a sanctioning mechanism is key here, however: it is this that changes the incentives for those who would otherwise free-ride. In the absence of a sanctioning mechanism, cooperation ends up unravelling in public goods games, because just a small number of selfish subjects will induce reciprocators to withdraw their cooperation and start free-riding themselves.[52]

Three key aspects of reciprocal behaviour

Beyond the basic point that a substantial proportion of the population are predisposed towards reciprocity rather than self-interest, what are the key aspects of reciprocal behaviour that are relevant to the design of welfare? Here, we pick out three.

Strong reciprocity, not long-term self interest

Some types of apparently reciprocal behaviour can in fact be explained in terms of long-term self-interest, particularly in repeated interactions – where repetition creates opportunities for future payback or for the formation of reputations (making others more likely to cooperate with you in future). Here, apparently non-self-interested behaviours, such as cooperation or costly punishment, could be *strategic*, because they increase the likelihood of benefits to you further down the line. This is indeed the premise of the standard account of cooperation in evolutionary biology (Trivers, 1971); blood-sharing by unrelated female vampire bats is the classic example. Such reciprocity – cooperation in expectation of future payback – is called *weak reciprocity*.

However, many reciprocal behaviours cannot be explained in this way, particularly non-strategic punishment. The ultimatum game described above, for example, is a 'one-shot' game (a single round) in which punishing a proposer at a cost to yourself cannot possibly bring you any future benefits. Yet people do this. Similarly, in versions of public goods games, it is possible to run multiple games simultaneously and mix the participants between each round so that no-one encounters each other in a game more than once (the 'perfect stranger' condition – see Fehr and Fischbacher, 2005). Yet sanctioning behaviour in perfect-stranger games remains similar to that in games in which participants stay together, despite the fact that participants cannot benefit in strategic terms from punishing other participants (the fact that you can't encounter the same person more than once precludes reputation formation).

The fact that people behave cooperatively in one-shot interactions and in 'perfect stranger' interactions is evidence that some reciprocal behaviours cannot be explained through self-interest.[53] This kind of reciprocity – cooperation without the expectation of future payback – is called *strong reciprocity*.

Intentions, not outcomes

Another important piece of evidence from these experimental interactions is that people, by and large, respond to what they perceive as fair or unfair *intentions* in exchanges, not fair or unfair *outcomes*. Falk, Fehr and Fischbacher (2003) conducted a set of 'constrained' ultimatum games in which the proposers could only choose from particular options (and the responders knew this). In one game, proposers could either offer 50-50 or 80-20 (in the first figure below). Around 44 per cent of responders rejected the 80-20 offer: the (approximately) half of the population who are strong reciprocators, who are prepared to punish an unfair offer at a cost to themselves. In another game, however, proposers could either offer 80-20 or 100-0 (in the second figure below). Here, however, hardly any responders (9 per cent) rejected the 80-20 offer.

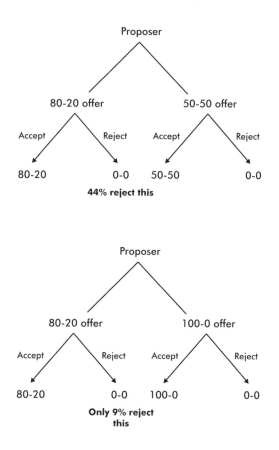

The reason is that the responders aren't simply responding to the material outcomes of the game (to the idea of receiving only 20 per cent of the total), but to the perceived intentions of the proposer. And, whereas 80-20 seems an unfair offer when the proposer could have chosen 50-50, in the second game, 80-20 is the fairer option when compared to the only available alternative of 100-0.

These results clearly contradict a 'consequentialistic' (outcome-based) view of fairness judgements, along with the consequentialistic assumptions of standard economic theory, which defines the utility of an action solely in terms of the consequences of that action. Rather, it suggests that the intentions we impute to others in cooperative endeavours will be of primary importance in our evaluations of the fairness of outcomes.[54]

Forgivingness: it's current behaviour that counts

In cooperation games, people tend not to hold grudges. In games with repeated interactions, reciprocators start out cooperating at the outset; free-riding is then met by either punishments being awarded in subsequent rounds (if available) or by the withdrawal of cooperation (if not available). However, crucially, many subjects also then behave in a *forgiving* way: if free-riders suddenly start cooperating, then so do reciprocators (see, for example, Fischbacher, Gachter and Fehr, (2001), in the context of public goods games).

So in evaluating how to respond to others, people seem to be concerned less by others' full record of past performance, than by their immediate behaviour – what they have just done in the immediately preceding round or what they are doing in the current round.

Interestingly, in some types of games, it is known that this property of forgivingness (a willingness to forgive past defections and cooperate in subsequent rounds if others do) is an optimal strategy for maximising returns. For example, in the 'iterated prisoner's dilemma' (Axelrod, 1984), the optimal strategy is to punish defectors in the next round, but then reward them for subsequent cooperation (the 'tit-for-tat' strategy). Whether or not the instinct to forgive previous un-cooperative behaviour (if individuals are now cooperating) reflects a strategic impulse is hard to know. Either way, the lesson is that past transgressions tend to be forgiven. It is what people do now that counts.

Returning to the real world: reciprocity and welfare

Laboratory experiments are all very well, but what does research into public attitudes towards welfare tell us about whether and how these sentiments figure in the real world? Here we look at evidence for the three aspects of reciprocity discussed above.

Strong reciprocity

Weak reciprocity clearly figures in support for welfare. Many people, for example, support the welfare state in terms of the principle of insurance. In a recent survey, 74 per cent agreed with the statement that, "The best reason for paying taxes now is that you never know when you might need benefits and services yourself" (Sefton, 2005).

But is support for welfare solely dependent on the anticipation of getting something back in return, or does strong reciprocity also figure here? One clue that it might is that many people seem to subscribe to an important *asymmetry* characteristic of strong reciprocity: a belief that it is legitimate for people to contribute without necessarily being repaid, combined with a belief that it is *illegitimate* for people to receive without a requirement also for them to contribute. So, for example, many people *don't* seem to think it's unfair that taxpayers might contribute towards services that they don't use personally. However, people *do* tend think it's unfair that people might benefit from services that they haven't personally contributed towards.

Research by Tom Sefton for the British Social Attitudes Survey (Sefton, 2005) found that, across the population as a whole, there was net disagreement with the statement that, "It's not fair that some people pay a lot of money in tax and hardly use the services they pay for" (39 per cent disagreeing and only 32 per cent agreeing), while there was net agreement with the statement that, "It's not right that people benefit from services that they haven't helped to pay for" (with 48 per cent agreeing and just 26 per cent disagreeing). These figures are shown in the table further below.

To explore this further, Sefton analysed the population into three clusters, on the basis of their motivations for supporting or opposing welfare.

- *Samaritans* (29 per cent of the population) believe people are entitled to help because they are in need, which does not depend upon then having contributed or 'deserved' help in some other way. Significantly, and contrary to the population as a whole, 67 per cent of this group do *not* think it unfair that some people benefit from services that they haven't helped pay for. (And a huge 71 per cent of this group do not think it unfair that some people pay tax without using services.)

- *Robinson Crusoes* (26 per cent of the population) are less wedded to the welfare state and more resistant to redistribution. Contrary to the predominant view within the population, 75 per cent think it is unfair that some people pay tax without using services. (And a huge 91 per cent think it is unfair that some people benefit from services they haven't helped pay for.)

- *Club Members* (45 per cent of the population), on the other hand, demonstrate precisely the asymmetry that is characteristic of strong reciprocity: welfare isn't necessarily conditional on those paying in getting something back personally, but it is conditional on those who do get something out putting back in again. So (along with Samaritans) Club Members don't think it unfair that some people pay tax without using services. But (along with Robinson Crusoes), Club Members do think it unfair that some people benefit from services that they haven't helped pay for.

So Sefton's Club Members are the locus of strong reciprocity within the population: their support for welfare is conditional on recipients having fulfilled their part of the bargain by contributing back what they reasonably can.[55]

Table: The different mix of attitudes between different groups within the population (from Sefton, 2005). As the asymmetry in their attitudes shows, Club Members are strong reciprocators.

	Whole population	Samaritans	Club Members	Robinson Crusoes
		(29% of population)	(45% of population)	(26% of population)
Net support for statement: *"It's not fair that some people pay a lot of money in tax and hardly use the services they pay for"* (% agree – % disagree)	DISAGREE -7	DISAGREE -61	DISAGREE -20	AGREE +66
Net support for statement: *"It's not right that people benefit from services that they haven't helped to pay for"* (% agree – % disagree)	DISAGREE +22	DISAGREE -54	DISAGREE +28	AGREE +89

Intentions, not outcomes

In one exercise in our focus groups, we sought to explore the factors behind perceptions of the 'deservingness' of benefit recipients. Participants were presented with a number of imaginary characters who were out of work and receiving unemployment benefit (or some other out-of-work benefit). They were then asked to rank characters in terms of the validity of their claim to unemployment benefit, and further questions were asked to probe what lay behind these judgements.

The exercise compared attitudes towards characters in different circumstances (and controlling for other differences): for example, comparing characters with and without savings; comparing a character who was born in the UK with another who had come to the UK and worked here; comparing a character who had lost their job through staff cuts with another who had been sacked for 'skiving', and so on. An example of the stimulus material is given below.

Example of stimulus material from exercise on the deservingness of benefit recipients

Gary (former security guard)
- laid off through cutbacks 9 months ago
- claiming unemployment benefit
- registered at Jobcentre
- wants security work again
- keeps turning down available jobs

Ian (former security guard)
- sacked 6 months ago for skiving off
- claiming unemployment benefit
- registered at Jobcentre
- regrets previous behaviour
- now looking hard to find new job

Interestingly, various factors often associated with judgements of desert seemed, in the final analysis, to make little difference to participants' views of the validity of each character's claim to unemployment benefit. What *did* make a difference was whether or not the character concerned was genuinely trying to get a new job – that is, the level of 'reciprocal effort' in return for receipt of unemployment benefit. Indeed, this was the 'deal breaker' for nearly all participants. A character who was seen to be turning down available jobs without good reason over a long period of time was always ranked last in terms of deservingness, and by a long way.

The reason was the character's imputed intention: by evading what participants perceived to be a shared obligation to put something back in, he was viewed as "not acting in good faith". By contrast, other characters who were felt to have a good reason for turning down available jobs (or not being in work altogether – like a single mother caring for her children) met with sympathy and support for their claim on benefits.

Where someone was indeed seen to be 'operating in good faith' and trying to get a job, this trumped other possible concerns one might imagine would affect judgements about fairness. One striking example of this was on the issue of immigration. Many participants entered discussions about immigration at the level of negative stereotypes, often leading initially to harsh and punitive attitudes being expressed towards 'immigrants'. What was interesting, however, was that, when presented with fictional characters in specific situations and asked to evaluate them (which moved people away from dealing in stereotypes), participants applied a very refined and consistent standard of fairness. A character who had come to the UK two years ago and worked since, but was now unemployed was felt by nearly every participant to have a perfectly fair claim to as much unemployment benefit as anyone else (and far more claim than the native Brit who was turning down available jobs).

The initial negative sentiments directed towards 'immigrants', it turned out, were not because people had some objection with the idea of people coming to the UK to work per se, nor because of views about race, ethnicity and culture, but because they had in their minds a stereotype of an immigrant who was someone who arrived in the UK and came straight onto the system of out-of-work benefits (something it is virtually impossible to do).

This finding, which we saw repeated in group after group, poses a strong challenge to the thesis, recently articulated by David Goodhart (Goodhart, 2004), that increasing ethnic and cultural diversity will necessarily undermine the sense of mutual obligation and fairness that underpins collective welfare. Our research suggests, by contrast, that while immigration may be the locus of these debates in popular consciousness, for most people it is the perceived lack of contribution of immigrants (via negative stereotypes) that drives harsh attitudes, rather than any aspect of racial, ethnic or cultural difference.

Table: Attitudes concerning eligibility for unemployment benefit (from Sefton, 2005)	
Under what circumstances would it be right to limit a person's access to unemployment benefit?	*% agree*
They were not actively looking for work	78
They had not paid much in taxes because they had been unemployed for a long time	25
They were not born in Britain, but settled here more than two years ago	22
They recently came to Britain because they were in danger at home	21
They had not paid much in taxes because they were bringing up children	9

These findings are backed up by data from the 2005 British Social Attitudes Survey showing people's views about what kinds of factors might justify *limiting* a person's access to unemployment benefit (Sefton, 2005). The circumstance in which the largest number of people (78 per cent) thought it right to limit access was if 'they were not actively looking for work'; this compares to just 22 per cent wanting to limit access if the individual only settled in Britain two years ago.

An important sentiment lying behind many public attitudes to welfare is *fear of being taken advantage of*. Strong reciprocity is in some respects a combination of non-self-interested generosity (where people are prepared to put in, even if the returns do not come to them personally) with a fear of being taken advantage of (which is why people nevertheless want to ensure those receiving welfare are also putting something back in). The suspicion that others might be taking advantage of you, relentlessly played on by the tabloid media, is the key driver of negative attitudes to welfare recipients. It is therefore something that is important for any policy framework to address if a generous welfare settlement for tackling poverty is to be possible.

Interestingly, while this suspicion can be a difficult sentiment for welfare debates, it does not necessarily place the bar very high in terms of what people demand of those benefitting from welfare. The emotion in question is a protective-defensive one, often satisfied by proof that an individual is acting in good faith. Being taken advantage of, after all, is about the *intentions* of the people you interact with. It is not the case, for most people, that they require others to contribute the same amount to the pot; rather they want proof that an individual is trying – that they are intending to contribute.

That intentions are the key is also why we see huge public sympathy for groups like the low paid and carers: people can see that they are trying. As the table below

shows (containing results from our survey research), policies which are seen to satisfy the demands of strong reciprocity – even highly redistributive policies – can garner a
huge depth of public support across party lines.

Table: Support for a higher minimum wage and more financial
support for carers. (The survey questions are paraphrased here.)

	All	Conservative supporters	Labour supporters
	% agree	% agree	% agree
Higher National Minimum Wage?	81	75	87
More financial support for carers?	85	86	88

This importance of intentions was seen particularly clearly in the focus group exercise described above, which discussed a character who had recently come to the UK, worked
for two years and was now unemployed and claiming
Jobseeker's Allowance. Participants had absolutely no problem with this, provided they were convinced the individual
in question was trying to get another job. Participants were
asked how long someone would have to have work in the UK
before being entitled to out-of-work benefits. Some volun-
teered a year or six months, but participants generally found
this a difficult question to think about. Then one participant
made clear he thought the question was missing the point, in
a statement that received agreement from the whole group:

"The point is not how long. I wouldn't mind if
someone had got a job in the UK and was travelling
here to take it up, but then the company immediately went bust and they needed support. But I'd want
to see a letter saying they had a job before they
came here. I'd bloody well want to see proof..."

(Male, London)

Forgivingness: it's current behaviour that counts

In the exercise described above – where participants judged the perceived validity of different characters' claim to unemployment benefit – an interesting finding cropped up again and again. The figure above gave an example comparing two characters. One (Gary) became unemployed through recession but was now turning down offers of available jobs; the other (Ian), was unemployed because he was sacked for misconduct, but was now looking hard to find a new job. Without exception, participants in our focus groups were fine with Ian getting benefits, but not with Gary.

The pattern was that people tended to forgive past mistakes, provided the individual in question was trying now.

This conclusion is backed up by an analysis of our survey results. The survey found strong net opposition to the proposal that "The Government should spend more money on welfare benefits for the poor, even if it leads to higher taxes for everyone else" (with 24 per cent agreeing and 49 per cent disagreeing). We also asked a series of questions to measure beliefs about those in poverty, beliefs which could be possible drivers of opposition to (or support for) redistribution. Through linear regression models, we then explored the strength with which these beliefs were associated with opposition to redistribution.

Some of the results are displayed in the chart below. The vertical bars each represent factors which might influence support for redistribution (in this case, reducing support for redistribution). The length of each bar is effectively a measure of the magnitude with which this factor reduces support for redistribution.[56]

The first bar measures the effect of the income band of the respondent – used here as a proxy for self-interest (since the higher your income, the less likely you would be to benefit personally from 'increasing welfare benefits for the poor'). The second bar measures the effect of the belief

Determinants of support for redistribution to those on low incomes: comparing the relative effect of different variables

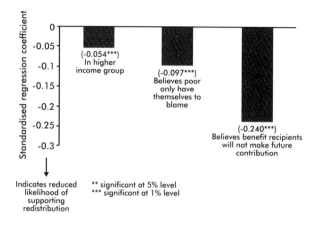

that 'Most of the people normally described as 'poor' in Britain today only have themselves to blame for not having a higher income', and the third bar measures the effect of the belief that 'Most people who receive benefits now will make a contribution back to society in future, through activities like employment or caring for others'.

In fact, despite widespread opposition to redistribution, these results are potentially positive for progressives for two reasons. First, a comparison of the first bar with the second and third shows that beliefs and values are more powerful determinants of attitudes to redistribution than self-interest. (If opposition to redistribution were driven by self-interest, it would be harder to do anything about it.)

Second, a comparison of the second and third bars shows that beliefs about the present and future (what benefit recipients will do now in return for benefits) are more powerful determinants of attitudes than beliefs about the past (whether they were responsible for getting into poverty in the first place). Again, this is good news: if opposition to redistribution were primarily driven by attitudes to past events, it would be harder to do anything about. On the other hand, we can do something about public perceptions of what those claiming benefits are currently doing, or will go on to do in future.[57]

This suggests that framing welfare policy in a way that gives people more confidence that those receiving benefits now are making (and will go on to make) a contribution back to society could play an important role in fostering support for welfare.

Conclusion: harnessing public attitudes to fight poverty

Attitudes to welfare are often difficult for progressives, with both punitive attitudes towards those in poverty or those receiving benefits, and opposition to important types of welfare policy. However, through these negative attitudes, some glimmers of hope emerge. Attitudes to welfare are not driven primarily by self-interest. Many people are happy to cooperate, provided the right conditions are in place. People think progressive tax and benefits are fair. And, as we have seen, where people feel that those on low incomes (such as the low paid or carers) are indeed making a contribution to society, there is huge public support for measures to help them.

Much more difficult is where a hard-nosed insistence on reciprocity in welfare seems to give rise to opposition to need-based allocation or results in negative views of welfare recipients. However, even here, an examination of what underpins attitudes produces some potentially optimistic results. People are worried about the intentions of others, not their earning power. And people seem more moved by whether or not welfare recipients are prepared to make a contribution back to society, rather than by their past behaviour. Crucially, then, there are significant ways in which existing attitudes would actually permit a *more* liberal, *more* generous and *more* inclusive welfare system than the one we have at the moment, one which would also 'resonate' more closely with people's underlying sense of fairness.

Ultimately, successful welfare strategies will be the ones which harness such public attitudes to work *for* poverty prevention, rather than against it.

While there is some cause for optimism, though, there is also a need for realism. It's great that opposition to welfare is not driven by self-interest. But, equally, much support for welfare is not driven by altruism either – an assumption which egalitarians often get wrong.

In fact, even egalitarians should be grateful for strong reciprocators. By punishing free-riders at cost to themselves, strong reciprocators enforce the cooperation of potential free-riders, leading to better collective long-term outcomes for everyone. Altruists don't do this. In a very important sense, the punishment of free-riders is a *public good* created by reciprocators which benefits us all. Without them, we might have evolved into a very different species.

6. In this together?
Why universalism matters

Earlier chapters have explored the importance of the coverage of welfare institutions for effective poverty prevention. In particular, Chapter 4 showed how different decisions about policy coverage can have profound implications both for public attitudes to welfare and for the underlying quality of social relations.

This chapter looks at how we might go about getting this dimension of policy right in practice. In the section that follows, we will briefly explore what universalism is, why it is important for welfare, and why getting this aspect of welfare wrong can lead to greater poverty and inequality. We then look at some policy reforms that would begin to address these issues in two areas where our welfare institutions are currently getting this wrong: social housing and taxation.

The importance of universalism in poverty prevention

Chapter 3 examined two key 'dilemmas' of welfare, one of which was the appropriate balance between universalism and targeting. Comparing the very different post-war histories of social housing and the NHS, it looked at how this aspect of institutional design can have fundamental consequences for the effectiveness and sustainability of social policy. At worst, getting it wrong can lead to vicious circles of residualisation and decline. Getting it right, however, if other circumstances permit, can lead to virtuous circles of generosity and sustainability.

Clearly, then, determining the appropriate coverage of policy is a vitally important part of the strategy of welfare. We will argue in this chapter that a more universalist approach will be needed in various areas if we are to entrench a poverty prevention settlement for the 21st Century.

What is universalism?

Universalism refers to both the coverage of institutions and the way in which individuals are treated by them. As a general principle it refers to an institutional design that encompasses all individuals equally, rather than separating off a particular 'need group' or treating them exceptionally. As such, the principle embodies a certain equality of treatment and equality of status.

More specifically, universalism can apply to both the question of who is *eligible* for a particular policy, and the question of *how much* each individual gets from it. Sometimes 'universalism' is used to describe a policy for which all citizens are eligible (like the NHS), while on other occasions it is used to describe a policy which allocates resources on a flat-rate basis (like Child Benefit).

In many ways, universalism of eligibility or coverage is more fundamental than universalism in the size of award.[58] There are numerous contexts in which 'equality of treatment' need not imply formal equality in how much everyone gets, but can allow for significant variation. When awards are income-related within universal coverage in this way, the design is often termed 'progressive universalism' – for example, with the Child Tax Credit or the Child Trust Fund.[59] Progressive universalism thus combines some of the efficiency of targeting (those in greater need get more) with universal membership (all are part of the same institutional structure).

However, it may also be the case that for universal membership to be meaningful, the size of awards cannot get too unequal. If, for example, benefit levels cease to be especially meaningful to middle-income households, the institution itself might lose its relevance, and the equality of status that membership brings will dissipate.

Why is universalism important?

Very generally, there are three types of reasons why universalism is important in welfare policy.

Normative arguments for universalism

As we shall see below, there are good policy reasons to advocate universalism as a more effective approach for helping those that need assistance most. But there is a deeper point of principle here: universalism is an expression of the core ideal of social equality.

Specifically, universal institutions express our *common membership* of society. This common membership, moreover, embodies a particular kind of *equality of status*: as the philosopher David Miller puts it, "there are certain social groups whose members are entitled to equal treatment by virtue of membership. The claim to equality flows from the very fact of membership" (1999).

The institutional division of people into different groups, on the other hand, while sometimes quite necessary, can create inequalities of status. The logic of targeting is that it must necessarily rely on a series of classifications of individuals, (whether poor v. non-poor, reliant v. self-sufficient, and so on). As explored in Chapter 4, once this happens it is all too easy for the disadvantaged to be treated as the 'undeserving', and subject to stigma. Universal institutions, by contrast, even where they must differentiate between the level of provision people are entitled to, do not do so in a way that forces a distinction between different groups.

Universal institutions do more than just define group membership and enshrine equality of status, though. They can also serve to strengthen the common bonds of membership – the social relationships that exist between individuals and groups. Conversely, Chapter 1 highlighted some important instances where the deterioration of relations within a society was part and parcel of people being institutionally segregated.

All of this is why, for example, the campaign to reintroduce universal free school meals in England is so important. Not simply because it would improve children's health and help family finances; but because it would help to foster social equality between school children, and remove any stigma from children in low-income families who claim free school meals.[60]

Universal institutions are thus based on the normative premise that we are all equal citizens. And it is partly this equality of citizenship that justifies the institutional analysis we offer here: welfare policy must proceed from the assumption that equal citizenship is an appropriate goal of a socially just society (though this is by no means a principle that is accepted by all).

Empirical arguments for universalism in poverty prevention

A good reason for advocating universalism is that – ironically – it can be more effective at reaching those who need help the most. A practical problem with targeting resources is that it can result in low take-up. Certainly there may be practical reasons for this, such as more complex administration, but the history of welfare suggests that – in some contexts, at least – the ethos of targeting may itself be part of the problem. As we have seen, dividing the population into groups of recipients and non-recipients can create the risk of stigma and a perception that it is somehow not respectable to claim the benefit or service in question, a perception that historically has been deeply embedded in Britain's welfare culture. Another more direct reason is that targeting often requires means testing (or income testing), which can itself discourage take up and cause resentment if it surrounds support to which people feel they are legitimately entitled.

Nowhere have these issues been more visible than in pensions policy. As we saw in Chapter 3, the low level of post-war pensions left many reliant on means tested National Assistance, and the perceived stigma and complexity of claiming prevented potential claimants from coming forward: in the mid-1960s it was found that approximately 15 per cent of pensioners eligible for assistance were not claiming it.[61] We see a similar problem with take up today, with approximately one third of all pensioners entitled to Pension Credit (1.4 million households) not taking it up, and almost half of all pensioners entitled to Council Tax Benefit (2 million households) not taking it up.[62] Indeed, older people seem to have particular problems with means tested benefits: take-up is often lower among pensioners than among working-age groups for benefits that both groups are eligible for, such as Council Tax Benefit (DWP, 2009).[63]

It is interesting to note that the take-up of income-related child support has increased as its coverage has increased, with around half of eligible families claiming the Family Income Supplement (1974-1987), around two thirds claiming the Family Credit (1988-1999), and over four fifths (currently 85 per cent) today claiming the Child Tax Credit. Take-up of universal Child Benefit has been estimated at 98 per cent.[64]

Whilst the segregating effects of the benefit system may seem invisible, there are other aspects of targeting that are highly visible. The clearest case here is the process of physical and social segregation in social housing – especially in the large council estate. Given its visibility, it is perhaps no surprise that this segregation has led to discrimination in the jobs market (as well as in other markets, such as household insurance). In particular, there is a growing body of evidence to support anecdotal accounts of postcode discrimination, in which job applications are 'filtered out' based on area (Fletcher et al., 2008).

And more general social discrimination in this area has become worryingly widespread, with the cheap laughs that come at the expense of 'chavs' and the sink estate. Regardless of the extent to which these estates may or may not be associated with anti-social behaviour, all are tarred with the same brush. Perhaps most of all, stigma and exclusion work against poverty prevention through their effect on the self-esteem and morale of those who are on the receiving end of it (Lister, 2004).

When is targeting justified?

The limitations of targeting strategies do not mean that it is always wrong to target resources. Indeed, when faced with immediate emergencies, targeting may well be necessary to maximise the impact of limited extra resources. With millions of pensioners in poverty in 1997, and the poorest living on just £70 a week, the targeting strategy of income support pursued by the Government almost certainly achieved a greater reduction in poverty in its first few years than a strategy of universalism would have done. Our point here is that there are both inherent limits to the effectiveness of such a strategy (as problems with Pension Credit take-up show) and that, *over the long term*, such a strategy will eventually prove less effective. That is why the gradual rebalancing of support towards the Basic State Pension that will take place over the coming years is the right direction to move in. More generally, it is important to make clear that targeting of this sort is a short-term measure, not a preferred institutional design.

Second, variable awards (which may require income testing or means testing) will often be necessary if individuals need different levels of support. One insight of a 'capabilities based' approach to equality is that individuals may require different

---

levels of support in order to compensate them for different levels of capability. Another issue is that some benefits should rightly reflect the actual costs that households face, rather than simply giving them equal amounts (as currently happens with financial support for housing and childcare). In both cases, doing more of this kind of *context-sensitive* redistribution is an important goal for the future welfare state. Our point here, however, is that it is infinitely preferable to do this within a system that everybody is part of, rather than a system that is targeted in coverage. There is therefore an important distinction to be made between means testing that limits the coverage of a policy and means testing that determines the size of award within a framework of wide coverage. Progressive universalism (the latter) will usually be more effective at reaching those who need help than targeting via restricting coverage (the former).

Ultimately, much will boil down to one's *motivation* for means testing. There is another legitimate distinction to be made between means testing to cut expenditure (which we often see under governments of the right) and means testing to ensure that *increases* in expenditure are targeted on those that need them most. The former is more likely to result in strategies of restricting coverage and will create a system where the ethos is to discourage claiming (with unfriendly and intrusive administration). By contrast, the latter is more likely to result in strategies of progressive universalism and will create a system where the ethos is to encourage claiming (as with the Government's recent Public Services Agreement target to increase the take-up of Pension Credit).

Dividing the population into groups on the basis of some institutional classification can also inadvertently create *barriers to exit* from poverty or disadvantage. One example of this is the withdrawal of benefits or services as income increases, which can subject the recipient to high marginal tax rates, potentially disincentivising people from earning more and creating a 'poverty trap'. Housing Benefit in particular has a very steep withdrawal rate (65p for every extra pound earned); combined with other benefits, it can produce effective marginal tax rates as high as 95 per cent, meaning only 5p is kept in each new pound earned. Another example is the possibility of the removal of benefits or services, creating uncertainty about what, say, accepting a job will mean for the support an individual gets. Very often employment opportunities are temporary or insecure; yet once off certain benefits – such as Housing Benefit – it can be difficult and slow to re-enter the system; many households have been driven into debt and poverty during the waiting period. This potential instability can make it rational to stay out of work. By contrast, a less targeted system, with the retention of support across important life transitions (particularly moving into work) would eliminate these barriers.

And such barriers exist spatially too, as when social housing is provided with little connection to local labour markets and poor access to services. Part of the reason for this is historical: many estates were built to service industries that are now defunct. But it is also the result of poor planning. Such physical isolation can be a particularly strong driver of social exclusion, with lack of access not just to jobs, but to social networks too.

Instrumental arguments for universalism in poverty prevention

A third – and crucial – factor is the role of universalism in shaping public support for, or opposition to, welfare policy. In Chapters 4 and 5, we looked at various ways in which the coverage of a policy interacts with public attitudes. One very important one was the way in which wide coverage can tap into middle-class self-interest as a source of support for the welfare state – and, in doing so, align the interests of middle-income and lower-income groups. As we saw when political pressure prevented the Conservative Governments of the 1980s from phasing out Child Benefit, universal coverage ensures that the 'sharp elbows of the middle class' are actually fighting to protect the services that the most vulnerable rely on. And people's willingness to pay tax for welfare depends on what they get back. So getting the generous welfare state we need will probably require a good deal more universality.

Moene and Wallerstein (2001) demonstrate this point through a range of ingenious economic simulations. Assuming voters are self-interested, they show that the preferred tax rates and benefit levels for the median voter rise with increasing universality of benefits. For benefits with narrow coverage, however, the preferred tax rates and benefits levels for the median voter are zero. When a degree of altruism is added into the model, the result is basically the same: while people are now prepared to pay *some* tax for benefits with narrow coverage, preferred tax and benefit levels still rise with increasing universality.

A deeper reason why universal services command more public support revolves around what the coverage of a policy implies for the perceived social identity of those receiving it. Earlier, we saw how in some contexts, the more we target a good, the more it becomes associated with a stigmatised 'out-group', thereby undermining its popular legitimacy. Over time, the result is that the politics of welfare reacts to popular sentiment with retrenchment. A vicious circle is then set up when this retrenchment creates even greater targeting, and an even sharper distinction between recipients and non-recipients.

In fact, polling reported in Chapter 5 showed a strong association between perceived social distance from council tenants (how much people thought they had in common with them) and support for welfare policy. What's more, this perceived distance was in part an institutional creation: the further one lived from council tenants, the less likely one was to feel you had anything in common with them. Targeting and segregation had created a sense of 'them' and 'us', wholly detrimental to the solidarity we need for welfare policy. Sadly, much social housing has been provisioned in a way that has tapped into neither the empathy nor the self-interest of the wider public.

Strong links between identity, social distance and support for redistribution have also been found in other (non-institutional) dimensions of difference. In the context of race, for example, Gaertner et al. (1996) found that US citizens who thought of themselves primarily as 'Americans' rather than 'white Americans' were more likely to support welfare policy targeted at black Americans than citizens who thought of themselves primarily as 'white Americans'. Similarly, white US citizens who thought of black Americans primarily as 'Americans' rather than as 'black Americans' were more likely to support policy targeted at black Americans.

The analysis above suggests that ensuring welfare institutions have sufficiently wide coverage, and that they unite rather than divide the population, will be key to the strategy of poverty prevention. In particular, the need to foster and maintain public support for generous welfare means that reshaping the design of some of our major benefits and services in order to generate virtuous, rather than vicious, circles of public sentiment should be a major reform challenge for the future.

We now turn to some of the policy areas discussed earlier, to show how the analysis above motivates particular programmes of welfare reform.

Integrating public and private housing

As we saw in Chapter 3, one of the British welfare state's key failings has been in the provision of social housing. Recent evidence, reviewed in Chapter 2, supports what many have long suspected: that living in social housing can also be a cause of poverty and inequality, and not just a symptom (Feinstein et al., 2008). But what is really striking is that the same body of evidence found that these correlations between tenure and disadvantage are not historically inevitable. For the generation of tenants born into social housing in 1946 there are no such correlations; the council house was typically a source of both pride and social inclusion. Fast-forward to 1970, however, and, for those born into social housing, the full range of disadvantages had kicked in.

What happened in between was the 'residualisation' of the social housing sector (also described in Chapter 3). By this we mean two processes. The first arose because of the ever increasing *targeting* of social housing only on those in most need, with the consequence that it came to be seen as a service only for 'the disadvantaged'. The second process of residualisation came from the *physical concentration* of public housing in large and often isolated estates. Chapter 2 also examined some of the problems that arise from this targeting and segregation. In this section, we look at reforms that would begin to address them.

Achieving real mixed communities

The ideal of mixed communities was a central part of the post-war welfare settlement. Bevan championed the vision of the 'living tapestry' of mixed communities, with housing tenure no longer being a marker of social status. As we have seen, this ideal was not honoured for long. But it is the ideal we should return to today. This, we must be clear, must be the full Bevan vision: 'mix' does not mean a smattering of social housing clustered together in the less desirable parts of private housing estates; it means the full dispersal and integration of social housing across our housing stock, and within all types of neighbourhood, affluent and poor.

But this will not evolve spontaneously. What is needed is robust regulation of the planning process. To date, even though mix has ostensibly been at the heart of government planning policy, the ideal far too often fails in practice. And it fails because central regulation of the planning process has been too loose. This does not mean that there must be inflexible central housing targets prescribing the exact numbers and tenure mix of a given area. But it does mean that there should be planning at the regional as well as the Local Authority level, and it does mean that this should be driven by more than 'guidance'. At present, Local Planning Authorities can require new developments to follow the principles of mix, but they are not obligated to do so. In practice this means that mix often does not happen at all in many areas. Moreover, when it does happen it has tended to come in a formulaic 'bricks and mortar' approach, focussing narrowly on a mix of *tenures* rather than the broader aim of a well-balanced mix of different *income* households in a neighbourhood. We will need the latter as well as the former if we are to return to Bevan's vision that society was not to be segregated by income or social status.

Local Authorities should therefore have an obligation to ensure that all new private and social housing is genuinely 'pepper-potted' and 'tenure blind'; that is, there should be no visible distinction between the tenures, and the presumption must be that this is best achieved by avoiding obvious clusters of different tenures. Moreover, it is crucial that the role of 'tenure' in planning is only a means to an end. If we are to do Bevan's ideal justice, then mixed tenure must be a *proxy* for mixed income – or, in the language of the past, mixed 'class'. Finally, we need to pursue the kind of measures necessary to ensure that mixed communities do not lose their balance over time. In particular, active area management is crucial in high-density mixed areas, as poor management can quickly lead to decline and the exit from the area of those with the means to do so. It also means that we must re-appraise the role of the 'buy to let' market, which has recently radically altered the intended balance of a number of mixed developments, with the 'owned component' becoming just another part of the rental sector.

The importance of 'ordinariness'

Recent evidence on housing mix (for example, Allen et al., 2005) has yielded the seemingly prosaic but in fact very important conclusion that residents of established mixed communities regard one another as 'ordinary people', with no stigma attached to tenancy. One interview-based study of the attitudes of homeowners on a mixed estate (Holmes, 2006) found that 89 per cent were satisfied with their neighbourhood; and when prompted to respond directly to the question of income mix, 77 per cent of owners either felt it made no difference to their satisfaction or had a positive view of mix. What did count in terms of satisfaction were quality homes, good services and a feeling that the neighbourhood was pleasant and safe.

We also know that these positive reactions are not just internal: good planned mix – both new developments and active interventions in older neighbourhoods – has generated positive perceptions from those living outside and those seeking to move in, often reflected in the property values of mixed areas. Open market price increases in some developments (for example, New Earswick) have outperformed the regional average. One review of seven case studies found there was no significant negative association in which mix drives down property prices (Rowlands et al., 2006). Again, in all cases, far more significant than mix for the attractiveness of the neighbourhood was the quality of the homes and the surrounding infrastructure and services.

What is of crucial importance here is the loss of stigma: these are neighbourhoods of choice, not of last resort. And there is ample evidence that both internal and external perceptions of such neighbourhoods, and the self-image of social housing tenants, can be significantly improved (Martin and Watkinson, 2003).

But mix is not merely about making tenants feel better: if mixed communities are popular and viable, we can begin to really tackle some of the deep spatial and social segregation that are part of the causal processes of poverty. It can also help to negate the more abstract but deeply entrenched perception that social housing is a devalued public good.

Reforming financial support for housing

Part of the residualisation of housing provision has been the residualisation of financial support for housing, especially Housing Benefit, with its narrow coverage, inflexibility, and steep withdrawal rate. So part of our 'de-residualising' agenda has to be to extend this system of financial support. One of the motivations here is to tackle the disincentives from benefit withdrawal, and to end the separation of people into different types of housing support. Another important motivation is to extend support to low- and middle-income homeowners, particularly those on low incomes struggling with mortgage payments, many of whom are victims of the same ideology of housing that has had such an adverse impact on the social sector.

During 2009, between 40,000 and 60,000 families will have lost their homes, and at present there are approximately 250,000 households that have fallen into arrears with their mortgage payments.[65] Many of these households will have to, in one form or another, rely on the assistance of the state. And many other households would also no doubt benefit greatly from doing so, rather than scraping by on the narrowest of margins. So here there is both a significant need for many property-owning low- and middle-income households to reconnect with the support of the welfare state, and also an important opportunity to challenge the underlying ideology behind the Right-to-Buy – that being a good citizen was somehow all about 'independence' from the state. In doing so, we can begin to break down widespread perceptions that tenure distinctions also bring with them a tacit moral distinction about the status of households.

One way of doing this could be through a Housing Cost Credit. This would, firstly, bring all forms of housing assistance into the same institutional structure, so that, for example, instead of recipients of Housing Benefit or Support for Mortgage Interest being filtered into separate categories, all would be part of the same system.[66] Secondly, through a more gradual taper, it would extend support further up the income spectrum than Housing Benefit usually reaches, helping a wider range of households and lessening the marginal tax rates faced by those currently receiving support.

This more generous progressive universalism would come at a cost. One way of paying for this would be to remove the exemption from capital gains tax on your principal primary residence (a tax expenditure which cost some £14.5 billion in 2007-08). Many of the families who have benefitted in the past from this highly regressive tax break would now get some support through the Housing Cost Credit; but they would now do so as part of the same system as everyone else, and in a distributionally fairer way too, with more support going to those on low incomes (whether in the social rented or private rented sectors or homeowners).

Breaking down tenure distinctions

As well as reducing the residualised nature of Housing Benefit, by covering households of different tenure a Housing Cost Credit would reduce the visibility and relevance of tenure distinctions. But what options are open for breaking down tenure distinctions themselves, which can prove so socially divisive?

One is the concept of shared ownership, which can blur the polarisation between outright ownership and non-ownership, potentially introducing a degree of universalism into tenure classification. Clearly in the current financial crisis, encouraging people to enter a falling market is not a good idea in the short term. Yet in the longer term, shared ownership can be a means of offering some of the advantages of subsidised home-ownership, without reinforcing the cultural belief that this is somehow a morally superior form of tenure.

The various forms of shared ownership schemes (in which a Housing Association typically owns part of a bought property) should be brought together into a far more fluid system, in which households who have made a move into ownership can rely on further support if they need it. Part of the core offer should be to enable tenants and owners to engage in 'reverse stair-casing': not only to move up into ownership with help, but also to move back down out of ownership, without undue penalty, if their circumstances change. One way of facilitating this approach would be to pursue a (qualified) 'right to sell', whereby in certain contexts homeowners could apply to sell all or part of their property to their Local Authority or to a local Housing Association, whilst remaining in the same home. Such a measure would go beyond existing 'emergency' measures of support, such as government-backed mortgage-payment 'holidays' and the very limited (and highly targeted) form of an option to sell that is currently on offer.

Sometimes such applications would be driven by deteriorating financial circumstances, but in other cases they might be for more positive reasons, such as a desire for more flexibility to pursue new opportunities in work or life. Whatever the motivation, though, the overall impact would be to create a more graduated housing system and to blur the current sharp distinctions between tenures that label public housing tenants as lesser citizens than owners. Whereas the Right to Buy greatly contributed to the process of residualisation, an option to sell would reconnect citizens to the welfare state as a positive protective mechanism.[67]

There is in fact scope for more radical reform to break down tenure distinctions by looking at the nature of tenure itself. One suggestion might be to scrap social housing as a tenure altogether, giving all who needed it direct financial assistance through Housing Benefit.[68] But existing attempts to extend the responsibility of the tenant through direct transfers (to be used in the open rental market) do not augur well. The Local Housing Allowance has in fact led to high levels of arrears for landlords and financial difficulties for tenants (Shelter, 2009). And it would be all too easy to simply transfer the problems of the social sector to a just-as-deeply-residualised private sector, as our history of 'slums' and landlordism shows.

But there is another possible approach to tenure, one which proceeds from the opposite direction. Instead of trying to herd people into home ownership (which may or may not be beneficial for them), all in the name of promoting an ideal of 'independence from the state', an alternative way of 'detoxifying' tenure distinctions would be to make more explicit the way in which homeowners are in fact dependent on society as a whole.

For the fact is that the very existence of private property is utterly reliant on the public laws, public bodies, public goods and public expenditures that support ownership: legal rights, along with agencies to monitor, adjudicate and enforce those rights; protection from theft, vandalism, arson, and other property crimes, along with the police and other public authorities to coercively prevent individuals from engaging in these activities and a system of courts and prisons too; protection from fire and flooding; and so on. If you lived in Bosnia in 1995 (coercive confiscation of property) or Hull in 2007 (flooding) you probably have a keener awareness of how little 'private property' means without a government that has the power to defend it (paid for, of course, by public spending).

What's more, the value of private property is also utterly reliant on the quality of surrounding public goods, from street lighting and transport access, to public services and the local environment.

Yet there is very little awareness of the public nature of private property, let alone the public costs involved. Encouraged in part by the ideology that was used to promote the Right-to-Buy in the 1980s, there is a widespread and rather naïve libertarian view that private property ownership is somehow about 'freedom from government'.

Stephen Holmes and Cass Sunstein sum up neatly what is wrong with this position:

> "A liberal legal system does not merely protect and defend property. It defines and thus creates property. Without legislation and adjudication there can be no property rights...Government lays down the rules of ownership specifying who owns what and how particular individuals acquire specific ownership rights. It identifies, for instance, the maintenance and repair obligations of landlords and how jointly owned property is to be sold. It therefore makes no more sense to associate property rights with 'freedom from government' than to associate the right to play chess with freedom from the rules of chess."
>
> (Holmes and Sunstein, 1999)

So property rights, in short, rely upon interdependence, not independence. And recognising this is the first step if we are to neutralise the heavily moralised distinction between tenures in this country. It is not just that social housing tenants are dependent on the state and other citizens for the existence of their housing; we all are.

We have already discussed how intermediate ownership has the potential to blur the distinction between ownership and rental status by introducing gradation into the system. A longer-term, but potentially more radical, solution might be to encourage a fundamental shift in the way that we conceptualise tenure itself. The central move here would be to treat *all* property as part of a kind of 'social leasehold' system. Rather than classifying tenures in terms of the ownership of bricks and mortar, we should think of them primarily in terms of their reliance on a surrounding set of public goods. In terms of this 'social component' of property, all properties would be treated as leaseholds, with the Local Authority as the 'landlord'.

None of which would mean a loss of rights. A freeholder could continue to sell both land and property, at will, in the open market. And there would be a contractual relationship with the 'landlord', setting out government's duties and responsibilities. Indeed, this approach could motivate an *increase* in homeowners' rights, such as a legal duty on government to protect properties from flooding.

Social leaseholding would be accompanied by the payment of a 'social rent' – not an additional charge, but a repackaging of that portion of income tax and council tax which is currently spent on maintaining the institutions that support property rights, and the local infrastructure which makes property existence possible. Social tenants would of course pay additional rent for occupation of the property as well, as would shared ownership households, while homeowners would pay no additional rent. The situation with private rental would be more complex, with two rental streams, one from tenant to the landlord and one from the owner to the Local Authority.

By making more visible the link between property rights and public goods, such a 'social rent' could well increase public acceptance of property-related taxation (and could potentially be an important part of council tax reform). More importantly, though, while there would still obviously be a distinction between owners and renters, bringing all dwellings into the same category for the purposes of a 'social rent' could help to reduce the social divisiveness of the owner-'non-owner' distinction that is so detrimental to tackling poverty and exclusion.

Trying to change the way we think about property and tenure in order to make our mutual interdependence explicit might sound abstract, but we believe it is the first necessary step to addressing both the underlying psychology and the public politics of housing policy. Doing so should be part of a cultural and ideological transformation of the way in which we think about the relationship between citizenship, home-ownership and social housing, with the latter no longer conferring a status of illegitimate dependence and second-class status.

Integrating tax and benefits

Why our tax system is bad at poverty prevention

The UK's system of income tax was initially conceived as a device for raising revenue, first introduced in the 1790s to finance the Napoleonic wars, and then re-introduced in the 1840s to deal with a growing budget deficit. During the first half of the 20th century, however, the income tax system evolved a new function. A variety of 'tax expenditures' were developed whereby the tax system was used to channel resources to particular groups (by reducing their tax bill) in ways that met the objectives of social policy. An early example was the introduction of the child tax allowance in 1909 to help families with children.

In his 1955 lecture, *The social division of welfare*, Richard Titmuss, reviewing the previous 50 years, noted "the remarkable development of social policy operating through the medium of the fiscal system", a phenomenon he termed 'fiscal welfare'. And today, our tax system is full of such expenditures, with tax breaks for things ranging from pensions saving to charitable donations to employer-supported childcare.

Viewed in retrospect, however, the use of the tax system for such welfare purposes is profoundly unfortunate for two reasons: its coverage and its distributional properties. Both of these features make it singularly unsuitable for poverty prevention.

Division from the benefits system

Through mechanisms like tax exemptions, allowances, deductions, reliefs and deferrals (henceforth 'allowances and reliefs'), government can allocate revenue to help household finances via the tax system. However, it's clear that using revenue on allowances and reliefs will not benefit those without sufficient incomes to be paying tax in the first place – including many not earning above the personal allowance threshold.[69] The Conservatives' current proposal for a tax break for married couples, to take one example, would not help around 600,000 or so married couples of working age without a taxable income above this threshold. And while it may be tempting to draw a distinction between government transferring resources to people, on the one hand, and government not taking resources in taxation, on the other, the reality is that tax breaks are discretionary expenditure decisions by government – just the same as decisions to spend resources on any other programme.

Of course, in such cases, individuals and households not helped by tax breaks can receive help separately through the benefits system. But separating these two groups into different systems is not only more complex, but socially undesirable too. Most obviously, it sets up a trade-off between helping one group or helping the other, pitting their interests against each other. And as Chapters 4 and 5 showed, separating individuals into different groups can impose social identities on them, potentially increasing social distance and generating stigma.

Of course, there will always be *net contributors* and *net recipients* in the welfare system: people with higher incomes will be contributing more than they receive back, and people with lower incomes will be contributing less than they receive back. However, this does not mean that we have to separate these groups out visibly in the organisation of the system itself.

Rather, in as many areas as we can, we should integrate tax and benefits together into a universal system that everybody is part of. This means net contributors receiving benefits (essentially deductions from their tax liability) and net recipients paying tax (essentially deductions from their benefit entitlement). We look at one method of doing this further below.

Though it would generate a lot of 'churn' (taxing benefits, for example, would simply return the money back to government coffers), this is all 'virtual' (money wouldn't literally be going back and forth). The result would simply be a new (and fairer) formula for calculating the 'tax-and-transfer position' of a household. In fact, under some possible designs, integrated universal systems such as this could be a lot simpler than what we have at the moment, which requires handling complex interactions between two different systems.

Most importantly, though, more integration of tax and benefits would better align the welfare interests of all citizens, reducing the stigma of benefits and generating a stronger set of relations between individuals by uniting them within a common institution.[70] That, in turn, is why such reforms would permit a far more generous welfare system.

We have seen this on various occasions throughout the history of tax and benefits. The box below looks at one important example: the organisation of financial support for families with children.

A history of division and integration: financial support for families with children

When Child Benefit was introduced in 1977, it amalgamated two previously separate systems of support: the child tax allowance, introduced in 1909, and Family Allowances (a universal payment to families with children, though not for the first child), introduced in 1946.

However, whereas the child tax allowance clearly was relatively more important to higher-income groups, the Family Allowance was relatively more important to lower income groups – and polling from the 1950s to the 1970s suggested

---

that Family Allowances had a degree of stigma attached to them (Klein, 1974). Despite increases in 1952 and 1956, the value of the Family Allowance had been allowed to stagnate through the 1950s, one of the factors that lay behind the 'rediscovery' of poverty in the 1960s (Abel-Smith and Townsend, 1965). The result was competition for revenue between the two schemes, which figured strongly in political debates of the 1960s and 1970s.

Child Benefit amalgamated these two separate systems into a genuinely universal flat-rate benefit, uniting lower and higher income groups within the same scheme, and with a distributionally more progressive result. The result was near-universal take-up. Furthermore, the value of the benefit for middle-income families was sufficiently 'meaningful' to ensure their political support. So there was a high degree of political fallout when the Thatcher Government froze Child Benefit in the late 1980s, with the Major Government forced to increase it again in the early 1990s.

History briefly repeated itself when the Labour Government created a Children's Tax Credit in 2001, which was a tax allowance and therefore only of value to taxpayers, and then – partly on distributional grounds – transformed this support into a payable credit via its incorporation into the Child Tax Credit in 2003.

Sure enough, many of those welfare states that are more effective at tackling poverty than the UK also have more of the kind of tax-benefit integration discussed here. Financial support is delivered to individuals and households through transfers, rather than tax allowances and reliefs; these generous transfers, in turn, tend to be quite heavily taxed.[71] For example, direct taxes paid on public transfers amounted to over 2 per cent of GDP in the social democratic welfare states (and over 4 per cent in Sweden and Denmark); they amounted to between 1-2 per cent of GDP in the Christian Democratic welfare states; and they amounted to less than 1 per cent of GDP in the liberal welfare states (and less than 0.5 per cent in Australia, Canada and the UK). Similarly, whereas the United States provides 'tax breaks for social purposes' worth over 2 per cent of GDP in value, the use of such tax breaks is virtually non-existent in Scandanavian countries. None of this is a coincidence.

Regressivity

Given that income tax was devised as a system for raising revenue, then making it progressive was an important step to ensure citizens contributed fairly to public expenditure. In its most recent incarnation, this happened in 1909 via the addition of a higher rate ('supertax').

But this also meant that the 'welfare function' that subsequently evolved within the tax system during the 20th century – of using tax expenditures to channel support to particular groups – was always going to be an ineffective tool for tackling poverty and inequality. This is because a tax structure that has been developed for *raising* revenue progressively will necessarily be regressive if the same structure is used as a vehicle for *transferring* resources to citizens.

Using rate cuts to transfer revenue to individuals will clearly be regressive since it will only benefit those who are paying tax, and those with larger tax liabilities will benefit more. A less obvious but equally serious problem, however, is that a progressive structure of tax rates also makes the impact of *allowances* regressive. This is because the effective value of a tax allowance is dependent on both an individual's potential tax liability and their marginal rate. The table below illustrates these points, looking at the effective value of the personal income tax allowance in 2008-09. As the first three rows show, because allowances can only reduce an individual's tax liability to zero, those earning less will benefit less than those earning more. As the last three rows show, allowances are also worth more to those with higher marginal rates, because the tax due on the pounds being exempted is higher for them than it is for those with lower marginal rates.

Table: Effective value of the income tax personal allowance. The basic rate in 2008-09 was 20 per cent, starting at £6,035; the higher rate was 40 per cent starting at £40,835.

Gross earnings (£)	Effective value of personal allowance at £6,035 (£)
0	0
5,000	1,000
10,000	1,207
37,500	1,747
50,000	2,414

By the same logic, straightforward *increases* in allowances and thresholds are also regressive. The resultant change will be worth more to those with higher marginal tax rates and those with tax liabilities above the new threshold. So more of the revenue that the government 'forgoes' goes to higher earners than lower earners. Whilst some of the regressive impact of increases in allowances and thresholds can be limited by manipulating other features of the system (such as simultaneously reducing other thresholds), the regressivity of foregoing revenue through these basic tax parameters is built into the underlying structure of a progressive tax system.

These features make tax expenditures such as allowances and reliefs in the direct tax system singularly unsuitable as an instrument of progressive social policy. Far better to use transfer payments that can be flat-rate or themselves progressive (by tapering them off at higher rates). For example, in 2008-09, £4.7 billion of expenditure on the Child and Working Tax Credits counted towards reducing recipients' tax liabilities; but the effect of this expenditure was not regressive because the value of credit available is reduced through a set of tapers as income increases.

So the problem is not just with the coverage of the existing tax system, but the regressive nature of using current tax structures (rates and allowances) for providing financial support. Having a progressive income tax system is important for raising revenue fairly and tackling inequality. But this also then places serious constraints on the use of the system as a vehicle for poverty prevention. Channelling support to people through the tax system is a truly terrible way of trying to tackle poverty and inequality.

To illustrate, the graphs below compare the impact of four different possible strategies for spending £4.1 billion. The first two of these are tax expenditures of the type discussed above; the second two are other possible types of transfers (direct flat-rate payments):

1. cutting the basic rate of income tax for working-age individuals by 1 per cent;
2. increasing the value of the personal allowance for working-age individuals by £750;
3. giving every working-age individual in the UK £114; and
4. giving every working-age household in the UK £170.

The first graph shows the amount of this £4.1 billion that would go to each working-age household income decile for each of the possible measures listed above (and the gradient of this distribution across the income spectrum). As can be seen, both the rate cut and the allowance increase are deeply regressive. With the rate cut, a whacking 86 per cent of the revenue goes to the richest half of households; with the allowance increase, 74 per cent of the revenue goes to the richest half of households. Expenditure on the flat-rate payment to individuals is much more balanced across the income distribution:

expenditure per decile does increase slightly as you move up the working-age household income distribution, but this is simply because there are more single households in lower deciles and more couple households in higher ones. Finally, expenditure on the flat-rate payment to households is obviously flat across the household income distribution, with £410 million spent on each decile.

The second and third graphs then show the average distributional impact (expressed as a percentage change in household income) of each reform by household income decile. The second graph shows the extent to which both the rate cut and the allowance increase are regressive, with working-age households in the middle and at the top of the income spectrum benefiting proportionately more than households at the bottom of the income spectrum. By contrast, the third graph shows that the flat-rate payments to individuals and households are progressive, with lower income households benefiting proportionately more than higher income households.[72] The flat-rate payment to households is especially progressive.

Expenditure gradient by working-age household income decile for possible fiscal reforms

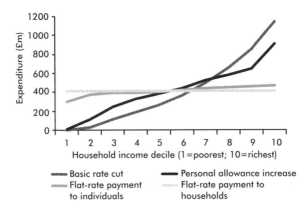

Distributional impact by working-age household income decile for possible fiscal reforms

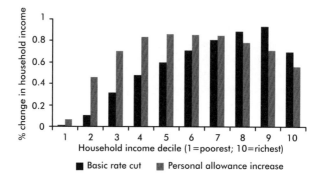

Distributional impact by working-age household income decile for possible fiscal reforms

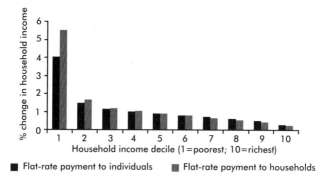

It is worth emphasising a point that such analysis highlights: whether via rate or threshold, simple tax cuts increase relative poverty. As can be seen from the second graph above, cutting the basic rate or increasing the personal allowance will, on average, increase the

income of the median working-age household by more than that of households at the bottom of the income spectrum.

Restructuring the system: creating a universal tax credit

Yet despite this analysis being well understood by policymakers for many decades, we have continued to rely on systems of reliefs and allowances within the tax system for welfare purposes. Today, the largest two tax expenditures within the income tax system are the £45.1 billion annual value of the income tax personal allowance, and the £17.5 billion annual value of income tax relief for registered pension schemes, but there are many more.[73]

There is a strong case for now replacing tax expenditures such as these with flat-rate transfer payments that can be similarly deducted from people's tax liabilities. Here we describe a route to doing this with the personal tax allowance for working-age adults, by introducing instead a *universal tax credit*, but the approach could apply in other areas too. Here we describe an approach that could be executed in several steps; each step, however, has validity independent of the others.

STEP 1: Replace the personal allowance for working-age adults with a tax-deductible flat-rate credit worth the same amount to basic-rate payers. For example, in 2008-09, replacing the personal allowance of £6,035 (in 2008-09) with a direct payment of £1,207 would have had no financial impact on basic-rate payers, whilst eliminating the regressivity of the system overall. This is shown in the third column of the table below. Analysis suggests this could save the government £3.9 billion (resources that are currently providing extra value for higher-rate payers).[74] Crucially, for the first time, this would give governments the ability to cut taxes for all in a non-regressive way – by lump sum, rather than by rate or by threshold.[75]

STEP 2: Make the credit payable to all. A more radical step would be additionally to make the resulting transfer payments 'payable' (refundable), which means that after an individual's net tax rate has been reduced to zero they get the remainder as a net payment (as with existing tax credits). This is shown in the fourth column of table below. Such a payment would be a *universal tax credit*, which – as the distributional analysis in the previous section showed – would be a powerful tool for tackling poverty. It would also end the historic segregation of taxpayers and non-taxpayers, creating a welfare institution that unites their interests. All of sudden, the vehicle that taxpayers would demand to be made more generous would be the very same one helping those in poverty. (And surely this would make those in the Taxpayers' Alliance feel better about their work?) To deal with issues of fairness and work incentives, we suggest further below that receiving the universal tax credit should be dependent on some kind of participation requirement.

Table: A comparison of different vehicles for tax expenditure

Gross earnings (£)	Effective value of personal allowance at £6,035 (£)	Value of tax-deductible flat-rate credit at £1,207 (£)	Value of payable flat-rate credit at £1,207 (£)
0	0	0	1,207
5,000	1,000	1,000	1,207
10,000	1,207	1,207	1,207
37,500	1,747	1,207	1,207
50,000	2,414	1,207	1,207

Tax relief on pensions and savings

Not only would replacing allowances and reliefs with payable flat-rate credits be fairer distributionally; for those allowances and reliefs which are designed as incentives, it would produce a fairer distribution of incentives too. For example, pensions tax relief incentivises higher-rate payers at a level of 40p for each pound saved; for basic-rate payers, the incentive is just 20p for each pound saved; and for those earning less than the £6,035 allowance in 2008-09, the Government topped up an individual's contributions as if they were eligible for basic rate relief, but only for the first £2,880 in contributions within the tax year. (This contrasts with an annual limit of £235,000 in contributions for which higher rate payers could benefit from tax relief!)[76]

Again, a fairer approach would be to scrap pensions tax relief and replace this with flat-rate credits to incentivise saving, again, making these payable for those not earning enough to pay tax. Through the Saving Gateway programme for low income households, the Government is already planning from 2010 to offer a programme of 'matched contribution' saving incentives (rather than tax-relieved saving incentives), providing a matching payment of 50p in the pound for every pound saved (up to a limit of £300 per year). And these are payable to those with no tax liability. But this principle should form the underlying structure of all of our expenditure on saving incentives, replacing regressive tax expenditures.[77]

STEP 3: Shift the credit onto a household basis. The steps described above would produce a universal tax credit on an individualised basis (because it would replace the personal allowance in the tax system, which operates on an individualised basis). Both distributionally and culturally, this would, of course, be a massive improvement in its own right. But as resources are shared within the household, poverty is a household phenomenon, not an individual one (the Duke of Westminster's wife would not be in poverty if she had zero income). And, for the same reason, poverty is best tackled at the household level (though the tax system itself should stay independent). So another important reform would be to shift the universal tax credit onto a household basis. In particular, this would mean adjusting the credit so that its value for single households was not half that for couples, but more like 63 per cent of it (which reflects the long-standing single-couple ratio in our benefits system).[78] By operating on an individualised basis, the personal allowance has historically been insufficiently generous to single households relative to couples, and this injustice should be corrected.

Some rationales for a universal tax credit

An addition to the welfare system

On a practical level, a universal tax credit would be an important addition to the fiscal system. For the purposes of poverty prevention, the aim would not be to replace the existing suite of benefits, but rather to complement them.

One advantage of this would be to take the pressure 'off' other benefits and tax credits a bit. On child poverty, the strategy of ploughing more and more into the child element of the Child Tax Credit, while effective in the short term, might prove unsustainable over the longer term. One question here is the potential effect on work incentives, which a universal tax credit of the type proposed here would overcome, since it would be flat-rate (and not withdrawn as income increased), as well as being conditional on some kind of participation requirement. Another question (as the 10p tax row showed) is whether or not it is politically feasible to target ever larger amounts of revenue on one particular subset of the population.

Here, another advantage of a universal tax credit is that it would support a variety of groups in poverty that are currently not eligible for existing tax credits, such as workless adults without children. Even a modest payable credit could – alongside existing tiers of support – significantly reduce the depth of poverty that many such groups are in.

New political choices on tax

Nevertheless, the universal tax credit advocated here is conceived primarily as a vehicle to replace existing regressive tax expenditures and to provide a new option to cut taxes non-regressively (by lump-sum, rather than by rate or by threshold).

In doing so, it would provide new political choices for tax strategy. There are a variety of reasons why governments may want to reduce direct taxation in some way – to improve household finances, to stimulate demand in the economy, to compensate groups for changes elsewhere in the system, and so on. A universal tax credit would enable this whilst avoiding the regressive distributional impact of conventional tax cuts, which set back progress towards greater equality. Provided it was designed appropriately, a universal credit would potentially provide greater benefit to a larger number of households than the equivalent expenditure on tax allowances and reliefs. This would certainly mean that anyone trying to cut rates or raise allowances in future would have a harder job to justify using revenue in this way.

Changing the evolutionary dynamics of the tax system

Furthermore, by providing another vehicle within the tax system that could be uprated continuously, a universal credit would have the potential to change the evolutionary dynamics of the system – the way its distributional impact evolves over time. The replacement of the allowance with a flat-rate credit would mean that all income is taxed. While the overall financial impact would be neutral for basic-rate taxpayers, what it would mean is that substantial amounts of revenue would be generated each year through 'fiscal drag' (whereby earnings grow faster than tax thresholds, resulting in an increased average tax rate for individuals), because the effective 'basic rate threshold' would remain at zero. To offset this tendency for individuals' tax burden to increase, we would use the proceeds of fiscal drag to uprate the universal credit. Distributionally, of course, such a strategy would get you to a very different place in 20 or 30 years' time than the strategy of raising tax thresholds (which are currently price-indexed).

Indeed, fiscal drag would be an important source of revenue for uprating the credit. Making the credit payable (as suggested in Step 2), and increasing its value for single households to 63 per cent of that for couple households (as suggested in Step 3) would be expensive. However, these are relatively small amounts compared to what would be raised over a few years through the 'non-uprating' of thresholds. Potentially, this strategy would allow the value of a universal credit to increase quite rapidly.

A new function for the tax system

The proposal in this section is partly motivated by the belief that the tax and benefits system should have a function beyond raising revenue, redistributing income, providing incentives and internalising costs. It should also have the function of *uniting individuals* in society, strengthening the relationships between them and articulating their equal citizenship. That requires ending the historic separation of taxpayers and benefit recipients and aligning their interests within the same framework.

Tax credits, which can be both tax deductions for some and transfer payments for others, have already begun to achieve this for particular groups. Our proposal is to universalise this mechanism.

Evidence suggests this could be effective for both policy and political reasons. Reducing the visibility of distinctions within the system can eliminate stigma; we have seen this, for example, with the inclusion of extra financial support for disabled workers within the Working Tax

Credit (rather than them having to claim separate payments through the benefits system). And this, in turn, can improve the effectiveness of financial support for tackling poverty. Furthermore, including middle-income and low-income households within the same policy aligns their interests – as we have seen with the Child Tax Credit, where the inclusion of 90 per cent of households with children within this framework has made the prioritisation of expenditure here popular and politically viable. Ultimately, a universal tax credit would align the strategy of increasing financial support for those in poverty with that of incremental tax reductions for low- and middle-income households.

A basic income?

Finally, it's worth observing that a universal credit of this type would essentially create a *basic income* within the tax and benefits system – a working-age equivalent of Child Benefit or a Citizens Pension. However, there are some important differences between what is proposed here and a basic income as classically conceived.

First, the credit proposed here is not supposed to be an adequate income that would, by itself, keep all above the poverty line (the personal allowance for basic-rate payers is currently effectively worth around £25 a week). Rather, the idea is to create *a foundational level of support* that would complement the current set of benefits and tax credits (much like Child Benefit for children).

Second, the credit proposed here would differ from the standard idea of basic income in being *centred on the household*, rather than the individual. This partly reflects differing motivations. A basic income is commonly proposed as a manifestation of individual rights, which obviously leads to an individualised system (van Parijs, 1995). Here, our interest in it is as a tool for tackling poverty, which is most effectively done at the level of the household.[79]

Finally, the standard notion of basic income is as an unconditional payment – a 'citizens' income'. But this is by no means the only option. Following Atkinson (1996), our preferred model – which fits well with the proposals in the following chapter – would be to make the credit conditional on participation in one of a range of socially useful activities, which could involve caring or training as well as paid employment (as well as, for those out of work, activities to prepare for and look for work). Not only would the conditionality involved in a participation credit provide a useful vehicle for maximizing participation in society, but it would also offset reductions in work incentives from replacing the personal allowance with a payable credit.

Making benefits and services meaningful to middle-class households

The opening section of this chapter explored some reasons why universalism is important in poverty prevention, from avoiding stigma and removing barriers to exit from poverty, to fostering common social identity and aligning the interests of key electoral groups.

This last point about aligning interests and identities is especially important when we consider the evolution of welfare states over periods of time. The evidence cited earlier suggested that – whether motivated by self interest, or caused by the perceived social distance between contributors and recipients – institutional structures that divide the population tend to reduce public willingness to contribute to the policy in question. However, the 'proof of the pudding' comes not from economic simulations or social psychology experiments, but from real-world welfare states. That targeting resources on those in poverty is not the best way to help them might sound totally counterintuitive. But it is what comparisons of welfare states show time and again.

The table below compares different welfare states in terms of their degree of low-income targeting and their efficacy in reducing poverty and inequality, measured over a period from the early 1970s to the late 1990s. Strikingly, the welfare states in those countries which target a substantial proportion of their benefits on the poorest (the 'liberal' welfare states like the US, the UK and Australia) do far *worse* at reducing poverty and inequality than the welfare states in countries which rely more on flat-rate or earnings-related benefits (particularly the 'social democratic' welfare states like Sweden and Norway).[80] The reason why can be seen in the final column of the table: the countries with more targeting end up with far less generous welfare states than those with less targeting.

And, sure enough, statistical analyses of welfare state performance tend to show a very significant association between poverty reduction and welfare state generosity (for example, Moller et al., 2003), but no independent association between poverty reduction and degree of targeting. Indeed, some studies show *negative associations* between poverty reduction and degree of targeting (Kim, 2000).

Note that the claim is not that countries which target resources on the poorest simply have more poverty and inequality, which could ultimately be due to other factors (and, indeed, could explain a short-term desire to target). Rather, as a comparison of the pre- and post-tax-and-transfer poverty rates in the table below shows, *it is that their welfare states actually do less redistribution than those which do not target resources on the poorest*. This is a phenomenon that the political scientists Walter Korpi and Joakim Palme have nicknamed the 'paradox of redistribution': "the more we target benefits at the poor only, the less likely we are to reduce poverty and inequality" (Korpi and Palme, 1998). The reason is that the degree of redistribution a system produces is not only determined by the 'vertical gradient' of its distributional profile (targeted, flat-rate, earnings-related, etc.), but by the volume of finance flowing through it. And, as we saw in Chapter 5, people are often less willing to contribute to more targeted systems.

Table: Welfare state performance from early 1970s to late 1990s. Figures refer to averages over the period (taken from Moller et al., 2003 and Bradley et al., 2003).

	pre-tax & transfer poverty	post-tax & transfer poverty	% reduction in poverty due to taxes and transfers	pre-tax & transfer Gini coefficient	post-tax & transfer Gini coefficient	% reduction in inequality due to taxes and transfers	scale of welfare generosity (taxes and transfers as a proportion of GDP)
Social Democratic welfare states							
Sweden	14.8	4.8	64.5	32.7	20.2	37.9	1.61
Norway	12.4	4	67.2	29.8	21.5	27.5	0.96
Denmark	17.2	4.8	71.5	32.5	21.5	33.6	2.17
Finland	12.1	3.4	69.1	31	20	35.2	1.35
Christian Democratic welfare states							
Belgium	19.5	4.1	78.8	33.7	21.6	35.6	2.34
France	21.8	6.1	57.9	39.4	29.4	25.4	0.88
Germany	9.7	5.1	46.9	32.2	26.2	18.7	-0.41
Netherlands	18.5	11.5	66.9	37.5	26	30.6	3.46
Liberal welfare states							
Australia	16.2	9.2	42.2	37.5	28.5	24	-1.97
Canada	17.1	11.9	29.9	35.8	28.2	21.3	-1.22
United Kingdom	16.4	8.2	48.7	38.2	29.3	22.7	-1.52
United States	17.2	15.1	12.1	39.8	32.8	17.6	-2.21

It may not be obvious that flat-rate and earnings-related benefits can be redistributive at all, but of course when combined with progressive taxation they can be. A system which collects revenue progressively and then spends it by giving everyone an equal amount will end up transferring resources from those paying more tax to those paying less.[81] And an earnings-related system (which gives out higher benefits to previously higher-earning households and lower benefits to previously lower-earning households) can be redistributive too, provided the gradient of expenditure out is 'shallower' than the gradient of expenditure in.[82] (For example, in the US pensions system, workers pay a percentage of their earnings, and benefits are then calculated on the basis of a progressive formula so that lower-paid workers get more pension per dollar of contribution than higher-paid workers.)

Of course, in terms of *redistribution per pound spent*, targeted systems are more efficient. But if non-targeted systems make people sufficiently more willing to pay into them, then the net result will be more redistribution of resources. And this is what we often see in practice. The change in Finland, for example, in the 1960s from flat-rate to earnings-related pensions (that is, giving more to richer households) significantly reduced poverty and inequality among the elderly over subsequent decades (Jantti, Kangas and Ritakallio, 1997).

This practical point about redistribution is one among a number of factors that explain a deep link between the differing *objectives* of welfare states and their differing efficacy in poverty prevention – again, a seemingly paradoxical one. Those welfare states whose main objective is *tackling poverty* have always done much worse at tackling poverty than those welfare states whose main objective is *wage replacement*.

The welfare state in the UK, with its legacy of the Poor Law, has historically been focussed on the relief of poverty – and, as we saw in Chapter 3, never entirely been able to lose that ethos. Continental social insurance systems, by contrast, formed at times of industrial upheaval and great mass insecurity, focus much more on wage replacement. And this partly explains the relative failure of the UK to tackle poverty when compared with its continental counterparts. For the result of pursuing a strategy of wage replacement is that benefits are paid out at levels that are genuinely attractive to middle-income households. The result is deep support for welfare provision in these countries across all sections of society, with a correspondingly generous system that is highly effective in tackling poverty.[83]

Perhaps the obvious area in which the tension between these different objectives has been felt within the UK has been within our pensions system, and this example is discussed further in the box below.

Institutional dynamics in the evolution of state pensions

Historically, the UK state pension would have achieved the buy-in of more middle- and higher-income households if it had simply been set at a more generous level from the start. Its relative lack of generosity arose from two aspects of Beveridge's original model (the Beveridge 'strait-jacket' – Fawcett, 1996). First, it was assumed that the aim of the pension should be subsistence (eliminating poverty), but no more, with any further income to come from voluntary provision. Pensions were thus set at a flat rate, immediately distinguishing Britain from continental schemes such as Germany and Sweden (whose objective was to replace earnings). Second, the National Insurance scheme was to be funded from *flat-rate contributions* from all, which meant that the resulting benefit levels were constrained by what the poorest could reasonably afford to contribute. This in turn meant that the benefits were never especially valuable to many middle-class households, especially for pensions, where many began to invest more in their own occupational and private provision instead.

Flat-rate pensions (and contributions) were subsequently abandoned in the 1959 National Insurance Act, which some viewed as a move towards a model of wage replacement (although the under-

---

lying motivation was really to make contributions progressive in order to raise more funds). However, the 1959-1964 Conservative Government also pursued a direction of reform that would deal a fatal blow to the future generosity of state pensions. Following the 1954 Philips Report, they formally abandoned Beveridge's objective of trying to provide pensions at subsistence levels (which the Report had described as an 'extravagant use of the community's resources'). So it was clear that private provision, on the one hand, and means tested National Assistance, on the other, would have to play increasing roles. In line with this, they devoted considerable resources and energy towards getting people to take up private and occupational pensions, particularly through the 'contracting out' facility – basically, encouraging employees to exit from the state scheme.

Abel-Smith and Townsend (1957), and subsequently the Labour Party, made a valiant attempt in the late 1950s to argue for the introduction of more genuine earnings-related provision, mindful of designing a scheme with sufficient public acceptability. Similarly, in order to try and rekindle more middle-class buy-in, Labour introduced the State Earnings-Related Pension Scheme (SERPS) in the late 1970s and increased the value of the basic state pension. But these attempts to rectify the problems with the system came too late. The fact that many workers were now more attached to occupational and private provision created a powerful set of interests against markedly increasing the generosity of the National Insurance scheme. And there was insufficient popular support for the model to stop the incoming Thatcher Government breaking the earnings link for the basic state pension and cutting SERPS. As Howard Glennerster (2004) puts it, "There was no large body of middle class pensioners who saw it as in their interests to defend the state scheme, as there has been in the US." The value of the basic state pension has subsequently declined and been overtaken by the value of means tested income support for pensioners.

In many respects, this story of the decline of the UK state pension, particularly when compared with the different trajectory of pensions in countries like Sweden (which had similar debates in the 1950s), is a classic example of the kind of path-dependent institutional evolution discussed in Chapter 4. Future decline was built into the initial structure of Beveridge's model and made inevitable by the subsequent Conservative response to the problems this caused.

Should the UK adopt earnings-related benefits? State earnings-related systems seem most likely to prosper when creating a new area of provision, or filling a gap in provision, rather than being introduced to compete with existing private provision. In the latter case, a necessary precondition for success would seem to be widespread public discontent at the costs or security of private schemes (as currently exists in the US health insurance market). It is not clear that the current landscape in the UK is ripe for a major expansion of earnings-related provision, though piloting public insurance schemes in a few localities could be a valuable way to explore what potential exists across a range of policy areas.

This is not to say that developing earnings-related schemes in future would not be a positive development. More importantly, though, if the key objective is securing middle-class 'buy-in', then the short- and medium-term focus has to be on getting benefit levels that are sufficiently meaningful to middle-income households. The gradient of payments – whether progressive, flat-rate or earnings-related – is a separate issue from the actual level of award received by those in the middle. For example, the current debate about the Child Tax Credit for middle- and higher-income households is about how high it should extend and how generous it should be, not whether or not the benefit taper should be progressive, flat-rate or earnings-related. Certainly, earnings-relatedness is one way to give middle-income households a stake in the system, but as Child Benefit shows, not the only one.

The history of social policy in the 20th century has very often been a case of the Labour Party versus the Treasury (yes, even since 1997 too). The reason is because the Treasury's approach to fiscal responsibility has often been through minimising expenditure, and then doing as well as you can with what you have – hence a predilection for targeting. By contrast, many of the civilising social reforms this country needs and has needed over the past century are ones where fiscal responsibility would be better practised through maximising willingness to contribute and then balancing larger volumes of revenue and expenditure.

The key problem resides in the internal structure of the Treasury. Spending envelopes are set at an aggregate level on the basis of economic, demographic and fiscal projections; how you design welfare policy is then treated as a second-order issue to be decided afterwards. Yet if the analysis in this section is correct, then social policy design is one of those factors that should form the basis of fiscal projections in the first place. Given that the structure of welfare programmes dramatically affects willingness to contribute through taxation, it is essential to factor this into considering the sustainability of public spending. (It is ultimately no less irresponsible to fail to take account of the effect of narrower targeting on future tax revenues than it is to fail to take account of population growth on demand for services.)

A key step would therefore be to set up a team within the Treasury that would monitor the dimensions of policy that underpin taxpayers' willingness to contribute – and which would scrutinise each reform proposal for its effect on this as hawkishly as the expenditure policy teams scrutinise departmental outturns.

Conclusion: ending the social division of welfare

As the analysis here and in earlier chapters has shown, the questions of *who is included* in policy and *how they are treated* relative to one another are fundamental for explaining the success or failure of welfare institutions. And investigating these questions in practice produces surprising answers. Perhaps counter-intuitively, redistribution to the poorest often seems to be most successful when policy frameworks do not attempt to identify them. Similarly, the long-term success of redistribution often seems to rely more on the value of a benefit or service to middle-income households than to low-income households.

We have argued here for universalising reforms that would reunite the population in key areas of social policy – housing and taxation – that are currently the site of damaging social division, division that not only hinders attempts to tackle poverty, but which actively reproduces and entrenches it. The paradox of welfare policy is that, for those policy instruments we so desperately need to tackle poverty, the key to making them more effective is precisely to shift their remit *away* from a focus on tackling poverty and towards articulating our equal citizenship.

7. Why we need a new welfare contract

Earlier chapters have explored the tensions between need and entitlement in welfare – an age-old dilemma. For the principle according to which welfare institutions distribute resources is of fundamental importance for the success and sustainability of social policy. In particular, Chapter 5 showed the importance of ensuring that reciprocity is enshrined – and seen to be enshrined – within the welfare system.

In this chapter, we look at how we might go about designing a welfare system in order to do this better. In the section that follows, we briefly review what reciprocity is, why it is important for welfare, and why failures of reciprocity can lead to ineffective welfare – and to poverty. We then explore how it might be possible to meet the twin challenges of making our social security system both more generous and more popular.

The importance of reciprocity in poverty prevention

Chapter 3 looked at the unhappy post-war history of social insurance – and particularly out-of-work benefits. The story was one of high ideals and initial popularity, with a widening of entitlement to social security contributing to a large reduction in poverty. But it was also a story of the exclusion of other social groups, inadequacy, flawed design and eventual popular backlash, which has contributed to a good deal of poverty today, as well as a public opinion landscape that often makes anti-poverty objectives seem even more intractable.

Three particular issues highlighted were:

- the way in which the historic exclusion of carers from a system of full, independent insurance led to large numbers of women without a full state pension in retirement;

- the way in which many people were effectively moved onto passive out-of-work benefits in the 1980s and 1990s and left there, with knock-on effects on subsequent employability, life chances and household incomes; and

- the way in which declining popular support for certain aspects of welfare – particularly out-of-work benefits – undermined support for expenditure in these areas, making possible benefits cuts in the 1980s (and a continuing relative decline in benefit values). As Chapter 2 showed, this has resulted in large numbers of working-age adults in poverty today.

On one level it could be argued that these problems simply reflect a failure by the welfare state to respond sufficiently to a variety of social needs. But while they do have this in common with many other failures of welfare provision, they also have an additional dimension which marks them out as especially pernicious: a failure by our welfare system to both recognise and require socially useful contributions on the part of citizens. It is the presence of this deeper dimension, a *failure of reciprocity*, that makes these failures of welfare provision especially unjust and harmful. And, we will argue in this chapter, it is in rectifying failures of reciprocity that we can have most impact on poverty over the long term.

What is reciprocity?

Reciprocity is about making a contribution in return for benefits received, or receiving benefits in return for contributions made. Often we think about reciprocity in terms of exchanges between individuals ('an eye for an eye'), but it is clear that as a principle it can operate in a collective context too, meaning that those who claim a share of collective resources also make an effective contribution to the creation and maintenance of those resources.

In the context of welfare, reciprocity can be instantiated in different ways. One interpretation is a requirement to make a suitably fitting productive contribution in return for drawing on public provision (White, 2003), such as working to increase national output or contributing to national well-being. A further dimension might be a requirement specifically to contribute financially to the pot of resources from which individuals draw, such as paying tax to the exchequer.

A 'looser' version of reciprocity might simply be a form of conditional exchange, so there are conditions attached to receipt of benefits. These might not be requirements to contribute back into the pot, but perhaps to demonstrate some other type of behaviour – welfare with 'strings attached'. Although one might want to draw a distinction between reciprocity and simply any type of conditionality, one can imagine conditions that entail a certain degree of effort or sacrifice on the part of the recipient; in such cases it may make sense to talk about 'reciprocity' since one can talk about the degree of 'fittingness' between the effort or sacrifice made and the benefits received.

Why is reciprocity important?

Very generally, there are three types of reasons why reciprocity is important in welfare policy.

Normative arguments for reciprocity

Some argue – persuasively, in our view – that the requirement of reciprocity in welfare is an independent claim of
justice (especially White, 2003). This is because 'free-riding'
– claiming a share of the fruits of others' labour without the
intention of contributing back – is morally objectionable. It
violates a norm of mutually respectful regard for one another. It is also exploitative, effectively setting up relations of
'aristocracy' and 'servility' between individuals. So free-riding is incompatible with equal citizenship.[84]

As well as ensuring that all individuals receiving benefits make a contribution back in return, reciprocity also
requires, conversely, that existing contributions to society
from which others benefit are properly recognised and
rewarded. Today, it is estimated that individuals perform
unpaid care work worth about £67 billion in value (in
England alone) and unpaid volunteering work worth over
£22 billion (including nearly two billion volunteer
hours).[85] Taking reciprocity seriously also means better
valuing such contributions, including with more financial
support for those making them.

There is a very practical dimension to these normative
arguments: the allocation of resources. The failure to
reward care work sufficiently, for example, has resulted in
an unfair distribution of resources: in 2001, economically
inactive working-age carers providing more than 20 hours
a week in care lost a potential £5.47 billion in income
(nearly three quarters of the estimated costs of substitut-
ing that care with formal care services) (Moulin, 2008).[86] Or
to take an opposite example: if, say, 50,000 people who
could work instead decided (let's say unreasonably) to
remain out of work for 15 months, rather than, say, three
months, the additional cost to the exchequer from
Jobseeker's Allowance alone would be £167 million –
money that could have been used to raise the child element of the child tax credit by around £20.

It is worth noting that an insistence on reciprocity will not necessarily have an equalising effect. Sanctioning an individual who refuses to participate in job search activities without good reason, for example, may well increase hardship. But, as we discuss below, it is our belief that an insistence on real reciprocity in welfare will more often act as a force for tackling poverty. For this to hold, however, government needs to meet its own side of the bargain to provide fairer chances for all.

Empirical arguments for reciprocity in poverty prevention

The normative arguments outlined above are really about enforcing one party's responsibility to others *for the benefit of others*. But there is also an argument that enforcing the requirement for an individual to make a contribution *is of benefit to the individual themselves*. This is a paternalistic argument (often associated with political theorists like Lawrence Mead) over which some degree of care needs to be taken.[87] In particular, for this argument to be made, the purported benefits to the individual themselves should correspond at some level with their own preferences for their life plan (White, 2003). And, there is also clearly a need to balance the advantages of conditionality against the potential harms to individuals that can result from the enforcement of conditions.

Nevertheless, paternalistic arguments for reciprocity do have some validity. One advantage of enforcing the requirement to make a contribution is that it can benefit individuals who would otherwise be unmotivated or who would not otherwise engage in activity that could be beneficial to their future life prospects. In requiring them to take up opportunities that they otherwise would not, conditionality and compulsion can actually be important drivers of equality of opportunity (White, 2004). Furthermore, by requiring individuals to maintain contact with the labour market, such requirements can prevent the disconnection from work that evidence shows can greatly impair future employment outcomes.

Instrumental arguments for reciprocity in poverty prevention

A third consideration is the role of reciprocity in shaping public attitudes to welfare. If reciprocity is felt to be a requirement of fairness, as Chapter 5 suggested it was, it follows that welfare systems that are felt to violate reciprocity will arouse public opposition, with all the consequences for the generosity, effectiveness and sustainability of welfare that have been highlighted in previous chapters. Specifically, the perception that recipients of welfare are 'free-loaders' can lead to support for welfare retrenchment or reactionary behavioural regulation which may harm vulnerable claimants.

Nor is this just about policy: a sense of grievance about the welfare system and the resulting negative judgements about the moral worth of those receiving welfare can directly affect claimants through stigma and discrimination. Given that the vast majority of claimants operate in good faith and play by the rules, the social security system actually does its beneficiaries a great disservice if it fails to cultivate the perception that the system is fair.

So reciprocity is necessary to create the sense of public legitimacy about welfare that will be needed to entrench a long-term welfare settlement. And these considerations feed back into policy in a very direct way. For a system with greater public legitimacy can generate higher levels of contribution through taxation than one with less. So reframing social security in a way that fosters greater public support will be critical in order to get the more generous welfare state we will need to prevent poverty.

This section has touched on two particular challenges for tackling poverty. First, there are a range of ways in which our system of social security will need to provide more help and support than it currently does – including, in some cases, higher benefits going to more people. But this will be expensive. So, second, people will need to remain willing – and, indeed, to be *more* willing – to pay taxation to finance this social security. And this, in turn, means they will need to see the system into which they are paying as fair.

At first glance, these two challenges seem quite dissonant. If there's opposition to welfare for the unemployed, then it seems unlikely we can both increase its generosity *and* improve perceptions of how fair the system is. Can we really square both of these objectives?

In this chapter we will argue that we can; these objectives needn't conflict at all. But squaring them requires redesigning the system to change how people look at it – and getting the politics of welfare right.

Raising the safety net

Chapter 2 highlighted significant and rising poverty among working-age adults, particularly working-age adults without children, and identified the low level of out-of-work benefits as a key driver of this. Ever since 1981, these benefits have only been uprated in line with prices, meaning their value has been falling relative to average earnings (and the poverty line). For example, the value of unemployment benefit for a single adult fell from 20.6 per cent of average earnings in 1979 to just 10.5 per cent in 2008, and for a couple from 33.4 per cent in 1979 to 16.5 per cent in 2008 (DWP, 2009).

The table below shows, for different household types, the amount by which a household with no adult in work would fall short of the Government's official poverty line of 60 per cent of median income (after housing costs).

Household type	Equivalised poverty line (60 per cent median income after housing costs)	Value of out-of-work benefits (excluding Housing Benefit)	**Shortfall between financial support and poverty line**
	£ / week	£ / week	£ / week
Working-age single adult, no children	£115	£78	**£37**
Working-age couple, no children	£199	£115	**£84**
Working-age single parent, two children (5 and 14)	£239	£207	**£32**
Working-age couple, two children (5 and 14)	£322	£244	**£78**

The value of out-of-work benefits given here excludes Housing Benefit so as to compare with the after-housing-costs poverty line. The benefits included here are Jobseeker's Allowance and Council Tax Benefit (allocated at £14 per week) for childless adults and Jobseeker's Allowance / Income Support, Council Tax Benefit, Child Benefit and Child Tax Credit for households with children. Note that the poverty lines are for 2007-08, since we do not yet know the poverty lines for subsequent years, while the benefit rates are for 2009-10. However, the poverty lines are only likely to have increased marginally since 2007-08, so the comparison here should nevertheless give an accurate picture.

In all cases, the standard of living for those having to rely on out-of-work benefits is appallingly low – and well below the poverty line. While the Government increased these benefits above inflation in the 2009 Budget, the current level of unemployment benefit and adult income support of £64.30 a week is still just £9 a day. And while housing and council tax costs are covered by other benefits, £9 a day is certainly not enough to cover food and drink, clothing and toiletries, household goods and services, or transport, let alone any activities that would allow an individual to participate in society. That's why the loss of a job is currently one of the main 'triggers' that push households into poverty (Smith and Middleton, 2007). And while many groups should not expect to have to live on out-of-work benefits for any significant length of time, this is no reason for them to have to live in poverty for these short periods.

Though it's not really the political orthodoxy of our times, it's hard to resist the conclusion that there needs to be a significant increase in the level of out-of-work benefits. An immediate move therefore should be to re-link the uprating of out-of-work benefits to earnings, stopping the value of these benefits falling further and further behind the poverty line. But a one-off increase in the value of these benefits will also be needed to redress the shortfalls highlighted in the table above.

If implemented, the universal tax credit proposed in Chapter 6 would plug a fair amount of this gap (at 2009-10 rates, £25 a week for a single working-age adult). But even with a new benefit like this, the remaining necessary rise in JSA / IS would need to be at least £12 for singles to bring them up to the poverty line. Keeping the same couple-single ratio would imply a rise of £20 for couples. Even this would still leave childless couple households £16 short of the poverty line; the necessary rise here would be £38 a week.

Given that such benefits constitute a large proportion of household income for many groups, such an increase could have a dramatic effect on poverty levels. Such an increase could also make the benefit more 'meaningful' to many middle-income households (since it would replace a larger proportion of their previous income). Though a small step, it might begin to get us back to a position where many households saw social security benefits as worth protecting.

The question of incentives

The question of incentives

Wouldn't raising out-of-work benefits disincentivise work? Not necessarily; it depends on how it is done. Here, we briefly discuss some relevant considerations.

More eligibility, not less: Anxiety over 'gains to work' has long been a feature of our welfare debates. The Poor Law was based on the infamous 'principle of less eligibility', which demanded that the position of the able-bodied 'pauper' must be kept inferior to that of the poorest independent labourer. The problem with this principle was not that there should not be a gain to work, but that the gain to work was to be maintained through downwards pressure on the living standards of those out of work. By contrast, sufficient gains to work should be maintained through a principle of *more eligibility* – combining more generous benefits for those out of work with upwards pressure on the incomes of the low paid.

In practice, this function is performed today by the Minimum Wage and Working Tax Credit. For all one reads in the right-wing tabloids about being 'better off on benefits than in work', these two policy measures (both bitterly opposed by the right) have substantially increased gains to work since 1997. As well as recommending that upwards pressure be applied to the Minimum Wage, we therefore propose that the increase in out-of-work support recommended above should be balanced with a corresponding increase in *in-work* support (such as a £12-a-week increase in the basic element of the Working Tax Credit). Not only would this help maintain the financial gain experienced when moving into work; it would also help to tackle in-work poverty too. And, given that our proposal to raise out-of-work benefits would also apply to young adults, we would also propose that entitlement to the Working Tax Credit be extended to childless under-25s, for whom the gain to work is just as important as for the over-25s.

Conditional generosity, not mean-spiritedness: Another way to ensure that more generous financial support for those out of work does not necessarily mean fewer in work is by imposing a *requirement* on citizens to work (or to participate in some way). By making being 'ready for work' (or preparing for work) a condition of receiving financial support, conditionality frameworks can override financial work incentives (Brewer et al., 2008).

Furthermore, attaching conditions to receipt of welfare is a much better way to ensure people meet their responsibility to contribute to society than applying downwards pressure to levels of welfare (Grubb, 2000). Providing a level of out-of-work support that means households are in poverty by no means hastens their transition back into work; indeed, it can actually be a substantial *barrier* to finding sustainable employment, shifting a household's focus from self-improvement to survival. In reality, meagre levels of support mean that households using out-of-work benefits will often end up taking on substantial debt to survive. The welfare system's focus must be on providing a sufficiently decent platform to help individuals turn their lives around, not to entrench crisis.

Promoting the work ethic: Finally, it would be wrong to assume that more generous benefits necessarily create a cultural aversion to employment. In fact, studies of attitudes across different welfare states tend to find precisely the *opposite* effect: people's employment commitment tends to be stronger in countries with more generous benefits than in those with less generous benefits. Ingrid Esser (2009), for example, finds that employment commitment is significantly higher in welfare states with more generous benefit levels (the Scandanavian welfare states) and weakest in those with lower benefit levels (such as the UK). She also finds that levels of employment commitment have not decreased over time in countries with more generous welfare states; nor have they increased over time in those with less generous welfare states.

One can imagine various reasons why this might be so. One is that citizens might be more willing to submit themselves to the forces of flexible labour markets if they know that there is a secure safety net in place should they need it. Another is that more generous benefits might themselves incentivise work by having contribution conditions attached to them (especially earnings-related benefits). Either way, it is clear that a more generous safety net is by no means incompatible with promoting the work ethic.

Fixing the holes in the safety net: from 'contribution' to participation

It is not simply that the level of social security benefits is too low for those receiving them, but that many others are not eligible to do so. They end up falling through the holes in the safety net. So we also need a much more inclusive system.

One solution would be to move to a system of residence-based benefits. Such a system could have various possible advantages (including some of those discussed in the previous chapter). We believe, however, in the context of social security, that the 'contributory ethos', with its formalised link between putting in and taking out, is important to maintain.

Not only are there important fairness arguments for maintaining this link; in terms of ensuring the welfare system is seen as legitimate, the psychological connection between putting in and taking out that the National Insurance system creates is 'gold-dust'. Ironically, many of the formal mechanisms that originally created this link have either withered away or were illusory to start with (as discussed in Chapter 3). But simply by making the link between contributing and receiving explicit, the National Insurance system is often looked at in a more benign way than income tax (Hedges and Bromley, 2001).

However, as discussed in Chapter 3, the post-war National Insurance system, many aspects of which are still with us today, was not an especially inclusive one. Beveridge's conception of contribution was firmly centred on paid work: that of a full-time employee paying a set amount into the National Insurance Fund each week throughout their working life.[88]

There were two main reasons behind this design. First, there was intended to be a tight link between the structure and financing of the scheme: Beveridge originally envisaged it running on an actuarial basis, whereby the funds paid in by individuals would partly finance the benefits paid out to them in future. Second, and perhaps more importantly, Beveridge believed that such an arrangement was required to satisfy public perceptions of fairness.[89]

But the organisation of the system that emerged from these objectives resulted in some profound injustices, some of which are still with us today. Frustratingly, very few of the problematic aspects of how our contributory system has been structured were necessary properties of a contributory system; many of them reflected quite a rigid conception of insurance.

In fact, the link between structure and financing was a sham from the start. Not paying pensioners a pension from day one would have been deeply unpopular, so it was always the case that current generations were financing pensions for the previous generation, not their own future pensions. The actuarial basis of the scheme was formally abandoned in the 1960s, with the National Insurance Fund now run on a pay-as-you-go basis. Even on this basis, however, there is still no coherent link between contributions paid in and benefits paid out: at times (like the early 1980s) the National Insurance Fund has run a deficit and had to be topped up with general tax revenue; at other times (like today) the Fund has run a large surplus, with funds effectively subsidising other programmes.

This is not to say that there is anything wrong with a purely symbolic link between contributions and benefits. But there is a sad irony here. For it was Beveridge's belief that this tight link between structure and financing was necessary – and that it was what would make the public regard the system as fair – that led to National Insurance excluding many citizens.

In this section, we look at three aspects of this exclusion: the types of activity recognised as valuable; barriers to entry into the system; and the issue of when you have to make your contribution with respect to your period of protection.

What counts as valued activity?

Perhaps the most controversial example of this was centring entitlement on paid employment, which immediately put the system beyond groups such as carers (mainly women) or the disabled.[90] The former gained entitlement as dependents of their partners, while the latter were primarily reliant on means tested National Assistance. The result was effectively to 'segregate' workers and non-workers within the welfare system, a fundamental breach of equal citizenship.

The effects of this are perhaps seen at their starkest in inequalities in pension entitlements today. Because of their historic role as primary caregivers, this system has very dramatically discriminated against women: many who have taken time out of work to have a child or care for a sick or elderly relative have found themselves in poverty in old age.

Reforms currently underway will very significantly improve the position of women.[91] Furthermore, the conversion of Home Responsibilities Protection into a system of National Insurance Credits in the 2007 Pensions Act also brings a degree of individual rights and independence to women and carers, who are now able to build up their own entitlement to a state pension *on the basis of their own activities*, rather than through their partner.[92] Crucially, it moves the notion of 'contribution' out of the domain of paid employment and into the domain of socially valued activity. In doing so, it clearly breaks the link between entitlement and finance paid into the system.[93]

These are principles we now need to make the basis of our entire social security system. For example, full-time education or training does not necessarily attract National Insurance Credits, despite the huge social benefits of a skilled population.[94] Nor does volunteering (though the Government said they might look into this in 2005). Volunteering is recognised in the benefits system in some ways.[95] But we should ensure that those engaged in certain types of intensive volunteering also have their contribution recognised. After all, you get National Insurance Credits while you're doing jury service, so why not for other unpaid activities we rely on too?[96]

Fixing these holes in the contributory system would not only make a further contribution to preventing future pensioner poverty, but would explicitly acknowledge the social value of a wider range of important activities – something the economist Tony Atkinson has described as *participation* to distinguish it from the Beveridgean notion of 'contribution' (Atkinson, 1996).

And as well as future entitlement to pensions, we should also ensure that those participating can get decent benefits today. The value of Carer's Allowance – currently £53 a week – is even lower than the out-of-work benefits discussed earlier, such that many carers have to top-up this benefit through Income Support. At the very least, carers should be entitled to the increased value of Income Support outlined above.

Finally, a more inclusive notion of participation would also resonate much more strongly with people's sense of fairness. In the focus group exercises conducted for the project, there was a huge strength of feeling that caring was under-recognised in society and that carers deserved more help and support – a view expressed by participants of all political stripes. Previous research also shows a strong desire amongst the public to recognise and reward care work and voluntary work in a similar way to paid employment (Stafford, 1998; Kelly, 2006; DWP, 2006).[97] So recognising a wider notion of contribution is one very important way in which *existing* public attitudes towards welfare would potentially permit a more inclusive and generous approach.

How high is the bar to join the welfare club?

The existence of 'floors' on the level at which people are able to contribute (and receive support) has been another way in which having too rigid a link between contribution and receipt has ended up excluding people.

The flat-rate contributions structure for National Insurance that Beveridge had originally created (discussed in Chapter 3) was eventually abandoned in 1961 and replaced with earnings-related contributions, which made sense in terms of fairness. However, a Lower Earnings Limit (LEL) was subsequently introduced – a weekly wage above which someone had to be earning in order to gain entitlement to insurance benefits.

While the National Minimum Wage has made this threshold less exclusionary in recent times, historically the LEL has been an important source of exclusion from social security and remains so for some groups today. In particular, it has prevented the low paid or those in part-time work from making National Insurance Contributions simply because they earn less than a certain amount each week (currently £95). In 2005 there were around 1.2 million women earning less than the LEL (Bellamy, 2007); the vast majority of these were in part-time work, balancing this with caring for young children.[98] Though the 'male breadwinner' model of the family might have been the norm in Beveridge's day, the National Insurance system has failed to keep up with the major changes that have happened since, especially the huge rise in women's employment, part-time work, temporary work and flexible working.

There is a particular injustice in the Lower Earnings Limit. Though it does not affect huge numbers of people, nobody who is fully participating in society should be prevented from building up entitlements because they earn too little – and especially not when this is the result of low paid part-time work or the result of balancing work with caring.

The cause of offence goes back to the distinction between intentions and outcomes, noted in Chapter 5. Provided people are 'operating in good faith', they should not be discriminated against because of low earning power; and provided they are engaged in legitimate forms of participation, they should not be discriminated against if the number of hours they can spend in employment is limited. Now that any pretence of a link between an individual's financial contributions and benefits paid out has been dropped, the Lower Earnings Limit should be abolished.

Arbitrary floors to entitlement, by-products of historical conceptions of how the National Insurance Fund should operate, do not necessarily correspond with popular ideas about what constitutes a fair system – particularly with the widespread belief that people should contribute resources in relation to their means (Hedges, 2005).

So National Insurance benefits *should* be funded progressively. And this progressive principle should now override those aspects of the structure of the scheme that are outdated remnants of its actuarial origins.[99]

This recommends a further change. The historical link between financing and structure also resulted in the application of an Upper Earnings Limit – a level of earnings above which you stop paying National Insurance Contributions (you are deemed to have 'financed' your future benefits). Although the one per cent increase in NICs in 2002 did go all the way up the earnings scale, the current structure is still deeply regressive. In 2008-09, employees paid 11 per cent on every pound of earnings above £5,460 (the Primary Threshold), and then only one per cent on every pound of earnings above £40,040 (the Upper Earnings Limit). This means those earning larger amounts pay a smaller proportion of their earnings in NICs than those earning smaller amounts (see graph below).

So the Upper Earnings Limit should also be abolished, making the system of financing social security fully progressive – and more closely aligned with public perceptions of fairness.

How much of your earnings are paid in National insurance Contributions?

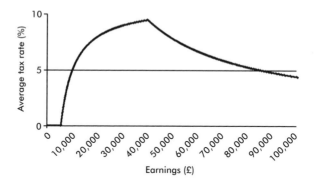

The average tax rate for National Insurance Contributions by earnings (employees' primary Class I rates, 2008-09). Without the Upper Earnings Limit, the average tax rate would gradually approach 11 per cent. However, under the current system it peaks at 9.5 per cent at earnings of around £40,000 and then gradually falls, approaching one per cent as earnings increase.

When do you make your contribution?

Another issue to consider here is the way in which benefit entitlement is tied quite tightly to past contribution records: entitlement today requires contribution yesterday. So those with insufficient contributions records are ineligible for contributory benefits.

We've already discussed the historic exclusion of carers from building up entitlement to the state pension. But this phenomenon also exists in eligibility requirements for the other social security benefits too (where entitlement to contributory out-of-work benefits is based on having made 26 weeks of contributions within the previous two years). Over the last ten years, for example, only around half of those moving onto incapacity benefit have been eligible for the contributory version of the benefit.[100]

One might argue that this doesn't matter much since people can instead get the equivalent income-based versions of these benefits, which are either set at the same level as the contributory versions (in the case of income-based Jobseeker's Allowance and incapacity benefit) or are set *higher* (in the case of Pension Credit).[101] But if we are concerned with the perceived legitimacy of the system, and its likelihood of being sufficiently generous in future, then it matters greatly. As we saw in Chapter 3 (and will discuss further below), the differences between social insurance and need-based social assistance have real consequences for the politics of welfare.

Linking entitlement too tightly to past contribution volumes is another way in which the design of National Insurance doesn't quite square with popular conceptions of fairness. Remember the result from the focus groups discussed in Chapter 5: the overriding factor in judging fairness in benefit receipt was not someone's previous record of activity but rather whether or not the individual was trying to get a job now (and, more generally, whether or not the individual would go on to make a contribution back to society in future). Current effort trumped previous activity. So getting a contributory system that invests more weight in current and future behaviour, rather than past behaviour, could be an important step in deepening its legitimacy.

Is there any way to get the goodness out of the contributory ethos without excluding people on the basis of past contributions records? Potentially, there is. Later, we go on to suggest how this could work, through a system of participatory benefits that can be paid in return for current activity. For now, we will simply note the principle at stake: no-one who is willing to participate now in socially valued activities should be excluded from support *on the basis of their participation*, and instead have to rely on support on the basis of need.

The reforms discussed in this section are all 'win-win': they would both tackle poverty *and* ensure the system operates in a way that is more closely aligned with public perceptions of fairness. Further below, we take on the harder challenge of how you would need to reshape the 'welfare contract' in order to deal with public attitudes that seem to work against poverty prevention objectives. First, we look at the other side of the coin: what it's reasonable to require those receiving social security to do.

From safety net to trampoline: conditionality for the right reasons

The other side of the bargain of improving and extending social security is what citizens themselves are required to do. Chapter 3 showed that, although 'behavioural conditionality' has always been a part of the British welfare system, over recent decades it has come to play a more and more prominent role in labour market policy (as it has in many other OECD countries).[102] And evaluations have shown that such conditionality has often been successful in increasing the numbers on out-of-work benefits moving into work.[103] Here we briefly review the role of conditionality in poverty prevention, and derive some principles for fair and appropriate conditionality.

As discussed in the first section of this chapter, conditionality can be justified in terms of fairness, with rights to welfare matched by responsibilities to participate in some way (or at least to move towards a state where one will be in a position to participate).[104] There is a strong argument, however, that for conditionality to be justified on fairness grounds it should also be the case that government is striving to provide all citizens with decent opportunities in the first place – a point we return to in the final section. But if reasonable opportunities are open for individuals, then there are indeed plausible fairness arguments for the principle of conditionality.

However, conditionality does pose a dilemma from the perspective of poverty prevention. It means there will be situations – rare ones – where individuals are sanctioned for a refusal to participate.[105] Provided this is done in a fair and humane way, with an underlying layer of support to protect against hardship and sufficient support for dependents, the application of sanctions is perfectly legitimate. However, in these cases conditionality can work against the objective of poverty prevention.[106]

In our view, the disadvantages of sanctioning are probably outweighed by the (paternalistic) ways in which an appropriate framework of conditionality can help to tackle poverty by connecting individuals with work and training and motivating them to take advantage of opportunities.

A potentially much bigger problem with conditionality is not the principle itself but the danger that, in practice, it becomes a tool for dealing with political pressure. The problem here is that a moment at which claimants are quite vulnerable becomes the focus of attempts to satisfy public demands for toughness. Such a situation introduces a whole new motivation for conditionality: not fairness, nor a paternalistic concern for claimants, but a desire to assuage public anxiety – and with it a dynamic that can be harmful for the welfare of claimants. So the *motivation* behind any framework of conditionality is often the key to predicting how it will fare for poverty prevention.

PRINCIPLE 1: For those claimants on whom it is suitable to place requirements, conditionality backed up by sanctioning as a last resort is legitimate. For public perceptions of fairness, *it is important to communicate that there is a requirement to participate and a framework of conditionality in place with the possibility of sanctions.*

PRINCIPLE 2: Beyond this, however, *the motivation behind a framework of conditionality should only ever be to help the claimant themselves.* **Changes to conditionality frameworks should only be made if there is evidence**

that they will benefit the prospects or welfare of claimants and never for the purposes of deterring claims or playing to public opinion.

There are some obvious applications of this second principle in current welfare debates. A particularly relevant one at the moment is the issue of mandatory work activity. Prolonged absence from the workplace can itself create barriers to moving back into work. For such individuals there is good evidence that participating in mandatory work activities ('intermediate labour markets', in policy jargon) can help 'reconnect' them with the world of work, increasing both skills and motivation.[107]

However, there is a difference between work experience and workfare. Workfare refers to regimes, often punitive ones, requiring work in return for receipt of benefits, typically with no further assistance with job search or training provided to help the individual move into mainstream employment. The evidence from workfare schemes around the world (Crisp and Fletcher, 2008) is that, while they can be successful in cutting benefit caseloads, they can actually *reduce* future employment chances by limiting the time available for job search and by failing to provide the skills and experience valued by employers. By contrast, an approach designed actually to help the claimant would be one that combines work experience with continued assistance (Gregg, 2008). As highlighted in the box further below, this is the subject of vigorous debate within current welfare reform proposals in the UK.

There are some further principles that follow from the first two. What is key for poverty prevention is that conditionality be part of an *enabling* regime. And this requires a combination of intensive support and generous benefits, combined with co-ownership of the process between claimants and advisers, and flexibility in applying requirements and sanctions.

PRINCIPLE 3: There should be *maximum co-ownership* of the return-to-work process between claimant and adviser.

In particular, conditionality must be operated sensitively if it is not to breach the principle of equal citizenship. While the relationship between the adviser and claimant will never be a symmetrical one, it must be a mutually respectful one. This is important for effectiveness too: when claimants feel cajoled or threatened, this can actually act as a barrier to them utilising support and taking up opportunities (Goodwin, 2008).

PRINCIPLE 4: Conditionality works best when combined with *generous financial support.*

For all the recent eulogising about US welfare reform, it is not the US but countries like Denmark and the Netherlands that provide the best examples of how to get labour market policy right. As countries that have consistently outperformed the UK and US on employment over the last decade, they show that high taxes, generous welfare and a strong union movement do not necessarily lead to the employment troubles of France and Germany (Schmidt and Wadsworth, 2005; Coats, 2006). In particular, they combine high levels of benefits with enabling but tight conditionality and intensive support and advice. By protecting families against a sudden drop in income, these generous benefit levels actively facilitate successful job search.

As well as more generous benefit levels, countries like Denmark also invest significantly in training and support with job search. And this is a key point: effective back-to-work programmes are expensive. Whilst the UK has been investing significantly more under programmes like the New Deal and Pathways to Work, we still lag behind the benchmarks of the best-performing countries and need to improve.

This observation should also make us suspicious of welfare reform proposals that are touted as saving large amounts of money.

PRINCIPLE 5: *The primary motivation behind condition-ality should never be to reduce expenditure.*

Earlier we suggested that getting the motivation behind conditionality wrong can not only produce ineffective pol-icy but can also risk substantial harm to claimants. And this is never more true than when the motivation is to cut spending.

The history of welfare reform is littered with examples of programmes whose primary aim was to 'reduce the welfare rolls'. Indiscriminately time-limiting benefits is a standard technique here. An example would be the infa-mous 'Wisconsin' welfare model: yes, these reforms did reduce welfare rolls, but that was partly a consequence of time-limiting benefits. The result was two million children in the US with parents out of work but receiving no state welfare (One Parent Families, 2007). Evidence suggests that indiscriminate conditionality solely motivated by a concern to get people off welfare can, far from integrating people into society, lead to large numbers of people and families 'disconnected' from both the world of work and the welfare system (Blank and Kovak, 2008).[108]

Particularly important in thinking about fair condition-ality is that the Government be clear about those groups who should not have an expectation placed upon them to be 'moving closer' to employment, and for whom it is per-fectly legitimate to have a long-term source of benefit income, including carers, the severely disabled, pension-ers and parents with young children.

PRINCIPLE 6: The Government should be clear about *those groups for whom there should be no expectation to work or prepare for work.* **In particular, it should state that**

caring for a relative or child who needs care is a perfectly legitimate reason not to be in work.

In this respect, the recent Gregg Review (2008) is surely right that the primary distinction in welfare policy should be the levels of requirement be placed on individuals rather than the specific benefit they are on. Following through this logic also allows us to separate out the different *welfare functions* of income benefits for different groups. As the figure below indicates, for those whose absence from work is regarded as temporary, benefits serve the function of *income replacement*. Importantly, this function should be distinguished from that of *income provision*: those benefits which support people who are rightly not regarded as temporarily absent from work, namely carers, parents of young children, students and so on. Finally, in-work support (like the Working Tax Credit) serves the function of *income supplement*, especially for those on low pay.[109]

There has been a lot of discussion recently about the potential of moving to a single working-age benefit (albeit with different categories within). And, indeed, there are many arguments to recommend this. In particular, a single working-age benefit could have an important 'universalising' function, reducing stigma and uniting those who were formerly divided into different client groups. (The lesson of the previous chapter is that a single benefit with three different subcategories is much preferable to three different benefits.)

Care would need to be taken, however, to ensure that moving to a single working-age benefit did not obscure the important moral difference between income replacement and income provision. While no-one should be categorised in terms of what they 'can' and 'cannot' do, it is important to be clear about what is legitimately expected of people and what this implies about the value of their current activities. Carers and parents should not be

The classification of benefit functions in terms of the requirements placed on individuals

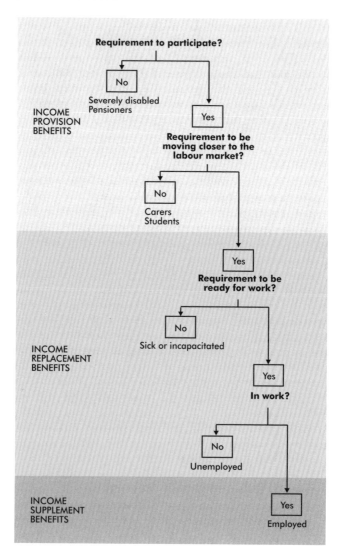

receiving financial support on the basis that in a few years' time they might be back in work; they should be receiving support because we value their caring activities. In this respect, Carer's Allowance is quite different to the group of out-of-work benefits it is often lumped with.

Provided such distinctions can be maintained within a single working-age benefit, however, we would propose expanding the idea to include in-work financial support too. Low pay, after all, is a contingency that we need to be protected against, just like unemployment and sickness. And bringing in-work support into social security would integrate those in work and those out of work into a single institution – much like the *French Revenu minimum d'insertion*, a benefit which can provide income support for both groups. Such a move could begin to put an end to the historic segregation of people within our welfare system by work status, perhaps the most damaging social division of all.

A final point is that having been explicit about those groups on whom there is no expectation to work or prepare for work, the Government should continue to explore the role that conditionality could play in maintaining options for individuals and improving life chances. One reason why conditionality has become menacing is that it is too often conflated with the idea of 'being on a journey towards employment'. But there is no necessary reason why it should be.

One particularly important phenomenon over the last decade has been the growth in 'soft conditionality' (the 'work-focussed interview' regime), which requires claimants to undertake certain actions, such as attending interviews and agreeing action plans, but does not require them to be available for work. Such regimes typically apply to those who are not in a position to move into work, such as those with a health condition or disability, or lone parents with young children, and the aim is to keep the claimant in contact with employment opportunities and encourage them to use voluntary initiatives if appropriate.

Importantly, requiring people to attend interviews and explore options imposes very little welfare cost on them (assuming it does not detract from caring responsibilities or that the individual does not have mobility problems). Yet evidence suggests it can be successful in connecting people with the world of work more generally, including increasing self-confidence and optimism about future work, motivating individuals to think actively about seeking work, and motivating individuals to undertake training.[110]

There are groups – for example, young, low-skilled carers – who should not be expected to be in work or preparing for work, but for whom a regular window onto possible work opportunities could be important to ensure they consider employment options at future stages of their life. Paternalistic though it would be, the Government should explore whether or not it would be appropriate to apply 'soft conditionality' to certain groups like this in order to improve life chances.

PRINCIPLE 7: *Government should separate the concept of conditionality from work expectations.* **It should then explore which groups might benefit from regularly exploring employment options even though there is no requirement to be ready for work or to prepare for work.**

The question of incentives

Perhaps the key insight of Beatrice Webb's critique of the Poor Law a century ago was that making the workhouse unattractive and demeaning in order to deter the illegitimate claimant was in direct conflict with the aim of helping people out of poverty and into work. By trying simultaneously to provide welfare and create deterrence within a single system, the Poor Law had been spectacularly ineffective at preventing destitution. Webb's solution was also simple: separate out the issue of how generously or ungenerously to treat the unemployed from the issue of

---

how to deter unfounded claims on the system. Replace ungenerous and punitive provision with generous and enabling provision that is underpinned by robust conditions.[111]

A century on, there is a real danger that the Government's proposal for a "work for your benefit" scheme (mandatory full-time work activity for those who have been unemployed for more than two years) risks mixing up these two ideas once again. On the one hand, the scheme is supposed to help claimants improve their work prospects and "employability skills". On the other, it is billed as a way of cracking down on those "playing the system". According to the recent White Paper: "The prospect of attending mandatory full-time activity for a substantial period of time would act as an effective deterrent" (DWP, 2008).[112]

But trying to conflate these functions within a single scheme risks missing the lesson of 1909. Any system which seeks to deter illegitimate claims by lessening the conditions of those who merit support will ultimately be self-defeating, and will fail the test of equal citizenship on which our welfare state depends. So, yes, let's have more support to help the long-term unemployed back into work, together with a framework of fair conditionality and sanctions to prevent exploitation of the system. But, as the Minority Report showed, you can't achieve both at once simply by making the experience of welfare unpleasant.

Making reciprocity explicit: giving the safety net more public legitimacy

The previous section looked at the problems with trying to use downwards pressure on the quality of welfare to deter unfounded claims on the system and incentivise work. Just as often in welfare history, however – including under the New Poor Law – such strategies have also been used to try to assuage public anxiety about welfare for able-bodied adults. Making the experience of out-of-work welfare meagre or even unpleasant, the thinking goes, should calm popular fears about people 'gaming the system'.

How attitudes to unemployment benefit have varied with the level of unemployment benefit

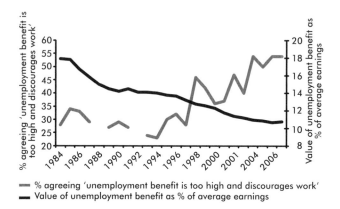

━━ % agreeing 'unemployment benefit is too high and discourages work'
━━ Value of unemployment benefit as % of average earnings

Data on unemployment benefit / Jobseeker's Allowance from DWP (2009). Data on public attitudes from NatCen's British Social Attitudes survey.

The trouble is, not only is such a strategy harmful for those on the receiving end. The truth is *it doesn't work.* The graph above shows an astonishing relationship. Ever since Margaret Thatcher broke the earnings link for the value of contributory benefits, the value of unemployment benefit has fallen and fallen relative to average earnings (and relative to some measures of prices too). But since the mid-1990s, the proportion of people agreeing with the statement that "unemployment benefit is too high and discourages work" has risen inexorably.[113]

At first, this looks completely paradoxical. How can anxiety about the generosity of unemployment benefit have risen at the same time as its relative value has declined considerably? In fact, there are perfectly simple reasons why this has happened.

What's gone wrong?

The problem is not the level of benefit at all. It's that people are concerned about the fairness of the policy underpinning it. And no amount of cutting the benefit would change this.[114] It's not that people think the level of benefits should be low, or that the welfare system should treat people badly. In the focus group exercise (described in Chapter 5) on who 'deserved' their benefits, nearly all participants thought those out of work and behaving responsibly should receive benefits (and a good many of these thought that £60 a week was far too low).[115] Rather, there is a concern – rightly or wrongly – that the system is also supporting people who do not intend to put something back in.

The hard truth, as we saw in Chapter 5, is that there is a widespread sense that those receiving benefits won't go on to make a reciprocal contribution back to society. This was by far the strongest driver of opposition to redistribution. Underlying all the angst is a sense that the welfare contract is broken.

How did we get here? The historical episodes reviewed in Chapter 3 and the evidence about public attitudes explored in Chapter 5 point us to some possible answers:

1) The first is a decline in the relevance of the contributory principle within our welfare system, which provided an important moral link between participation and welfare (however unjust and exclusionary particular historical manifestations of it have been). The shift, in the 1980s and 1990s, away from a reliance on contributory working-age benefits and towards income-based benefits profoundly altered the nature of the welfare system – and, with it, the relationships between those receiving benefits and everyone else. Need-based allocation, in turn, opens up a range of questions about the extent to which individuals are justified in receiving benefits.

2) The second is a subtle change in how people came to view those receiving welfare, one that followed from this downgrading of the contributory system. The shift from out-of-work benefits being conceived primarily as insurance to being conceived primarily as transfers to a particular need-group meant they went from being about 'all of us' (since the risks we insure ourselves against apply to everyone), to being about 'other people' (since only a minority are actually workless at any one time). By dividing them from the rest of the population, this change further accentuated questions about the 'deservingness' of recipients.

3) Once the focus of the welfare system became contemporaneous need (rather than life-cycle insurance), this placed the burden of enforcing a 'contract' on the very moment of claiming welfare. And this burden has been a feature of the growing emphasis on welfare conditionality over recent decades. Not only does this shift mean the system has become less concerned about what citizens are doing when they're *not* claiming benefits, and what their rights and responsibilities should be during these times. Much more importantly, it has focussed all of the political pressure on the single moment when individuals are at their most vulnerable. This sets up a direct trade-off between protecting claimants, on the one hand, and attempts to assuage public anxiety about welfare, on the other.

4) A fourth problem is that neither the contributory system nor current conditionality frameworks are especially good at allowing people to demonstrate good intentions in a positive way. The contributory system of course demonstrates past activity. But that is not sufficient: in our focus groups many participants were angry about a Jobseeker's Allowance claimant not trying to get a new job, even when the character in question had a sufficient contributions record. Current conditionality frameworks, via client-

adviser 'agreements', do have a vehicle to demonstrate intentions, though not much beyond basic compliance. What would be more effective would be if reciprocity itself formed the basis of allocating resources. Too often our major benefits and services, from incapacity benefit to social housing, have been framed in terms of what the recipient *cannot* do or *cannot* afford, rather than their intention to participate.

5) A fifth problem, also shared by both the contributory system and conditionality frameworks, is that by being too employment-centred they do not put nearly enough emphasis on rewarding other ways of participating. Inconsistent though it may seem, some participants in our focus groups spoke about lone parents in quite harsh terms when they were presented as out-of-work benefit claimants, yet spoke about them much more warmly when they were presented in the context of their caring responsibilities. That's why we badly need to move to a system that grounds entitlement in a broader range of participatory activities.

The analysis above suggests why we need a new welfare contract, and, by implication, what some of its features should be. Two key challenges stand out in particular:

- **We need to restore the link between welfare and participation in society**, though in a way that avoids both the exclusionary features of the old contributory system, and the 'negative-sum' approach of current conditionality frameworks.

- **We need to 're-universalise' social security, making the welfare system about all of us once more.** Among other things, this would get us away from a conception of rights and responsibilities that focuses simply on the moment of claiming welfare.

In the final section of this chapter, we explore some ways of implementing these objectives.

Before embarking on this, it's worth noting that this analysis begins to explain the seemingly paradoxical relationship between attitudes and benefit levels, illustrated in the graph above. As the benefit has become less and less meaningful to middle-income households and more and more focussed around a particular need-group, questions about the 'worthiness' of recipients have become more and more salient. The resulting public anxiety has not been addressed by further deterioration in benefit levels, whilst making harder the necessary reforms to get out of this strait-jacket.[116]

This dynamic has had a further negative reinforcement from New Labour's story about welfare reform. Over the last twelve years the Government has developed welfare conditionality in ways that have not only provided much welcome help and support for claimants, but could also have been used to restore confidence in the integrity of the system. Sadly, however, these developments have been accompanied by a narrative about 'cracking down' and 'targeting benefit thieves' that has actually *reinforced* people's concerns about the integrity of the system. The result has been a vicious circle of further public anxiety and political pressure, met with further crackdowns, and so on.[117]

This also explains the similar trend in the graph below, showing how concern about benefit fraud has gone up and up at the same time as the level of benefit fraud has come down and down. People are concerned about the intentions of claimants, not the cost of fraud. So telling people that fraud is low because you've cracked down on benefit cheats focuses their attention on people trying to play the system, thus increasing their concerns about fraud. (Much better to say that fraud is low because people are basically honest and the integrity of the system is intact.)

It's not just that 'get-tough' auctions can't deal with the problem, then. They make matters worse.

How fears about benefit fraud have varied with the level of benefit fraud (for Income Support and Jobseeker's Allowance)

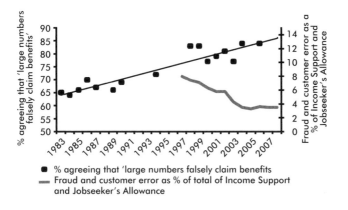

- % agreeing that 'large numbers falsely claim benefits
- Fraud and customer error as % of total of Income Support and Jobseeker's Allowance

Data on public attitudes from NatCen's British Social Attitudes survey. Data on benefit fraud and customer error from DWP (2009). Fraud and customer error across all benefits account for just 1.3 per cent of expenditure, and have followed a similar trend to that in Income Support and Jobseeker's Allowance given here.[118]

How to fix it: a new welfare contract to tackle poverty

So the long-term interests of the most vulnerable in our society will not be served by strategies that play to people's fears about welfare, but rather by re-framing our welfare system in a way that addresses the key challenges described above.

Enshrining reciprocity within the welfare system: a participatory principle

A move of the most fundamental importance would be to create a set of benefits that could formally restore the link between eligibility for welfare and participation in society. This would move much of the system of out-of-work benefits away from entitlement based on need to entitlement based on reciprocity. Few reforms, over the long term, could have a more profound effect on the way in which we think about welfare.

Support would be given in return for immediate participation (or preparation for participation) in socially useful activities, effectively replacing the old 'contributory principle' with a 'participatory principle'.[119] The new higher rates of out-of-work benefits proposed earlier in this chapter would be participation-based benefits (though there would still be the existing lower tier of income-based benefits to protect from extreme hardship those individuals who were in a position to participate but not doing so).[120]

Note that the aim here is not to exclude anyone. All of those who have the intention to participate in socially valuable activities (virtually all claimants) would qualify for the participatory system. The point is quite the opposite: a participatory system would allocate resources in return for activity in a way that did not exclude people in the way the old contributory system did and still does (because of insufficient past contributions records, or because of engagement in activities outside the labour market).

At a stroke, this reform would transfer the vast majority of those out of work and engaged in worksearch or work-preparation activities onto a participatory benefit that was awarded to them specifically for these activities. To take an example, in February 2008, 75 per cent of the 824,000 Jobseeker's Allowance claimants were on an income-based benefit, and only 25 per cent were on a contributory benefit. Yet the Department for Work and Pensions (see Gregg, 2008) estimate that in 2008 only around 0.1 per cent of Jobseeker's Allowance claimants (about 1,200 people) had multiple sanctions to their name – what might be deemed 'playing the system'. If this was taken as the mark of a refusal to participate, then the new situation would be 99.9 per cent of claimants receiving support on the basis of their active participation and intention to get a job, with 0.1 per cent on a lower income-based benefit.

So while talk of moving away from need-based allocation and towards participatory-based allocation might sound dangerous, it is not intended to be. The point is not that the welfare state would not be responsive to need, but rather that this is not how welfare transfers would be characterised for the vast majority of claimants.

Though perhaps a subtle difference, we think it would have a transformative effect on the culture of welfare. Take another example: it has been a scandal that, in recent history, lone parents caring for their children have been on a need-based benefit called Income Support. Nothing could have been better designed to whip up angst about lone parents and welfare. If we value family caring duties (which we do), then someone should be supported on the basis of discharging these duties. We're prepared to bet that if Income Support for lone parents had instead been called Family-Caring-Responsibilities Recognition, then lone parent welfare might have received a rather different press.[121]

We think that such a system could also deal more effectively with controversies about immigration, asylum and welfare. Those recently arrived in the UK who need financial support should receive support in return for participation in appropriate activities rather than receiving income-based versions of benefits (that, for those with no income, are equivalent in value to the contributory versions of those benefits). This would mean lifting any restrictions on their ability to search for and move into work (though this is not incompatible with government controlling the flow of inward migration for reasons of labour supply, nor applying strict controls on residence and citizenship). As our focus groups suggested, for most people the issue is not racial, ethnic or cultural difference, but what they perceive to be the intentions of those arriving in the UK.

So a participatory principle would be an opportunity to shift away from basing entitlement to non-income-based benefits solely on past contribution records and instead allow a consideration of claimants' current participation and intention to participate. This is how to square the circle of moving away from need-based allocation, whilst ensuring that no-one who is willing to participate in socially useful activities is excluded from receiving support.

Precisely what 'participation' involves would depend on which of the categories of benefits outlined in the table below was applicable. For income-supplement benefits (like the Working Tax Credit), the participation would be through paid employment. For income-replacement benefits (like Jobseeker's Allowance), participation would involve activities that move one closer to employment, such as worksearch, preparing for work, rehabilitation programmes, and so on. For income-provision benefits (such as Income Support for lone parents), participation would involve the relevant non-employment activities, such as caring for a child.

Pensions

While entitlement to a range of working-age benefits would be based on current activity, one's previous record of participation throughout life would still be the basis for determining state pension entitlement. Since an individual's state pension represents a significant expenditure during a period where there are declining opportunities to participate, it remains right that both eligibility and size of pension should still be linked to past participation records. However, one would now receive participation credits throughout life for the full range of activities discussed above: financial contribution through paid work, participation in worksearch, training or work preparation activities, and participation though caring or certain recognised types of volunteering.

In terms of past participation record, the current level of 30 years seems reasonable. However, even this could be less rigid if combined with increasing opportunities to build up one's participation record post-65. The old contributory system was designed for a time when reaching state pension age really did mean an exit from active life. This is no longer the case: well over a million people are now working beyond state pension age, while a third of the carers caring for more than 50 hours a week are over 65 (DWP, 2005). Indeed, in future we will rely increasingly on over-65s participating more actively.

So individuals should be facilitated in further building up entitlement through participation after 65. The announcement in the 2009 Budget that grandparents can gain National Insurance Credits for grandparental care from 2011 is a real breakthrough in this respect (and a long overdue recognition of this important caring work). A broader participatory principle would let this trend rip, with the opportunity to build up entitlement from appropriate types of volunteering or active community involvement as well.

On the other side of the coin, in return for a more liberal system of building up entitlements we should also abandon the arrangement that employees over 65 do not pay National Insurance Contributions on earnings. If longer active life is a reality, and if we are genuinely going to make the social security system progressive (by removing those structures that once reflected the idea that individuals were contributing narrowly towards their own provision), then age limits on the payment of National Insurance Contributions are just as arbitrary as earnings limits.

Table: The set of participatory benefits. The shaded cells identify those client groups on which there is a requirement to participate, and who would receive financial support in recognition of their participation.

Function of benefit	Type of benefit	Typical client group	Basis for eligibility
Income provision	Non-participatory income provision benefits	Severely disabled	Appropriate qualifying criteria (residence based)
	Participatory pensions	Pensioners	Past participation record
	Participatory income provision benefits	Carers	Current participation in appropriate activities
Income replacement	Participatory income replacement benefits	Unemployed / incapacitated	Current participation in appropriate activities
Income supplement	Participatory income supplement	Employed	Current participation in appropriate activities

From risk pooling to burden sharing

Earlier we observed that a key measure to get out of the situation we're currently in would be to shift the concept of welfare away from being about a contemporaneous need-group and back towards being about all of us again. One option for this would be to rejuvenate the classical notion of social insurance. And there is a lot to be said for re-framing welfare back around the notion of pooling risks. As discussed earlier, the notion of risk immediately 'universalises' the system, since the major life risks apply to all of us, and we can readily imagine possible futures where they might befall us.

But there are alternative ways to re-universalise the ethos of social security. One option would be a notion of *burden sharing across the life course*, which would involve an awareness of how resources are pooled to support each individual at critical moments in their life. This arrangement could, in turn, be formalised through the idea of a *lifetime welfare contract*, setting out the benefits and services that each citizen could expect at different stages of their life, and the types of participation that would be expected in return. A narrow version of this contract would be one that simply involved the major social security benefits, on the one hand, and specified the requisite financial contributions or qualifying participatory activity, on the other. A wider and potentially more exciting version would be one that also incorporated a wider range of services and contributions (discussed in more detail below).

The idea of burden sharing across the life course would in fact be much closer to describing how National Insurance actually works than a narrow conception of social insurance is. As we've seen, with earnings-related contributions for flat-rate benefits, there is only a limited link between the amounts paid in by individuals and the benefits received. And with the entire scheme run on a pay-as-you-go basis, then – given the substantial variation in benefits and services received by age group, as we saw in Chapter 2 – the reality is one of substantial intergenerational burden sharing.

Indeed, the concepts of 'insurance' and 'risk' are inaccurate for describing some of the events covered by the social security system. Unemployment, sickness and bereavement are certainly risks. But, in the 21st Century, old age is a certainty, not a risk, and so state pensions are more like social 'assurance' than insurance. Other events, like having a child, are not usually a matter of risk but choice, so it is also hard to construe maternity pay in this way. Rather, social security is really about providing protection during life events and transitions that would otherwise disrupt living standards and could mean a household moving into poverty.

None of this, however, is to say that the contract proposed here couldn't still be conceptualised in terms of 'insurance'. Though it is stretching the concept of insurance a bit to apply it to the participatory system set out above, if the ethos of insurance is what many citizens feel comfortable with, then we could continue with this branding.

But we should also be aware of how the reciprocal sentiments that underpin many people's views about welfare, explored in Chapter 5, potentially support a stronger notion of collective provision than simply insurance. Strong reciprocity implies the issue is less what you might personally get back from the system than whether or not those who are drawing on support are also putting something back in. So even if we retain the insurance 'branding' of the system, we should also be confident about breaking out of the fairness constraints a narrow concept of insurance imposes.

Advantages of a lifetime welfare contract

Though the idea of a lifetime welfare contract might sound unnecessarily formal, we think making the deal explicit would have many advantages. Here we focus briefly on four issues: (i) the educational role of a contract; (ii) the potential to widen the notion of rights and responsibilities; (iii) the potential to foster intergenerational solidarity; and, (iv) the necessity of clarifying the Government's side of the bargain.

(i) A lifetime welfare contract would be an important step towards 're-universalising' welfare because it would show every individual how they fit into the complex set of transactions that constitute our welfare state. Among other things, it would highlight the points in their lives when they have received, or might receive, benefits and services, even if they currently were receiving none. As the graph in Chapter 2 illustrated, people tend to be net recipients from the welfare state at some ages and net contributors at others. Yet the separation of the tax and benefits systems tends to label people as either 'taxpayers' or 'claimants', concealing this underlying pattern of financial relationships between citizens and the state throughout their life.

An explicit contract could therefore have an important educational function. It was certainly the case in our focus groups that looking at graphs of net contribution and receipt throughout life made participants (who were all of working age) feel a lot better about what they might be getting back for all the tax they pay: they simply hadn't thought about the distribution of this over their lifetime. For this reason, any welfare contract should extend beyond social security to embrace the variety of services and support that the welfare state provides.

(ii) As the graph in Chapter 2 illustrated, people enter their adult life already substantially in 'debt' to the welfare state, having benefited hugely from health and education services in childhood. We think it would be symbolically quite important in any lifetime contract for the first few years of adult work or participation to be effectively 'paying back' this service usage (with the number of years of participation for state pension entitlement reduced accordingly). In particular, framing taxation partly as reimbursement for services already used would potentially be very powerful for promoting the idea that paying your fair share of tax is an important social responsibility. Tax avoidance constitutes just as much a breach of the welfare contract as a failure to comply with benefit conditions.[122]

The responsibility to pay tax is one example of what should be a broader agenda with a lifetime welfare contract: to expand the notion of 'rights and responsibilities' away from simply the moment of claiming welfare, and towards what we expect of citizens across their lives (a bit like Beveridge's original vision). Another example might be a requirement for young people to engage in particular kinds of socially valued activity. Some countries organise this in terms of National Service; another option would be to make it compulsory to participate in one of a set of activities – including studying and employment, but also formal volunteering programmes. A lifetime welfare contract could therefore also play an important part in the socialisation of young people.

The broadening of rights and responsibilities in this way is in fact already happening in the context of immigration. The Government's proposal to create a pathway to 'earned citizenship' for people recently arrived in the UK is a very important one – and, provided it is implemented in a responsible way, could be a very effective way of dealing with controversies over immigration and welfare. And it is quite easy to see how this could be a gateway into a broader welfare contract for individuals who wished to remain in the UK. Though there would be important differences between our lifetime contract and the process for migrants, our point here is that a framework of 'earned entitlement' to welfare is something that should apply to the country as a whole.

(iii) Seeing the differential patterns of receipt and contribution across their lives also made the participants in our focus groups think very clearly about intergenerational responsibility. In one exercise, participants became angry with a character (a motor-racing driver) who had benefitted considerably from the welfare state in his youth, but had since moved to Switzerland for tax purposes. They felt that he now had a responsibility to put money back in for kids today.

Given population ageing, it will become increasingly important for people to accept that it is fair to be supporting the expansion of welfare services for older people. And an awareness of how they themselves will also be reliant on such services in old age, and a confidence that such services will still be available when they reach retirement, will be a crucial part of this. A welfare contract could play an important role in this process. Indeed, provided it was sufficiently robust, there is no reason why the Government could not make a fairness argument for supporting the creation of a National Care Service out of National Insurance.

(iv) Finally, and perhaps most importantly, as well as clarifying each individual's rights and responsibilities across their lifetime, a welfare contract could also be explicit about government's side of the bargain. As Stuart White has argued (White, 2003), it is only fair to place requirements on individuals if they have a set of fair chances open to them in the first place. Enforcing conditionality in the face of wide inequalities of opportunity risks exacerbating inequality and undermining life chances.

Certainly, the help and support on offer to those on out-of-work benefits has improved dramatically since 1997 and could be bolstered further still. But here we're talking about government's side of the bargain beyond the narrow confines of job search and preparing for work. When resources allow, a more generous skills and training offer for young people and adults should very much be part of this, with options for adults to re-enter education and training where they've missed out the first time around. Similarly, economic regeneration responsibilities for disadvantaged areas, or the direct provision of jobs through public works projects, would enable those out of work to have more of a choice.

Conclusion: re-linking welfare with participation in society

In this chapter we have argued for a fundamental over-haul of our social security system to make it fit for poverty prevention in the 21st century. The proposals include a sharp increase in the level of out-of-work benefits, matched by a corresponding increase in in-work support, along with a merger of these benefits into a genuinely unified working-age benefit. It is time once again to reassert the principle that the welfare system should guarantee a basic minimum of security that protects people from poverty. In particular, we have got to get away from the idea that there is something illegitimate about claiming out-of-work benefits. Provided someone is living up to their responsibilities (whether looking for a job, caring for a young child or rehabilitating themselves from ill health or injury), they should be supported.

Achieving and sustaining this will require a major shift in our public culture of welfare: in how people view it and those claiming it, and in how our politicians talk about it. To meet this 'popular legitimacy' challenge, we propose a 're-framing' of social security around a new participatory model. In some respects this amounts to a revitalisation of the concept of social insurance, but in a way that would be both more inclusive and resonate more closely with public perceptions of fairness than the old contributory system. We also suggest formalising the new system in terms of a lifetime welfare contract, which could make a positive contribution to getting us out of our current predicament where 'rights and responsibilities' only ever seems to apply to benefit recipients.

An important lesson of welfare history is that support to lift the most vulnerable out of poverty will not only be more effective if it encourages them to be full, participating members of society; it will be much more sustainable if it is seen to be given to them for being full, participating members of society, rather than simply because they are in need. We have tried to argue here that it is possible to have your cake and eat it: there is a space between unconditional need-based allocation, on the one hand, and a narrow contributory system, on the other. And it's a space we badly need to get into.

A participatory system such as the one proposed here would not only rectify a variety of injustices in the current contributory system, but, we believe, could help re-build public confidence in the welfare system once again. Perhaps the most dangerous thing in welfare – as the Poor Law taught us – is for the level of benefits or the character of provision to become the lever with which to address public concerns about the integrity of the welfare system. But too often that is where we still seem to be today. That is why designing a generous welfare system that can nevertheless address those concerns could scarcely be more important.

Conclusion

In this book, we have looked at two 'paradoxes' of welfare. Each paradox resides in a different aspect of how welfare institutions allocate resources. Both challenge a 'commonsense' approach to anti-poverty policy.

The first paradox lies in the coverage of welfare policy, and can be articulated as follows: targeting resources on the poorest is by no means the best way of redistributing to the poorest. Over the long term, policies with wider coverage, and with benefits and services set at levels that are meaningful to middle-income households, will often be more effective. In practice, this will mean championing universalism and integration, and understanding that resources invested in welfare for middle- and higher-income households can nevertheless be investments in poverty prevention when those welfare programmes also encompass the poorest.

The second paradox, closely related to the first, lies not in the coverage of policy but in the distributive principle underlying it: giving out resources on the basis of need is often not the best way of redistributing resources to those in need. History teaches us that, over the long term, welfare will often be more effective at tackling poverty if it is given to people for being full, participating members of society. And it will certainly be more sustainable if it is *seen* to be given to them on this basis. Taking this seriously will require a profound shift in how we conduct welfare policy, away from simply responding to need and back towards reciprocity once again – the idea of earning entitlement to welfare through social contributions.

The analysis in this book also shows why these two 'paradoxes' arise. In short, they arise because of a tension between the 'distributional' and 'relational' dimensions of policy. Targeting and need-based allocation can, if implemented insensitively, actively undermine the social relationships between citizens – particularly between poor and non-poor – that are needed to sustain generous welfare in democracies over long timescales. In Chapter 4, we put forward a model showing how tensions between these distributional and relational dimensions of policy can set up particular kinds of social dynamics, dynamics which, in turn, influence the paths along which welfare institutions evolve (whether expansion or residualisation).

Our analysis draws on, and has been influenced by, recent work in 'institutionalist' political theory. But whereas work in this tradition often traces the causative power of institutions to the explicit social behaviours they nurture – like the campaigning of interest groups, the decision making of bureaucrats, and so on – we see the key causal influence as residing more straightforwardly in the public attitudes of electorates, and the implicit responsiveness of governments to such attitudes. Welfare institutions, through the design of particular policies, structure the social contexts in which people evaluate the fairness and desirability of policy. And it is the dynamic interaction between the design of policy and the relevant public attitudes that ultimately determines the success and sustainability of anti-poverty programmes.

It is worth emphasising how deeply related these two 'paradoxes' are. Whereas universalism in policy can often 'close down' questions about the worthiness of recipients, selectivism can often open them up – thereby putting more pressure on the 'welfare contract' and perceptions of fairness in distribution. Reciprocity, on the other hand, can itself be a 'universaliser', by linking contributors and recipients together in relationships of equal (or more equal) status. And the absence of reciprocity puts more pressure on the coverage of a policy to foster public legitimacy.

Another important claim of our argument has been that welfare institutions themselves can create and nurture the social relationships between individuals and groups – whether in a helpful or harmful way. It is often said that the reason Scandanavian countries can support generous universal welfare estates is that they have more solidaristic societies than Britain. But our argument is that it is partly the universal institutions themselves that nurture and sustain that solidarity – just as the workhouses and slum concentrations of the Victorian era did so much to harm social relations in Britain.

The analysis offered here has led us to propose various reforms in areas where key welfare institutions currently seem to be structured in the wrong way for tackling poverty, notably tax, housing, social security and welfare-to-work. But the argument in this book is not limited to these domains; far from it – it is a blueprint for institutional reform that can be applied to any area of welfare policy, from transport to legal aid. Indeed, if asked to name an area of policy which entrenches social division and inequality, many would reach instinctively for education. Applying our analysis here would involve looking at how our education institutions segregate chidlren into different groups and 'filter' them into different developmental pathways, and exploring how to restructure our institutions to reconcile educational principles like meritocracy and choice with the principle of comprehensiveness that protects equal citizenship (see Bamfield, forthcoming).

What does the analysis in this book tell us about our current politics? One theme has been a sense of regret that, since 1997, Labour has accepted far too many of the institutional constraints that it inherited, which have created a variety of political 'strait-jackets' that it has had to struggle against.

Perhaps Labour's biggest failing here was not to have spent more energy (and resources) during the boom years on institutional restructuring to align the interests of low- and middle-income groups, which would have max-imised willingness to contribute to key anti-poverty poli-cies and provided the best defence against future retrench-ment.

From a political perspective, it is perhaps remarkable that it took Labour 12 years to introduce a new higher top rate of income tax. By creating a rate of 50 per cent for income above £150,000, the Government has effectively created a new social 'cleavage' at a point in the income spectrum that generates no political problems for it whatsoever (indeed, quite the opposite), but huge prob-lems for its opponents. And in doing so it has trans-formed the politics of 'the top rate of tax'. Indeed, it is astonishing that the Government struggled through a whole decade with the previous highest rate kicking in right in the middle of a vocal and electorally-sensitive group (upper-middle-class earners). Nothing could bet-ter symbolise the anxiety and acquiescence to the rules of previous Conservative governments that characterised New Labour in the late 1990s than turning in on itself about what it would or wouldn't do to the existing top rate of tax, rather than realising that it didn't have to accept this dilemma, and that with a bit of strategic restructuring it could have transformed the political cal-culus of the problem.

It isn't just the missed opportunities either, but the self-inflicted harm. Perhaps the worst way imaginable of struc-turing financial support for childcare was to create one system (the childcare element of the Working Tax Credit) for helping low-income households, and another (tax relief on childcare vouchers) primarily of importance to middle-income households. It's the kind of thing you might have expected a mischievous right-wing government to have done had it deliberately set out to create a conundrum for the left. And now that the Government is trying to extricate itself from this situation, it finds itself facing a powerful lobby – one that it created – organized to campaign against it.

The Government is absolutely right that tax relief is a bad way of providing financial support for childcare. But while it should be moving away from this model, it does not follow either that the right thing to do would be to target the same resources only on the poorest. What needs to happen – indeed, what should have happened in the first place – is to use the available resources to bring middle-income households further into the same system as low-income households. That would mean extending childcare support in the Working Tax Credit further up the income spectrum (if the resources were used on the demand side) or extending the entitlement to free early years' care and education (on the supply side). Indeed, even if merging the two systems brought about no net redistribution of resources in year 1, what it would mean is that in ten or even five years' time we would be in a totally different situation.

Whatever happens in the current debate, though, the episode will still be of value if progressives remember the basic lesson: never try to do social policy through tax breaks.

If the analysis in this book provides grounds for criticism of Labour's record in government, it also points us to perhaps its most remarkable achievement: effecting a 'sea change' in how we protect and nurture the welfare of children. And this has been precisely because of a breadth of coverage in key policy developments. The Child Tax Credit covering 90 per cent of families makes it far more durable than the Working Tax Credit or Educational Maintenance Allowances.

Or take Sure Start. Many progressives reacted with dismay when evidence emerged a few years ago that the Sure Start provision introduced by Labour had been used quite heavily by middle-income households ('not those for whom it was intended'). In fact, the 'invasion' of Sure Start and Children's Centres by the middle class is a cause for celebration: it is what will secure their future. And it will mean that governments will ultimately be able to do much more through them to help the most disadvantaged than if they were 'special measures' only for the poorest. (It is why, for example, the Tories have gone from wanting to abolish them to simply wanting to rename them 'Family Hubs'.)

The result of this agenda has been a significant and positive shift in public attitudes towards welfare directed at children. Go back sixty years and there was in fact a good degree of stigma associated with Family Allowances in the post-war welfare state (Klein, 1974), partly because they were primarily of importance to low-income households, and also perhaps because, being only for second and subsequent children, they were often associated with large families. Universal Child Benefit did change this a bit. But, nevertheless, until recently, child-centred welfare in the UK has sadly often attracted the attitude that 'they chose to have children, so it's their fault'.

In fact, over the last ten years, there has been a real strengthening in public support for this aspect of the welfare state. For example, when presented with a range of options, the proportion of people wanting to prioritise investment in 'child benefits' has increased from a fifth in the mid-1980s to two-fifths today (Taylor-Gooby, 2008). In decades to come, it is this expansion of provision and underlying change in the culture of child welfare that will be seen as the key legacy of this Labour Government.

In many ways, from breaking the earnings link in the uprating of benefits to selling shares in privatised utilities, the right has been much better at strategic institutional restructuring than the left. As discussed in Chapter 1, this has usually taken the form of removing all but the poorest from the coverage of welfare policy, especially through encouraging middle-class 'exit' from the welfare state (such as through the Right-to-Buy or private pensions). While provision for the poorest often gets less generous under governments of the right, its structure usually remains intact; reviewing welfare retrenchment in Britain and America in the 1980s, Paul Pierson (1994) observes that the welfare institution that underwent the least change under Thatcher and Reagan was means-tested social assistance. Rather, a libertarian desire to shrink the state tends to lead to the removal of all but those in the most dire need from scope of welfare.

And today this remains the key ideological distinction between left and right on welfare. "We mustn't see this effort at getting public spending down... as some dreadful catastrophe," said David Cameron recently; "We've got to see it as a big opportunity... to totally reform our government and put people back in control" (Andrew Marr show, 26/07/09). It doesn't take a huge amount of imagination to work out what's being planned.

The analysis in this book challenges the right's libertarian ideology, an ideology that sees taxation and spending as a problem. Chapter 6, in particular, illustrated that the key factor in explaining welfare states' success in reducing poverty and inequality was 'welfare generosity' – the size of social spending as a proportion of GDP – not the efficiency with which resources were targeted. Ever since large cross-national datasets about welfare and inequality became available in the mid-1980s, comparative analyses have shown time and time again what to many will seem the most obvious link: that welfare spending reduces poverty, and the volume of this welfare spending is a (if not 'the') key determinant of success (see, for example, Kenworthy, 1999; Moller et al., 2003). Far from 'big government' or 'state welfare' causing poverty, as David

Cameron recently argued, precisely the opposite is true. The problem is that the right's libertarian ideology makes it impossible for them to acknowledge any of this evidence.

Our proposal to shift benefits as much as possible away from a need-based framework (income-based benefits) to a reciprocity-based framework (participatory benefits) will sound controversial to many. The point here is not that we wish to de-legitimise 'need' in welfare or suggest that the objective of progressive welfare policy should not be to respond to unmet need. Far from it. But as a quick comparison of Income Support (need-based) with successful benefits such as Child Benefit (citizenship-based) or the Basic State Pension (contributory) shows, the objective of meeting needs will often be met *least* successfully when resources are actually distributed on the basis of need. And this is in no small part because need-based social assistance will, politically, never be able to mobilise the investment necessary to prevent poverty.

So reframing welfare as participatory will be key to getting the effective and generous welfare state we need. The trick is to do it in a way that remains inclusive, taking the best of Beveridge's original ideal, but fashioning it a way that does not unfairly exclude many.

This argument poses a challenge to a variety of political perspectives. An insistence on reciprocity in welfare challenges a purist notion of 'welfare rights', arguing that enshrining 'responsibilities' within the system is not only a good thing in its own right, but also important if we are to prevent poverty.

But it also challenges New Labour's culture of conditionality and crackdowns, arguing instead for a system that positively values effort and social contributions of all kinds. It would get us out of the vicious circle we're in, where anxiety about welfare is met with stricter rules and rhetoric that only deepen our anxiety.

Many here would place the blame on the 'communitarian' turn New Labour took after 1994. Our view is that it was less the values of communitarianism that were the problem, but rather the way they have been operationalised in practice – through a very 'negative sum' approach that has succeeded in increasing opposition to out-of-work benefits in a way that the Conservatives never managed. To drive progressive change, Labour will need not just a new policy framework, but a new and more positive story about welfare. But this will only ever happen if we can prioritise the longer-term prize of a fundamental change in our culture of welfare over the short-term temptation to get a 'hit' with tomorrow's tabloids through a crackdown story that reinforces their readers' prejudices.

Perhaps most of all, though, an insistence on reciprocity – making welfare about 'good citizenship' once again – would challenge the right's notion of 'welfare dependency', reinvigorated under Thatcher, but, in truth, with us ever since the Poor Law. Only with a fundamental rethinking of what welfare is about will we ever be able to shake off this toxic historical legacy.

The left has often been accused of confusing means and ends, most particularly in its historical commitment to the common ownership of industry and services. One way of looking at the argument of this book – which is that the design of welfare institutions matters – is to see it as going beyond the objective of tackling poverty and inequality to specify the form that the means for tackling them should take.

In fact, by arguing that different values underpin different institutional designs, we are saying that how policy is structured is partly a normative question and that getting this right should be an end in itself. Take, for example, a targeted policy that required the presentation of vouchers in public settings in a stigmatising way. We would argue that, even if it were possible to generate exactly the same long-term distributional outcomes through this policy as through a universal policy funded through progressive taxation (a highly implausible assumption), nevertheless there would be something wrong with the policy in its own right.

But a different way of looking at the argument of this book is that it challenges the idea that tackling poverty should be the objective of the welfare state in the first place. For it is precisely the way in which policies focused on those in poverty construe the social relationships between poor and non-poor that can ultimately work against their long-term effectiveness.

Rather, a welfare state whose objective is to provide social protections and services for all, in return for contributions from all, will ultimately prove much more effective at poverty prevention.

And this is what lies behind the 'paradoxes' of welfare discussed here: those welfare states, like in America, whose policies are most designed to target poverty, end up being much *worse* at this than those welfare states, like in Sweden, based on equal citizenship.

Writing several years after the publication of the 1909 Minority Report on the Poor Law, Beatrice Webb explained its objective as follows: "to secure a national minimum of civilised life...open to all alike, of both sexes and all classes, by which we mean sufficient nourishment and training when young, a living wage when able-bodied, treatment when sick, and a modest but secure livelihood when disabled or aged" (1926). Nothing could better express the value of equal citizenship to which our welfare state needs to aspire again today.

Endnotes

1   Note that basket-of-goods approaches ('budget standards' or 'minimum income standards') are sometimes wrongly conflated with the idea 'absolute poverty', that is, measuring poverty lines against a fixed price level (Piachaud and Webb, 2004). But of course, what constitutes a 'necessary' basket of goods can evolve over time, relative to what people come to regard as necessities. And what people regard as necessities, in turn, tends to increase with average incomes (Kilpatrick, 1973). Nor is it the case that budget standards are more focussed on 'severe' poverty than income-based measures; despite the transition from the former to the latter across the 20th Century, Piachaud and Webb observe that the value of poverty lines adopted throughout the century – while they vary from study to study, hindering comparisons – have on average only risen a little relative to average expenditure levels. Comparing the poverty line that Rowntree used in his 1899 study of York (Rowntree, 1901) with the modern measure of 60 per cent of median income, they find that, for a single adult, the 1899 line was 36 per cent of consumer expenditure per capita, while the 2001 line was 42 per cent. Today, modern budget-standards approaches to defining necessities can produce results that are *higher* than the 60 per cent of median income measure – suggesting households that fall below this line really cannot

afford basic necessities. For example, Bradshaw et al. (2008) calculate minimum income standards for households (on the basis of public views about basic household necessities) and find that the minimum income standards for a single working-age adult, a couple with two children and a lone parent with one child are all above 70 per cent of median income (after housing costs).

2   Though impossible to know how valid it is to compare poverty levels for York to those of the whole country, many social historians suggest that York has been fairly representative of Great Britain throughout the 20th Century.

3   Cited in Hills (2004a). One crucial change was a huge rise in worklessness amongst older men as a result of economic restructuring, particularly those with low skills and also those with health problems. The inactivity rate for men aged 55-64 with low skills rose from 14 per cent in 1978 to 36 per cent in 1998 (Faggio and Nickell, 2003).

4   Rowntree recorded in his 1899 survey that 52 per cent of those below his 'primary poverty line' were in regular work but at a low wage. Today, more than half of children and working-age adults who are in poverty live in families where someone is in paid work (see poverty.org.uk).

5   The proportion of employees whose wages were below two-thirds of the median rose from 12 per cent in 1977 to 21 per cent in 1998 (McKnight, 2002). This was mainly because economic restructuring led to an increasing premium on skills (Machin, 2001), but also because the labour market institutions that could have restrained growing wage inequality (such as unions and regulatory bodies) were weakened, as were the social and reputational norms that had in the past restrained excesses of high and low pay (Atkinson, 2002).

6   Quoted in John Ranelagh, *Thatcher's People: An Insider's Account of the Politics, the Power, and the Personalities*, London: HarperCollins, 1991.

7   As she put it in her famous 1975 speech 'Let our children grow tall', "the pursuit of equality is a mirage"; what mattered was "the right to be unequal".

8   In 1979, 87 per cent thought it was 'very' or 'fairly important' to put more money into the NHS (as opposed to 7 per cent who thought more money shouldn't be put in) and 80 per cent thought it was 'very' or 'fairly important' to put more money into getting rid of poverty (as opposed to 8 per cent who thought more money shouldn't be put in). In all cases, there had been no change or negligible change since the same questions were asked in 1974.

9   Taylor-Gooby's survey also found strong support for statements such as 'the welfare state helps people who don't deserve help' (71 per cent to 17 per cent) and 'the welfare state causes bad feeling between taxpayers and people who get benefits and services' (68 per cent to 25 per cent).

10   Several statistics in this section are taken from the New Policy Institute's excellent Poverty Site at: poverty.org.uk

11   Indeed, widening the focus to adults may actually be an important development for tackling child poverty. To take an example: recent concern with child poverty and later life chances has led to social policy extending further backwards into childhood and beyond that into pregnancy (where, for example, poor maternal nutrition can stunt later cognitive development). But while a £190 grant in the 25th week of pregnancy is a welcome development, the fact is that it is the very first days and weeks of pregnancy that are most critical for a child's development (Bamfield, 2007). And this development occurs before the pregnancy is typically identified. The only way to ensure children get the best start in life is therefore to tackle adult poverty.

12   Office for National Statistics, Social Trends, vol.38 (2008).

13   It was perhaps only with the abolition of the 10p income tax rate that this group (who were not initially compensated by offsetting measures) received major political attention.

14   This is because out-of-work benefits are only uprated by the ROSSI inflation index, which tends to be lower than other measures of inflation.

15   When it comes to financial support for households with children we are in the middle of the pack, while for those in work on low pay our benefits system is at the very top of the pack (OECD, 2007).

16   ONS, 2006 population projections

17   The Personal Social Services Research Unit estimates that the number of over 65s with a care need will increase from around 2.5 million now to around 4 million by 2026 (Cabinet Office, 2008).

18   One in six adults still do not have the literacy skills expected of an 11 year old (Leitch, 2006).

19   While this thesis is contested, recent evidence (Bell and Blanchflower, 2008) seems to support it.

20   And if employees find it more satisfying to receive their entire income through their employer, then there is no reason why we should not look again at the possibility of in-work financial support being paid via employers.

21   Goodhart (2004) quotes David Willetts articulating the issue powerfully as follows: "The basis on which you can extract large sums of money in tax and pay it out in benefits is that most people think the recipients are people like themselves...If values become more diverse, if lifestyles become more differentiated, then it becomes more difficult to sustain the legitimacy of a universal risk-pooling welfare state."

22 Ipsos Mori, 'Effect of the Budget', Fieldwork results 1976-2007

23 Described in more detail in Gregory (2009).

24 Cited in Timmins (2001)

25 The concept of social insurance is one possible framework for instantiating reciprocity in welfare, though, as we discuss in Chapter 7, not the only one.

26 As his famous 1942 report put it: "Insured persons should not feel that income for idleness, however caused, can come from a bottomless purse...Whatever money is required for provision of insurance benefits, so long as they are needed, should come from a fund to which the recipients have contributed and to which they may be required to make larger contribution if the Fund proves inadequate" (Beveridge, 1942, paragraph 22).

27 By 1954 there were already 1.8 million on National Assistance and this would rise to 4 million in the 1970s (Lowe, 1999).

28 In Chapter 7, we further argue that these features are not even particularly resonant with popular conceptions of fairness.

29 In the 1948 National Assistance Act and the implementation in July 1948 of the 1946 National Health Service Act, respectively.

30 While it would be unfair to accuse Marshall of naïve determinism – his account was a good deal more nuanced than this – the over-optimism of many progressives at this time about the arrival of the welfare state did smack a little the complacency; as an election agent put it in the 1955 election campaign, "Issues? There are no issues. This is a census".

31 There were only two OECD countries where there was a significant reduction in spending in the 1980s and 1990s: the Netherlands and Ireland (and in the latter case this is partly because increases in welfare spending during this period didn't keep pace with Ireland's remarkable pace of economic growth). Castles (2004) calculates that the average change was an increase in social expenditure of 4 per cent of GDP between 1980 and 1998.

32 Brooks and Manza (2007) – discussed further below.

33 And there is good evidence that policy preferences do actually figure in voters' choices (Knutsen, 1995).

34 This is a good candidate for the most devastating election defeat in history. Key issues of public dissatisfaction were the Progressive Conservatives' approach to managing the budget deficit, and controversial spending on military helicopters.

35 Similarly, support for private alternatives to public provision tends to be higher in countries with a greater reliance on private provision.

36 Discussed further in Chapter 3.

37 Brook et al. (1998) show that people tend to be more supportive (than the population on average) of spending on social groups that they themselves are part of.

38 In their enlightening book, *Not only the poor: The middle classes and the welfare state* (1987), Robert Goodin and Julian Le Grand discuss the role of middle-class interest in the defence of key planks of the welfare state from retrenchment.

39 This will ultimately depend on how people perceive the 'value' of marginal reductions in need to vary with the intensity of need (see Miller, 1999).

40 Discussed in more detail in Horton (2008).

41 How people allocate resources in group settings depends very much on what they have been told about the character of the group in question (Miller, 1999). For example, how people allocate bonuses to successful sports performers depends on whether the activity is seen as an individual event (like long-distance running) or a team event (like football) (Törnblom and Jonsson, 1987).

42 As Castles (2004) puts it, "There is no sign here that Western welfare states are marching in tune to the beat of a single drummer…Indeed, the story is one of a slight accentuation of existing welfare regime biases."

43 Here, the Webbs can arguably lay as much claim to being the founders of modern political institutionalism as Weber (1922). And the 1909 Minority Report can perhaps lay a claim to being one of the first documents to practically apply such institutionalist insights in the service of actual policy reform.

44 In another exercise, reported elsewhere (Bamfield and Horton, 2009), participants were shown the structure of existing income-related benefits and tax credits, like the Child Tax Credit. Many liked their progressive structure and thought it perfectly fair. And in exercises where participants were asked to design their own income-related benefit (usually a general benefit 'to help with living costs'), the vast majority gave it a progressive distributional structure. Similarly, when participants were shown how income tax liability varied with income, and were asked how they would change it if given the chance, most made it more progressive, reducing the burden at the lower end of the income spectrum and increasing it at the top end.

45 Figures refer to taxes as a percentage of gross income for non-retired households. Figures for 2006-07 (Jones, 2008)

46 Figures from Jones (2008)

47 A further important source of negative attitudes to welfare recipients, not pursued here, was a widespread belief that adequate opportunities exist for all (not that opportunities are equal, but that there is enough opportunity to get on if you really want to). This belief in the ready availability of opportunity results in highly 'individualised' explanations of poverty and disadvantage: people attribute success and failure to the individual themselves and tend to downplay the significance of structural causes of poverty. This view is also clearly part of the broader phenomenon discussed here: a view that the primary beneficiaries of welfare policy are somehow not deserving of support.

48   In most of these exercises, the benefit was an individualised, rather than a household, one. Many participants drew benefit coverage up to incomes of £40,000-£50,000, even though they had been told that £43,000 was the 90th earnings percentile (in 2007).

49   The discussion here and in this section draws on Bowles et al. (2005). For a review of ultimatum games, see Güth and Tietz (1990).

50   For a review of public goods games, see Ledyard (1995).

51   For a review of different attitudes sets within populations, see Kahan (2005).

52   It's worth noting here how important the design of institutions is in shaping the dynamics of cooperative behaviour. We have seen how the presence of a sanctioning mechanism fundamentally changes the nature of the cooperative endeavour. Also crucial is the sequencing of interactions. In a one-shot simultaneous interaction (where people know each other's type), the presence of free-riders will induce reciprocators to withdraw cooperation (so no-one cooperates), since all know the free-riders will behave selfishly. However, in a sequential interaction, where a sanctioning mechanism is available, the presence of reciprocators will induce free-riders to cooperate (so all cooperate), since the latter know they will be subsequently punished. In this way, subtle features of the way we structure our institutions can lead to the development of cooperative or non-cooperative equilibria.

53   Some (for example, Binmore, 1998) have suggested that that strong reciprocity is not really a deviation from self-interest but rather reflects an 'inability' by

humans to adapt to artificial conditions like one-shot interactions and 'perfect stranger' scenarios – in other words, a type of behaviour that appears other-regarding when exercised in situations for which it did not evolve. Evidence casts doubt on this interpretation, though, particularly evidence showing that subjects do in fact understand the strategic differences between different types of interaction (Fehr and Fischbacher, 2005). Either way, however, it is not especially important which of these interpretations is correct as it is a type of behaviour that humans *do* exhibit, and so it is relevant for thinking about welfare, whatever its evolutionary origins.

54   And a further clue is provided by the fact that, if an offer in an ultimatum game is generated by a computer rather than a human (and respondents know this), or by the roll of a dice, low offers are very rarely rejected (Blount, 1995). There's no intention involved.

55   Like Robinson Crusoes, Club Members are prepared to distinguish between 'deserving' and 'undeserving' recipients and are more likely than Samaritans to have concerns about welfare fraud.

56   Note that these tests only identify a correlation between these factors, not a causal link. However, we picked these beliefs for survey investigation precisely because our deliberative research had suggested that they were causal factors in driving opposition to redistribution.

57   The view of contribution or desert evidenced here is a forward-looking, dynamic one, slightly different from the traditional 'backward-looking' conception of desert in moral philosophy, where it tends to be based on the evaluation of some past performance (Sher, 1987). For many, what people deserve when it comes to welfare depends on what they will do now and in future (not too dissimilar from the kind of judgements seen in experimental games which emerge from repeated interactions).

58 The public attitudes research in Chapter 6 suggested also that people *judge* universalism of eligibility as more fundamental too.

59 Strictly speaking, the Child Tax Credit is 'near-universal', open to around 85-90% of families with children.

60 It is estimated that around a third of a million children entitled to free school meals do not claim them. See: http://gmb.live.rss-hosting.co.uk/Templates/Internal.asp?NodeID=99101

61 See, for example, Lowe (1999) and Bridgen and Lowe (1998)

62 Figures from: http://www.poverty.org.uk/66/index.shtml

63 In fact, take-up 'by expenditure' tends to be higher than take-up 'by caseload' – showing that those entitled to larger awards (those more in need) are more likely to take them up. But in all cases there is a large tranche of people in need who, for one reason or another, do not take up these benefits.

64 Figures from HMRC and the Child Poverty Action Group website.

65 http://www.cml.org.uk/cml/media/press/2357

66 Existing tax credits already meet a range of needs through one and the same vehicle, providing, for example, extra support for disabled workers through the Working Tax Credit.

67 Importantly, a right to sell could also be a direct vehicle of housing mix when the properties concerned were in areas that have a relatively low proportion of social housing.

68 Recently suggested by Greenhalgh and Moss (2009).

69 In 2004-05, around 30 million of Britain's 47 million adults (63%) were paying income tax (Brewer et al., 2008).

70 The political consequence of separating people into groups, depending on whether the tax or benefits system is of primary importance to them, is to create competition for resources. In a very practical way –

given that taxation funds benefits – the result is a trade-off between tackling poverty, on the one hand, and helping the people that provide the resources for you to tackle poverty, on the other.

71 To take an example, in Sweden in 2003 a recipient of unemployment benefit who lives in a couple family with two young children received annual income support of 20,900 euros, but paid 6,100 euros in income tax and social security contributions, so the net benefit income was 14,800 euros (OECD, 2007).

72 Note that even though the flat-rate payment to individuals is worth more on average in cash terms to working-age households in higher income deciles than lower income ones (because households in higher income deciles are more likely to be couple households), the reform is nevertheless progressive because the amounts received are still a higher proportion of overall income for lower-income households than they are for higher-income households.

73 Figures for 2008-09.

74 Analysis by the Institute for Fiscal Studies. There are signs that the Government are cottoning onto this, with the announcement in the 2008 Pre-Budget Report that the value of the personal allowance would be restricted for those with incomes over £100,000 (and eventually withdrawn completely over £112,000). This is welcome, but really only a drop in the ocean when set alongside the regressive nature of the allowance across the whole income spectrum.

75 As such, this system would resemble the system of 'tax rebate' cheques that the US Internal Revenue Service sometimes sends out to American taxpayers (such as the $600 rebate that was part of Bush's 2008 Economic Stimulus Act).

76 Figures for 2008-09.

77 Again, the toothpaste is already out of the tube here, with the Government's announcement in Budget 2009

that it would restrict pensions tax relief for those earning over £150,000. In fairness terms, why not go the whole hog and have the same incentives for everyone?

78   The equivalisation ratio of (approx) 1/1.6 for singles/couples reflects the fact that couples pool resources and risks within the household, and benefit from economies of scale. That is why the welfare system does not give a couple twice what a single person gets.

79   One administrative drawback to the model proposed here would be that it requires everyone to file a tax return, much as currently happens in the US. This would be a minor administrative burden on households (though the hassle could be minimised if well designed). The blunt truth, however, is that if poverty is a household phenomenon, then we are never going to be able to tackle it effectively until HM Revenue and Customs has a direct relationship with every household.

80   In various measures of welfare states' reliance on means-testing between the 1970s and 2003 (Abe, 2001; Esping-Anderson, 1990; Eurostat New Cronos Database; OECD, 2007), Australia, Canada, the UK and the US rank as among the most reliant on means testing, with Sweden and Belgium the least reliant. Norway, Germany, the Netherlands, France and Denmark generally rank in the middle. A further measure of targeting (Mitchell et al., 1994), which looks not simply at the degree of means testing, but at how much of what's transferred actually goes to the 'pre-transfer poor', shows a similar ranking. Sweden is the least targeted; Canada, the UK, the US and Australia are the most targeted; and in between lie the Netherlands, France, Norway and Germany.

81   And this is simply looking at net redistribution of resources. In reality, we measure the distributional impact of a policy by looking at the proportionate

change in household income, not the absolute amount transferred. So it is clear that flat-rate benefits can be highly progressive in their impact, since they will produce a larger proportionate increase in household income for a low-income household, than for a middle-income or high-income household.

82   Also, in earnings-related systems, benefit levels are usually capped at some upper limit, ensuring that individuals earning considerably more than most of the population do not necessarily benefit in proportion to this.

83   As well as being instrumentally useful for poverty prevention, wage replacement actually addresses a separate welfare 'function', namely consumption smoothing (see, for example, Barr, 2001). We do not discuss this function further here.

84   As Stuart White puts it, to take advantage of the cooperative endeavours of others without making a reasonable effort to ensure they are not burdened by your membership of the community is to treat them in an offensively instrumental way (White, 2003).

85   Figure for care work from Moullin (2008). Figure for volunteering from http://www.volunteering.org.uk

86   Moullin estimates that almost a third of economically inactive carers experience relative poverty.

87   See, for example, Mead (1986).

88   In fact, Beveridge did think a good deal about the rights of carers (Harris, 1997), although many of his ideas here did not make it into policy.

89   "Benefit in return for contributions, rather than free allowances from the State, is what the people of Britain desire...Whatever money is required for provision of insurance benefits, so long as they are needed, should come from a fund to which the recipients have contributed and to which they may be required to make larger contribution if the Fund proves inadequate." (Beveridge, 1942, paragraphs 21-22).

90   In this chapter, we generally use the term 'carer' to refer both to people caring for children and to people caring for a sick, disabled or elderly adult.

91   Cutting the number of contributing years needed to qualify for a basic state pension to 30 and removing the requirement that one must have at least ten years contributions to get any state pension at all will substantially increase the entitlement of many women approaching retirement. And cutting to 20 the number of hours needed to be spent in caring each week in order to get National Insurance Credits will help many who provide a substantial amount of care each week – often at the expense of their own employment opportunities – but are not doing so full time.

92   Home Responsibilities Protection did not give you any more National Insurance Contributions; it only reduced the number of years you would have to have paid contributions in order to get the full amount of benefit.

93   In fact, there are precedents for this. Those on maternity leave can get National Insurance Credits. And if you are out of work through unemployment or illness you can have contributions paid in for you.

94   You can get credits if you're doing an 'approved training course' (16-19 year-olds in certain types of work-related training). But given that continuing education and re-training look set to become central aspects of any viable future economic strategy then we should ensure that any employment-oriented training (up to a certain amount) should qualify for credits too.

95   Importantly, one can volunteer whilst claiming one of the main out-of-work benefits (provided one is also meeting the relevant job search / work preparation requirements), and in many cases one can gain National Insurance Credits whilst on these benefits. But many volunteers are not covered by this, including those on formal volunteering programs (such as the recent national youth volunteering scheme).

96 One unavoidable consequence of giving caring and some types of volunteering the same contributory status as work is that it would probably be necessary to tighten up the criteria for being defined as a carer or volunteer, and to do more checking up on these groups.

97 For example, in a 2006 survey for the Department for Work and Pensions (Kelly, 2006), four-fifths of respondents thought that carers for sick or disabled relatives should receive the same amount of State Pension as somebody who has worked all their life.

98 McKnight et al. (1998) observe that men earning below the LEL are only likely to do so for a short time, whereas women tend to be in low-paid jobs for more extended periods and so the impact on their benefit and pension entitlements is more pronounced.

99 To take another example – a ludicrous situation – because for most people National Insurance is administered through employers, it is your earnings in individual jobs that counts, not your total earnings. The result is that if your employment is divided between two jobs, you only become entitled to contributory benefits if your earnings in *one of the jobs* exceed the LEL; your combined earnings do not count. The Department for Work and Pensions estimates that 'less than 50,000 people' are in this situation, among them 25,000 women (DWP, 2006). But that is not the point. These are not the workings of a mature welfare state fit for purpose in the 21st Century. In addition to abolishing the LEL, the administration of income tax and National Insurance should therefore be merged, to put an end to this kind of injustice.

100 Calculated from the Department for Work and Pensions' Tabulation Tool.

101 Although the income-based versions are means tested, so eligibility for these amounts depends on having no other sources of income.

102 By 'conditionality' we mean simply behavioural requirements focussed around the period of claiming benefits, backed up by sanctions for failure to comply.

103 See, for example, Manning (2005).

104 In fact, as White (2003) points out, all of the supposed progenitors of 'welfare rights' – from Tawney to Beveridge to Marshall – believed in a reciprocal duty to contribute in return.

105 For example, the vast majority of Jobseeker's Allowance (JSA) claimants are never sanctioned, and virtually none require more than one sanction. Recent DWP figures (Gregg, 2008) suggest that in 2008 only 1.8 per cent of JSA claimants behaved in a way that means they were sanctioned more than once, and only 0.1 per cent have multiple offences to their name – what might be deemed 'playing the system'.

106 Perhaps ironically, an important advantage of a more generous level of out-of-work benefits, as recommended earlier, is that sanctioning (a cut in benefits) can take place with less risk of harm to individuals and therefore can potentially play a more important role. This is an important reason why generosity and robust conditionality are actually quite good bedfellows (as we see in Danish labour market policy, for example).

107 See Gregg (2008) for a review.

108 One way to reduce the temptation of using conditionality to cut expenditure would be to have a presumption that any savings from reducing the claimant count should be hypothecated back into improving the support available in welfare-to-work programmes.

109 Note that this classification is designed to clarify the functions of different benefits on the basis of the requirements that it is justifiable to place on different groups. It is not intended to specify what individuals 'can' and 'cannot' do, which would be

counter-productive. If individuals want to participate more intensively than the requirements and
expectations placed on them, they should be
encouraged to do so.

110 See Gregg (2008) for a review of the evidence.

111 And, for the Webbs, this conditionality was indeed
robust: those refusing work or training were to be
shipped off to a detention colony.

112 As the Child Poverty Action Group has pointed out,
full-time work for just £64.50 a week works out at a
wage of £1.84 an hour (compared to the current minimum wage of £5.73 an hour).

113 This is also the time when there have been substantial increases in behavioural conditionality attached
to out-of-work benefits, including the introduction of
Jobseeker's Allowance in 1996, which requires an
individual to actively seek work, and mandatory
work-focussed interviews for new Incapacity Benefit
claimants and lone parents on Income Support.

114 Although such a trend in many ways seems profoundly depressing, what it implies is in fact remark-
ably good news: *fears about welfare seem to have
nothing to do with the actual level of unemployment
benefit.* So you cannot assuage concerns about out-
of-work benefits through downwards pressure on
benefit levels.

115 A US study by Farkas and Robinson (1996) found that,
while 93% of Americans (and 88% of those receiving
welfare) wanted the welfare system overhauled, "the
public's strong level of discontent stems from their
dissatisfaction with the system itself, not from the
costs or the fraud perceived to be associated with it."
When given a list of several reforms they could make,
cutting benefits ranked last in terms of popularity
(with only 19% supporting this), well below measures
such as compulsory training or better checking up on
claimants.

116 The diverging relationship between benefit generosity and concern about welfare illustrated above is precisely an example of the type of path dependency described in Chapter 4.

117 Sefton (2009) convincingly demonstrates that much of the hardening of attitudes towards welfare recipients took place since 1994, and particularly among Labour supporters. He concludes that the change in welfare rhetoric that occurred under New Labour is centrally responsible for the pattern of change.

118 Strangely, the Conservative government before 1997 declined to measure the extent of benefit fraud, despite it being a major part of their political narrative about welfare. (A cynic might suggest that inaccurate perceptions of widespread fraud might have been instrumentally quite useful to a government with retrenchment objectives.)

119 This suggestion has also been put forward by others (see, for example, Harker, 2005; Reed and Dixon, 2005).

120 In the vision outlined here, these participatory benefits, like contributory benefits, would not to be means tested (at least for a certain period of time), and would be taxed. It is worth noting, however, that means testing is not *necessarily* incompatible with the idea of entitlement through participation; it is just that, in the case of means tested benefits, the 'right' gained through participation would be a right to a minimum income guarantee.

121 On the other hand, we also think it is problematic to migrate lone parents of young children onto Jobseeker's Allowance, as the government is proposing to do (albeit a different form of Jobseeker's Allowance). Lone parents should be recognised for their caring contribution, not for jobseeking.

122 Tax avoidance also costs a good deal more than benefit fraud. The Department for Work and Pensions calculates

the amount lost to benefit fraud is £800 million (NAO, 2008), while most studies suggest the scale of tax avoidance is well into the billions; one recent calculation of the amount lost to personal tax avoidance (Murphy, 2008) puts the figure at £13 billion. So reforming the tax system to remove the opportunity for avoidance – such as through a set of minimum tax rates (Lansley, 2008) – would not only reaffirm the responsibility of all citizens to pay tax, but could also be a very important source of revenue.

Bibliography

Abe, A. (2001). 'Universalism and targeting: An International comparison using
the LIS Database'. Luxembourg Income Study Working Paper No. 288.

Abel-Smith, B. and Townsend, P. (1955). *New pensions for the old*. London: Fabian Publications.

Abel-Smith, B. and Townsend, P. (1965). *The poor and the poorest*. London: Bell.

Ajzen, I., Rosenthal, L. and Brown, T. (2000). 'Effects of Perceived Fairness on Willingness to Pay'. *Journal of Applied Social Psychology*. Vol. 30 (No.12).

Albanese, F. and Baxendale, A. (2009). *Campaigns briefing: Local housing allowance and direct payments - giving claimants a choice*. Shelter.

Alcock, P. (1984). *Poverty and state support: Social policy in modern Britain*. Harlow: Longman Group.

Alesina, A., Glaeser, E. and Sacerdote, B. (2001). 'Why doesn't the United States have a European-style welfare state?' *Brookings Papers on Economic Activity*. Vol. 2001 (No. 2). pp. 187-254.

Alesina, A. and Glaeser, E. (2006). *Fighting poverty in the US and Europe: A world of difference*. Oxford: Oxford University Press.

Allen, C., Camina, M., Casey, R., Coward, S. and Wood, M. (2005). *Mixed tenure 20 years on – nothing out of the ordinary*. York: Joseph Rowntree Foundation.

Atkinson, A. (1995). *Incomes and the welfare state: Essays on Britain and Europe*. Cambridge: Cambridge University Press.

Atkinson, A. (1996). 'The case for a participation income.' *The Political Quarterly*. Vol. 67 (No. 1). pp 67-70.

Atkinson, A. (1996). 'Income distribution in Europe and the United States'. *Oxford Review of Economic Policy*. Vol. 12 (No.1). Oxford: Oxford University Press.

Atkinson, A. (2002). *Social indicators: the EU and social inclusion*. Oxford: Oxford University Press.

Atkinson, A. (2008). *Top incomes over the 20th century: a contrast between continental European speaking and English speaking countries*. Oxford: Oxford University Press.

Autor, D., Levy, F. and Murnane, R. (2003). 'The skill content of recent technological change: An empirical exploration'. *Quarterly Journal of Economics*. Vol. 118 (No. 4). pp.1279- 1333.

Axelrod, R. (1984). The evolution of cooperation. New York: Basic Brook.

Barr, N. (2001). *The welfare state as piggy bank: Information, risk uncertainty and the role of the state*. Oxford: Oxford University Press.

Bamfield, L (2007). *Born Unequal: Why we need a progressive pre-birth agenda*. London: Fabian Publications.

Bamfield, L. and Horton, T. (2009). *Understanding attitudes to tackling economic inequality*. York: Joseph Rowntree Foundation.

Bell, D. and Blanchflower, D. (2009). 'What to do about rising unemployment in the UK'. *SCOTECON working paper*.

Bellamy, K., Bennett, F. and Millar, J. (April 2006). *Who benefits? A gender analysis of the UK benefits and tax credits system*. London: The Fawcett Society.

Binmore, K. (1998). *Game Theory and the Social Contract*. Vol. 2: Just Playing. Cambridge, MA/London: MIT Press.

Beveridge, W. (1942). *Social insurance and allied services*. London: HMSO.

Blank, R. and Kovak, B. (2008). *The growing problem of disconnected single mothers*. Madison, WI: Institute for Research on Poverty.

Blount, S. (1995). 'When social outcomes aren't fair: The effect of causal attributions on preferences'. *Organizational Behavior and Human Decision Processes*. Vol. 63 (No. 2). pp 131-144.

Bowles, S., Boyd, R., Fehr, E. and Gintis, H. (2005). *Moral sentiments and material interests: The foundations of cooperation in economic life*. Cambridge, MA: MIT Press.

Bradley, D., Huber, E., Moller, S., Nielsen, F. and Stephens, J. (2003). 'Distribution and redistribution in post-industrial democracies.' *World Politics*. Vol. 55. pp 193-228

Bradshaw, J., Middleton, S., Davis, A., Oldfield, N., Smith, N., Cusworth, L. and Williams, J. (2008). *A minimum income standard for Britain: What people think*. York: Joseph Rowntree Foundation.

Brewer, M., Saez, E. and Shephard, A. (2008). 'Means-testing and tax rates on earnings', in Mirrlees, J., Adam, S., Besley, T., Blundell, R., Bond, S., Chote, R., Gammie, M., Johnson, P., Myles, G. and Poterb, J. (eds.) Dimensions of Tax Design: The Mirrlees Review, OUP for IFS. Oxford: Oxford University Press.

Brewer, M., Sibieta, L. and Wren-Lewis, L. (2008). *Racing away? Income inequality and the evolution of high incomes*. Briefing Note no. 76. London: Institute for Fiscal Studies.

Brewer, M., Browne, A., Joyce, R. and Sutherland, H. (2009). 'Micro-stimulating child poverty in 2010 and 2020'. London: Institute for Fiscal Studies.

Brewer, M., O'Dea, C., Paull G. and Sibieta, L. (2009). 'The living standards of families with children reporting low incomes'. *Research Summary Child Poverty Unit*. London: Department for Work and Pensions.

Brewer, M. B. and Kramer, R. (1986). 'Choice behaviour in social dilemmas: Effects of social identity, group size and decision framing'. *Journal of personality and Social psychology.* Vol 3. pp.543-549.

Bridgen, P. and Lowe, R. (1998). 'Welfare policy under the Conservatives 1951-1964: A guide to documents in the public record office'. London: Public Record Office.

Brook, L. (1998). 'What drives support for higher public spending' in Taylor-Gooby, P.F. (ed.) *Choice and public policy.* London: Macmillan.

Brooks, B. and Manza, J. (2007). *Why welfare states persist: the importance of public opinion in democracies.* Chicago: The University of Chicago.

Butler, D. and Stokes, D. (1974). *Political change in Britain: The evolution of electoral choice.* 2nd ed. London: Macmillan.

Cabinet Office. (2008). *Realising Britain's potential: Future strategic challenges for Britain.* London: Cabinet Office.

Castles, F. (2004). *The future of the welfare state: Crisis myths and crisis realities.* Oxford: Oxford University Press.

Clasen, J. and Clegg. D. (2007). 'Levels and levers of conditionality: measuring change within welfare states', in Clasen, J. and Siegel, N. (ed.) *Investigating welfare state change: the 'dependent variable problem' in comparative analysis.* Cheltenham: Edward Elgar.

Coats, D. (2006). *Who's afraid of labour market flexibility?* London: The Work Foundation.

Cole, D. and Utting, J. (1962). *The economic circumstances of old people.* London: Codicote Press.

Crisp, R. and Fletcher D. (2008). *A comparative review of workfare programmes in the United States, Canada and Australia.* Department for Work and Pensions Research Report No.533.

Dean, J. and Hastings, A. (2000). *Challenging images: Housing estates, stigma and regeneration.* York: Joseph Rowntree Foundation.

Deacon, A. (1978) 'The scrounging controversy: public attitudes towards the unemployed in contemporary Britain'. *Social and Economic Administration*. Vol. 2 (No. 2).

Deutsch, M. (1985). *Distributive justice: A social psychological perspective*. New Haven: Yale University Press.

Dorling, D., Vickers, D., Thomas, B., Pritchard, J. and Ballas, D. (2008). *Changing UK: The way we live now*. London: Report for the BBC.

DWP (Department for Work and Pensions). (November 2005). *Women and pensions: The evidence*. London: DWP.

DWP (Department for Work and Pensions). (May 2006). *Security in retirement: towards a new pensions system*. London: DWP.

DWP (Department for Work and Pensions). (May 2006). *National pensions debate: Final report*. London: DWP.

DWP (Department for Work and Pensions). (2008). *Raising expectations and increasing support: reforming welfare for the future*. London: DWP

DWP (Department for Work and Pensions). (2009). *Fraud and error in the benefit system: October 2007 to September 2008*. London: DWP.

DWP (Department for Work and Pensions). (2009). *The abstract of statistics for benefits, national insurance contributions, and indices of prices and earnings 2008 edition*. London: DWP.

DWP (Department for Work and Pensions). (2009). *Income related benefits estimates of take-up in 2007-08*. London: DWP.

DWP (Department for Work and Pensions). (2009). *Households below average income: An analysis of the income distribution 1994/ 95 – 2007/ 08.* London: DWP.

Elder, G. and Bernard, C. (1977). *The alienated: growing old today*. London: Writers & Readers Publishing.

Esping-Anderson, G. (1990). *The three worlds of welfare capitalism*. Cambridge: Polity Press.

Esser, I. (2009). 'Has welfare made us lazy? Employment commitment in different welfare states', in Park, A., Curtice, J., Thomson, K., Phillips, M. and Clery, E. (ed.) *British Social Attitudes: The 25th Report*. London: Sage.

Falk, A., Fehr, E., and Fischbacher, U. (2003). 'On the nature of fair behavior.' *Economic Inquiry*. Vol. 41(No. 1). pp 20-26.

Faggio, G. and Nickell, S. (1977) 'The rise of inactivity among adult men', in Dickens, R., Gregg, P., and Wadsworth, J., *The labour market under New Labour: The state of working Britain*. Basingstoke: Palgrave Macmillan.

Farkas, S. and Robinson, J. (1996). *The values we live by: What Americans want from welfare reform*. New York: Public Agenda.

Fawcett, H. (1996). 'The Beveridge strait-jacket: Policy formation and the problem of poverty in old age'. *Contemporary British History*. Vol. 10 (No 1).pp. 20-42.

Fehr, E. and Fischbacher, U. (2005). 'The economics of strong reciprocity', in Gintis, H., Bowles, S., Boyd, R. and Fehr, E. (eds.) *Moral sentiments and material interests*. Cambridge, MA: MIT Press.

Feinstein, L., Lupton R, Hammond, C., Mujtaba, T., Salter, E. and Sorhaindo, A. (2008). *The public value of social housing: a longitudinal analysis of the relationship between housing and life chances*. London: The Smith Institute.

Fiegehen, G., Lansley, P. and Smith, A. (1977). *Poverty and progress in Britain, 1953–73*. Cambridge: Cambridge University Press.

Fischbacher, U., Gachter, S. and Ernst, F. (2001). 'Are people conditionally cooperative? Evidence from a public goods experiment'. *Economics Letters*. Vol. 71 (No. 3). pp 397-404.

Fletcher, D., Gore, T., Reeve, K. and Robinson, D. (2008). *Public housing and worklessness: Key policy messages*. Department for Work and Pensions Research Report 482.

Fone, D., Dunstan, F., Williams, G., Lloyd, K and Palmer, S. (2007). 'Places, people and mental health: A multitundinal level analysis of economic activity'. *Social Science & Medicine*. Vol. 64 (No. 633).

Fong, C. (2001). 'Social preferences, self interest and the demand for redistribution'. *Journal of Public Economics*. Vol. 82. pp 225-246.

Fong, C., Bowles, S. and Gintis, H. (2005). 'Reciprocity and the welfare state', in Bowles, S., Boyd, R., Fehr, E. and Gintis, H. (eds.) *Moral sentiments and material interests: The foundations of cooperation in economic life.* Cambridge, MA: MIT Press.

Gaertner, S., Dovidio, J., Anastasio, P. and Bachman, B. (1993). 'The common ingroup identity model: Recategorization and the reduction of intergroup bias'. *European review of social psychology.* Vol. 76. pp 388 - 402

Gazeley, I. (2003). *Poverty in Britain, 1900 – 1965.* Basingstoke: Palgrave Macmillan.

Glennerster, H. (2007). *British social policy: 1945 – the present.* Oxford: Blackwell.

Glennerster, H. (2004). 'Poverty policy from 1900 to the 1970s', in Glennerster, H., Hills, J., Piachaud, D. and Webb, J (eds.) *One hundred years of policy and poverty.* York: Joseph Rowntree Foundation.

Glennerster, H., Hills, J., Piachaud, D. and Webb, J. (2004). *One hundred years of policy and poverty.* York: Joseph Rowntree Foundation.

Golding, P. and Middleton, S. (1982). *Images of welfare: press and public attitudes to poverty.* London: Basil Blackwell/Martin Robertson.

Goodhart, D. (2004). 'Discomfort of strangers'. *The Guardian*, February, 2004.

Goodin, R. and Le Grand, J. (1987). *Not only the poor.* London: Allen and Unwin.

Goodwin, V. (2008). 'The effects of benefit sanctions on lone parents: employment decisions and moves to into employment'. Department for Work and Pensions Research Report No. 511.

Goos, M. and Manning, A. (2003). 'McJobs and MacJobs: The growing polarisation of jobs in the UK', in Dickens, R., Gregg, P. and Wadsworth, J. (eds.) *The labour Market under New Labour*. London: Palgrave.

Greenhalgh, S and Moss, J. (2009). *Principles for Social Housing Reform*. London: Localis.

Gregg, P. and Wadsworth, J. (2001). 'Everything you ever wanted to ask about measuring worklessness and polarization at the household level but were afraid to ask'. *Oxford Bulletin of Economics and Statistics*. Vol. 63 (special issue).

Gregg, P. (2008). 'Realising potential: A vision for person-alised conditionality and support'. Norwich: Department for Work and Pensions/TSO.

Gregory J. (2009). *In the mix*. London: Fabian Publications.

Grubb, D. (2000).'Eligibility criteria for unemployment benefits'. *OECD Economic Studies*. Vol. 31. pp 147-183.

Güth, W. and Tietz, R. (1990). 'Ultimatum bargaining behavior : A survey and comparison of experimental results'. *Journal of Economic Psychology.* Vol. 11 (No. 3). pp 417-449.

Harker, L. (2005). 'A 21st century welfare state' in Pearce, N. and Paxton. W. (eds.) *Social justice: building a fairer Britain.* London: Politico's.

Harris, J. (1997). *William Beveridge: A biography* (2nd ed.). Oxford: Oxford University Press.

Hasluck, C. and Green, A. (2007). 'What works for whom? A review of evidence and meta-analysis for the Department of Work and Pensions'. Department of Work and Pensions Research Report No. 407.

Hatton, T. and Bailey, R. (2000). 'Seebohm Rowntree and the post-war poverty puzzle'. *Economic History Review*. Vol. 53 (No. 3).

Heatherton, T., Kleck, R., Hebl, M. and Hull, J. (2000). *The social psychology of stigma*. London: Guilford Press.

Hedges, A. and Bromley, C. (2001). *Public attitudes towards taxation.* London: Fabian Publications.

Hedges, A. (2005). 'Perceptions of redistribution: Report on exploratory qualitative research'. LSE STICERD Research Paper No. 96. London: London School of Economics.

Hills, J. (2004a.). *Inequality and the state.* Oxford: Oxford University Press.

Hills, J. (2004b). 'Inclusion or insurance? National insurance and the future of the contributory principle'. *Journal of Social Policy* Vol. 33.

Hills, J. (2004c). 'The last quarter century: From new right to New Labour', in Glennerster, H., Hills, J., Piachaud, D. and Webb, J. (eds.) *One hundred years of policy and poverty.* York: Joseph Rowntree Foundation.

Hills, J. (2007). *Ends and means: The future roles of social housing in England and Wales.* CASE Report 34. p 5.

Hills, J., Sefton, T. and Stewart, K. (eds.) (2009). *Towards a more equal society?: (CASE Studies on poverty, place and policy).* Bristol: Policy Press.

HM Treasury. (2008). *Long-term public finance report.* (2008). London: HM Treasury.

Holmes, S. and Sunstein, C. (1999). *The cost of rights: Why liberty depends on taxes.* New York: Norton & Company.

Homes, C. (2006). *Mixed communities: Success and sustainability.* York: Joseph Rowntree Foundation.

Horton, T. (2008). *Equal citizenship: avoiding residualisation by welfare institutions.* Unpublished Fabian Research Paper.

Hyman, P. (2005). *1 out of 10: from Downing Street vision to classroom reality.* London: Vintage.

Jantti, M., Kangas, O. and Ritakallio, V. (1997). 'From marginalism to institutionalism: distributional consequences of the transformation of the Finnish pension regime.' *Review of Income and Wealth.* Vol. 2 (No. 4). pp 473-491.

Jarvis, S. and Jenkins, S. (1996). 'Changing places: Income mobility and poverty dynamics in Britain'. ESRC Working Paper 1996-19.

Jones, F. (2008) 'The effects of taxes and benefits on household income 2006-07'. *Economic & Labour Market Review*. Vol. 2 (No.7).

Kahan, D. (2005). 'The Logic of Reciprocity: trust, collective action and law', in Gintis, H., Bowles, S., Boyds, R. and Fehr, E. (eds.) *Moral sentiments and material interests: the foundation of cooperation in economic life.* Cambridge: MIT Press.

Kelly, M. (2006). 'Public attitudes to pension reform'. *Department for Work and Pensions Research Summary*.

Kenworthy, L. (1999). 'Do social-welfare policies reduce poverty? A cross-national assessment'. *Social Forces*. Vol. 77 (No. 3). pp 1119-39.

Kilpatrick, R. (1973). 'The income elasticity of the poverty line'. *Review of Economics and Statistics*. Vol. 55 (No. 3). pp 327–32.

Kim, H. (March 2000). *Anti-poverty effectiveness of taxes and income transfers in Welfare States.* LIS Working Paper No. 228.

Klein, R. (1974). 'The case for elitism: Public opinion and public policy.' *Political Quarterly*. Vol. 45 (No. 4). pp 406 – 417.

Knutsen, O. (1995). 'Party Choice' in van Deth, J. and Scarbrough, E. (eds.) *The Impact of Values.* Oxford: Oxford University Press.

Korpi, W. and Palme, J. (1998). 'The paradox of redistribution and strategies of equality: Welfare state institutions, inequality and poverty in Western countries'. *American Sociological Review*. Vol. 63 (No. 5). pp 661-687.

Kosenen, P. (1995). 'European welfare state models: Converging trends'. *International Journal of Sociology.* Vol. 25. pp 81-110.

Lansley, S. (2008). *Do the super-rich matter?* TUC Touchstone Pamphlet.

Larsen, C. (2008). 'The institutional logic of welfare attitudes: How welfare regimes influence public support'. *Comparative Political Studies*. Vol. 41. pp145-168.

Ledyard, J. (1995). 'Public goods: A survey of experimental research', in Kagel, J. and Roth, A. E. (eds.) *Handbook of experimental economics*. Princeton: Princeton University Press.

Leitch, S. (2005). 'Skills in the UK: the long-term challenge. Interim report'. *The Leitch review of skills*. London: HM Treasury.

Leitch, S. (2006). 'Prosperity for all in the global economy — world class skills: Final report'. *The leitch review of skills*. London: HM Treasury.

Lister, R. (2004). *Poverty*. Cambridge: Polity Press.

Lowe, R. (1999). *The welfare state in Britain since 1945*. Basingstoke: Macmillan

Lupton, R. and Power, A. (2002). 'Social exclusion and neighbourhoods', in Hills, J., Le Grand, J. and Piachaud, D. (eds.) *Understanding social exclusion*. Oxford: Oxford University Press.

Machin, S., Dickens, R., Gregg, P. and Wadsworth, J. (2003). *The labour market under New Labour*. Basingstoke: Palgrave Macmillan.

Manning, A. (2005). 'You can't always get what you want: The impact of UK Jobseekers allowance'. Centre for Economic Performance, LSE.

Martin, G. and Watkinson, J. (2003). *Rebalancing communities: Introducing mixed incomes into existing rented housing estates*. York: Joseph Rowntree Foundation.

Marshall, T.H. (1950). *Citizenship and social class*. Cambridge: Cambridge University Press.

McKnight, A., Elias, P. and Wilson, R. (1998). 'Research findings: Low pay and the national insurance system: A statistical picture'. Manchester: Equal Opportunities Commission.

McKnight, A. (2002). 'Low-paid work: Drip-feeding the poor', in Hills, J., Le Grand. J. and Piachaud. D. (eds.)

Understanding social exclusion. Oxford: Oxford University Press.

Mead, L. (1986). *Beyond entitlement*. New York: Free Press.

Miller, D. (1999). *Principles of social justice*. Cambridge, MA: London: Harvard University Press.

Mitchell, D., Harding, A., Natsem and Gruen, F. (1994). 'Targeting welfare'. *The Economic Record*. Vol. 70 (No.210). pp 315-340.

Moene, K. and Wallerstein, M. (2001). 'Targeting and political support for welfare spending'. *Economics of Governance*. Vol. 2(No. 1). pp 3-24, 03.

Moller, S., Bradley, D., Huber, E., Nielsen, F. and Stephens, J. (2003). 'Determinants of relative poverty in advanced capitalist democracies'. *American Sociological Review*. Vol. 68. pp 22-51

Montada, L. and Schneider, A. (1989). 'Justice and emotional reactions to the disadvantaged'. *Social Justice Research*. Vol. 3. pp313-344.

Moullin, S. (2007). *Care in a new welfare society: Unpaid care, work and welfare*. London: Institute for Public Policy Research.

Murphy, R. (2008). *The missing billions: The UK tax gap*. London: TUC

Musterd, S. and Andersson, R. (2006). 'Employment, social mobility and neighborhood effects: the case of Sweden'. *International Journal of Urban and Regional Research*. Vol 30.

NAO (National Audit Office). (2008). *Department for Work and Pensions: Progress in Tackling Benefit Fraud*. London: NAO

North, D. (1990). *Institutions, institutional change, and economic performance*. Cambridge: Cambridge University Press

National Consumer Council. (2004). *Why do the poor pay more...or get less? Consultation pack*.

OECD. (2007). *The Social expenditure database: An interpretative guide, SOCX 1980–2003*. Paris.

OECD (2007). *Benefits and wages: OECD indicators.*

Ohmae, K. (1995). *The end of the nation-state: The rise of regional economies.* New York: Simon and Schuster Inc.

One Parent Families. (2007). *Adopting US welfare reforms would mean more poverty, not less.* Press release. 12 Dec. 2007.

ONS (Office for National Statistics). (June 2008). *2006-based long term subnational population projections for England (SNPP).*

ONS (Office for National Statistics). (2008). *Effects of taxes and benefits.*

ONS (Office for National Statistics). (2008). *Social trends.* No.38, 2008 edition. Basingstoke: Palgrave Macmillan.

Opotow, S. (1990). 'Moral exclusion and injustice: an introduction'. *Journal of Social issues.* Vol. 46 (No. 1). pp 1-20.

Orloff, A. (1993). *The politics of pensions: A comparative analysis of Britain, Canada, and the United States.* Wisconsin: The University of Wisconsin Press.

Pfaller, A., Gough, I. and Therborn, G. (1991). *Can the welfare state compete?* London: Macmillan.

Piachaud, D. (1988). 'Poverty in Britain 1899 to 1983'. *Journal of Social Policy.* Vol. 17 (No. 3).

Pierson, P. (1994). *Dismantling the welfare state?* Cambridge: Cambridge University Press.

Pierson, P. (2000). 'Increasing returns, path dependence, and the study of politics'. *The American Political Science Review.* Vol. 94 (No. 2).

Power, A. and Houghton, J. (2007). *Jigsaw cities, big places, small places.* Bristol: Policy Press.

Ranelagh, J. (1991). *Thatcher's people: An insider's account of the politics, the power, and the personalities.* London: Harper Collins.

Reed, H. and Dixon, M (2005). 'National insurance: does it have a future?' *New Economy.* Vol.12 (No.2). pp 102-110. London: Institute for Public Policy Research.

Rendall, M. and Salt, F. (2005). *Focus on people and migration: The foreign-born population.* Basingstoke: Palgrave.

Rothstein, B. (1998). *Just institutions matter: The moral and political logic of the universal welfare state.* Cambridge: Cambridge University Press.

Rowlands, R., and Murie, A. and Tice, A. (2006). *More than tenure mix: Developer and purchaser attitudes to new housing estates.* York; Joseph Rowntree Foundation.

Rowntree, B. S. (1901). *Poverty: A study of town life.* London: MacMillan

Rowntree, B. S. (1937). *The human needs of labour,* new edn, revised and rewritten. London: Longmans Green.

Rowntree, B. S. and Lavers, G .R. (1951). *Poverty and the welfare state: A third social survey of York dealing only with economic questions.* London: Longmans.

Sarlvik, B. and Crewe, I. (1983). 'British general election study, 1983: Cross-Section Survey'.

Schmitt, J. and Wadsworth, J. (2005). 'Is the OECD jobs strategy behind US and British employment and unemployment success in the 1990s?' in Howell, D. R. (ed.) *Fighting unemployment: The limits of free market orthodox.* Oxford: Oxford University Press.

Sefton, T. (2002). *Recent changes in the distribution of the social wage,* CASE Paper 62. London: London School of Economics.

Sefton, T. (2005). '*Give and take: attitudes towards redistribution*' in Park, A. Curtice, J. and Sefton, T. (eds.) *British Social Attitudes.* New Delhi: SAGE Publications.

Sefton, T. (2009). 'Moving in the right direction? Public attitudes to poverty, inequality and redistribution', in Hills, J., Sefton, T. and Stewart, K (eds.) *Towards and more equal society: poverty, inequality and poverty since 1997.* Bristol: Policy Press.

Sher, G. (1987). *Desert.* Princeton: Princeton University Press.

Singleton, N., Bumpstead, R., O'Brien, M., Lee, A. and Meltzer, H. (2000). 'Psychic morbidity survey among adults living in private households' cited in Royal College of Psychiatrists, Mental Health and Work, 6. London: HSMO National Statistics.

Smith, N. and Middleton, S. (2007). 'A review of poverty dynamics research in the UK'. York: Joseph Rowntree Foundation.

Sriskandarajah, D., Cooley, L. and Kornblatt, T. (2007). 'Britain's immigrants: An economic profile'. London: Institute for Public Policy Research.

Stafford, B. (1998). *National insurance and the contributory principle (DSS social research branch in-house report 39)*. London: DSS.

Svallfors, S. (1997). 'Words of welfare and attitudes to redistribution: A comparison of eight Western nations'. *European Sociological Review*. Vol. 13. pp 283-304.

Swank, D. (2001). 'Political institutions and welfare state restructuring', in Pierson, P (ed.) *The new politics of the welfare state*. Oxford: Oxford University Press.

Tajfel, H. & Turner, J. C. (1986). 'The social identity theory of inter-group behavior', in Worchel, S. and Austin, L. W. (eds.) *Psychology of Intergroup Relations*. Chicago: Nelson-Hall.

Taylor-Gooby, P. (1982). 'Two cheers for the welfare state: Public opinion and private welfare'. *Journal of Public Policy*. Vol. 2 (No. 4), pp. 319-346.

Taylor-Gooby, P. (1985). *Public opinion, ideology, and state welfare*. London; Boston: Routledge & Kegan Paul Books.

Taylor-Gooby, P. and Martin, R. (2008). 'Sympathy for the poor, or why New Labour does good by stealth', in Park, A., Curtice, J., Thomson, K., Phillips, M. and Clery, E. (eds.) *British Social Attitudes: the 24th Report*. London: Natcen.

Thane, P. (2006). 'The 'scandal' of women's pensions in Britain: how did it come about?' in Pemberton, H., Thane, P. and Whiteside, N. (eds.) *Britain's pensions crisis: history and policy*. Oxford: Oxford University Press.

The Daily Mail. (2009). '£1bn tax raid on middle classes as Cameron warns they must share pain of spending cuts'. 27 July 2009.

The Daily Express. (1976). 'Get the scroungers'. 15 July 1976.

Thomas, A. (2007). 'Lone parents work focused interviews: synthesis of findings'. Department of Work and Pensions Research Report No. 443.

Thomas, A. and Griffiths, R. (2008). 'Evaluation of the first 18th months of lone parent personal advisor meetings: findings from the qualitative research'. Department for Work and Pensions Research Report No. 166.

Timmins, N. (1996). *The five giants: A biography of the welfare state*. London: Fontana Press.

Titmuss, R. M. (1955). 'The social division of welfare: some reflections on the search for equity', in Titmuss, R. M. (ed.) *Essays on the Welfare State*. (1958). London: Allen and Unwin.

Titmuss, R. M. (1957). National superannuation: Labour's policy for security in old age. London: Labour Party.

Titmuss, R. M. (1967). 'Universal and selective social services'. *New Statesman*, 15th September, 1967.

Törnblom, K. and Jonsson, D. (1987). 'Distribution vs. retribution: The perceived justice of the contribution and equality principles for cooperative and competitive relationships'. *Acta Sociologica*. Vol. 30 (No. 1). pp 25-52.

Townsend, P. (1979). *Poverty in the United Kingdom: A survey of household resources and living standards*. London: Allen Lane and Penguin Books.

Trivers, R. L. (1971). 'The evolution of reciprocal altruism'. *Quarterly Review of Biology*. Vol. 46 (No. 3557). Chicago: University of Chicago press.

Tsoukalis, L. and Rhodes, M. (1997). 'Economic integration and the nation state?' in Rhodes, M., Heywood, P. and Wright, V (eds.) *Developments in West European Politics*. Basingstoke: Macmillan.

van Oorschot, W. (2000) 'Who should get what and why?' On deserving criteria and the conditionality of solidarity among the public'. *Policy and Politics*. Vol. 28. pp 33-48.

van Parijs, P. (1995). *Real freedom for all: What (if anything) can justify capitalism?* Oxford: Oxford University Press.

Watkin, B. (1975). *Documents on health and social services: 1834 to the present day*. London: Methuen.

Webb, B. (1926 / 1975). *Our partnership*, 2nd edition. Cambridge: Cambridge University Press.

Webb, J. (2002). *Always with us? The evolution of poverty in Britain, 1886–2002*. Oxford: D. Phil Thesis.

Weber, M. (1922 / 1968). *Economy and society*. London.

Wilensky, H. (1975). *The welfare state and equality: structural and ideological roots of public expenditures*. Berkeley: University of California Press.

Wilkinson, R. and Pickett, K. (2009). *The spirit level: Why more equal societies almost always do better*. London: Allen Lane.

White, S. (2003). *The civic minimum: On their rights and obligations of economic citizenship*. Oxford: Oxford University Press.

White, S. (2004). 'A social democratic approach to welfare conditionality: Finding a framework for evaluation', in Stanley, K. and Lohde, L. *Sanctions and sweeteners: Rights and responsibilities in the benefits system*. London: Institute for Public Policy Research.

British Muslims and the politics of fairness

In 'Fairness not Favours', Sadiq Khan MP argues that an effective agenda to provide opportunity and tackle extremism across all communities must go beyond a narrow approach to security, and sets out new proposals for a progressive agenda on inequality and life chances, public engagement in foreign policy, an inclusive Britishness, and rethinking the role of faith in public life.

The pamphlet puts the case for an effective agenda to provide opportunity and tackle extremism across all communities must go beyond a narrow approach to security, and sets out new proposals for a progressive agenda on inequality and life chances, public engagement in foreign policy, an inclusive Britishness, and rethinking the role of faith in public life.

How to defend inheritance tax

Inheritance tax is under attack, and not just from the political right. The critics of this tax have dominated the debate over recent years but, as the authors of 'How to Defend Inheritance Tax' argue, this tax is one of the best tools we have for tackling inequality and kick starting Britain's stalled social mobility.

Defending inheritance tax is not just the responsibility of politicians – there must be a citizen-led campaign too. In this Fabian Ideas pamphlet, Rajiv Prabhakar, Karen Rowlingson and Stuart White provide progressives with the tools they need to win this argument.

They set out the evidence on inheritance and inequality, tackle the common objections to the tax, and demonstrate the moral and pragmatic arguments for an inheritance tax.

'The Fabians ask the most difficult questions, pushing Labour to make a bold, progressive case on taxation and the abolition of child poverty.'
– Polly Toynbee

How to narrow the gap and tackle child poverty

One in five children still grows up in poverty in Britain. Yet all the political parties now claim to care about 'social justice'. This report sets a litmus test by which Brown, Cameron and Campbell must be judged.

'Narrowing the Gap' is the final report of the Fabian Commission on Life Chances and Child Poverty, chaired by Lord Victor Adebowale. The Fabian Society is the only think tank with members. Join us and help us put poverty and equality at the centre of the political agenda.